JESUS IN THE THEOLOGY OF
ROWAN WILLIAMS

T&T Clark Studies in English Theology

Series editors
Karen Kilby
Michael Higton
Stephen R. Holmes

JESUS IN THE THEOLOGY OF
ROWAN WILLIAMS

Brett Gray

LONDON · NEW YORK · OXFORD · NEW DELHI · SYDNEY

T&T CLARK
Bloomsbury Publishing Plc
50 Bedford Square, London, WC1B 3DP, UK

BLOOMSBURY, T&T CLARK and the T&T Clark logo are trademarks of
Bloomsbury Publishing Plc

First published in Great Britain 2016
Paperback edition first published 2018

A catalogue record for this book is available from the British Library.

ISBN: HB: 978-0-5676-7017-5
PB: 978-0-5676-8163-8
ePDF: 978-0-5676-7018-2
ePub: 978-0-5676-7019-9

A catalog record for this book is available from the Library of Congress

Series: T&T Clark Studies in English Theology

Typeset by Deanta Global Publishing Services, Chennai, India

To find out more about our authors and books visit
www.bloomsbury.com and sign up for our newsletters.

CONTENTS

Acknowledgements

This work, a revision of my doctoral thesis, would not have been possible without the help and friendship of numerous people. Ben Quash and Susannah Ticciati encouraged a then parish priest, pursuing what he thought would be a professional doctorate, to set his sights on a more ambitious target. Mike Higton, as a doctoral supervisor, showed me what academic friendship and mentoring truly means – and he has continued to do so as a series editor. David Ford graciously stepped in to shepherd my PhD to its happy conclusion. Hugh Shilson-Thomas and Selwyn College were an immense support, both financially and in terms of providing a community of worship and friendship these last few years. The community that gathered around the Cambridge Interfaith Project opened my eyes in unexpected ways, and provided some of the best coffee breaks a researcher could ever have. I also owe a great debt to my family. My wife Alison has shown extraordinary patience with this project, and has been a constant support. My son Thomas has given me the gift of delight, and the excuse I needed to watch baseball games and movies which involve superheroes. This book is for them. The third, and part of the fourth, chapter of this book is an expansion of material that first appeared as the article 'Clones, Princes, and Beautiful Parodies: Rowan Williams's Negative Literary Christology' in the journal *Literature and Theology* 29, no.3 (2015): 284–97. I am grateful to the editors of that journal for giving a novice scholar his first chance at publication, and exposure to the refining fire of peer review. Elements of this work were also given an airing in papers for the Society for the Study of Theology's annual conference, as well as in a paper for the Christian Theology Seminar at the Faculty of Divinity in Cambridge.

INTRODUCTION

In the fraught lead-up to the 2008 Lambeth conference, Rowan Williams did something that was both striking and counter-intuitive: he wrote a book on Dostoevsky. As a piece of literary criticism, it stands on its own. It is a book about an author and his fiction that is sensitive to the concerns of Dostoevsky's context, and the questions that animated his work. Yet, it is also, arguably, the most serious *theological* text of Williams's tenure as Archbishop. It is the occasion for what can be described as an oblique essay in Christology, as I will show in my third and fourth chapters. In his book, Williams also speaks evocatively of Christ as the 'last word', an important intuition that will be explored and explicated at multiple points throughout this book. Williams's Christology, oblique or not, is this book's subject, and there is perhaps no better way to get to grips with a Christian theologian than to grapple with his understanding of Jesus Christ. It is an investigation that, in Williams, leads one through numerous other theological locations and conversations, and into the heart of a number of tensions (both creative and problematic) within his work. If Jesus is the 'last word', he is also a 'word' that animates Williams's concerns at every point. Unpacking this will be the burden of what is to come.

The reader will quickly realize that this book is not primarily a work of theological biography; it is not, in the first instance, the story of Williams's theological development, nor is it an account of his impact, as a thinker, upon the church. Rather this work seeks, through the close reading of multiple texts in relation to one another, to inhabit the theological logics implicit within Williams's writings. Yet, this book is also not a work of simple textual exegesis. In inhabiting Williams's logics, it will, at times, attempt to say *more* than Williams himself might. It will sometimes engage in a faithful expansion and illumination of what is implied by those logics. Attempting to say *more* is arguably necessary because of the dialogical and allusive nature of much of Williams's work. Much of it proceeds through conversations with others (Dostoevsky being a prime example) in which Williams inhabits the voices and concerns of his interlocutors. This dialogical way of proceeding is arguably a theological practice very similar to a tendency Williams himself notes in an essay on Thomas Merton. Merton, to Williams, was reluctant 'to commit his deepest identity to one voice only'. While this is potentially a 'deeply ambiguous' trait, Williams argues that Merton's habit of adopting the registers of those he dialogued with enabled him to 'discover *something else*, something not knowable or expressible in one consistent voice alone'.[1] In terms of

---

1. Rowan Williams, *A Silent Action: Engagements with Thomas Merton* (Louisville: Fons Vitae, 2011), 66. Emphasis mine.

theological methodology, this could be self-description on Williams's part. While occasionally displaying a frustrating diffidence and evasiveness, *his* dialogical habit of mind results in a certain theological polyphony, a multiplicity of registers and conversations within the corpus of Williams's writings that points to 'something else', to more than is evident in any one isolated dialogue or essay. Inhabiting these multiple voices in Williams's work, in order to say more, is implicitly demanded by that very multiplicity.

What also demand it are the textual forms Williams's work takes. While he has produced some substantial monographs, such as his books on Arius and Dostoevsky, much of his work has appeared as short essays, journal articles, published occasional lectures, forewords and afterwords to others' books, and even sermons and devotional texts. The student interested in a broad survey of Williams's thought will need to pursue a lot of widely dispersed, and disparately written, material. Nevertheless, the sense that Williams's polyphonous multiplicity of texts and conversations is not a cover for mere dissonance or incoherence is confirmed by what might be termed the 'fractal' nature of his work. Across the numerous dialogues and explorations that make it up, certain forms and formal moves reappear and replicate themselves within different registers and idioms. A prime example of this is explored in my first chapter, in the multiple voicings of divine difference that, for all their disparity, share a certain logic. It is this sense of formal repetition that gives one the intuition that a coherent vision underlies Williams's wide spread writings. But it is a coherence only found by attending to the polyphony. To try and enforce it before time risks losing that sense of excess, of 'something else' being implied through these multiple voices and dialogues.

In tracing these conversations and repeating forms, this book is perhaps an essay in what Williams has called 'celebratory' theology. It is 'an attempt to draw out and display connections of thought and image so as to exhibit the fullest possible range of significance in the language used'. It does not so much argue (although sometimes it will) as seek to 'evoke a fullness of vision'.[2] By necessity, this will entail a certain discursiveness, a following of multiple traces and a recurrent drawing of connections between different discourses. Sometimes we will even leave Williams's idioms and resort to the speech of others such as Dostoevsky, Donald MacKinnon and Gillian Rose. But, in this exploration of Williams's Christology, the vision 'evoked', in all its fullness, is of a Christ deeply implicated in human tragedy, and yet skilfully performing a healing and divine discontinuity within it. That performance opens up a field of almost unspeakable possibility, a never-ending and divinizing journey of the whole created order into God. This, it will be seen, is something of the content of what it means to cast Christ as the 'last word'. But such a celebratory theological discourse does not preclude conceptual rigour.[3] There are tensions in Williams's presentation that must also be attended to. The very impetus to implicate Christ in creation's tragedy – in order to heal creation – threatens to undo the possibilities of Christological mediation and much else

---

2. Rowan Williams, *On Christian Theology* (Oxford: Blackwell, 2000), xiii–xiv.

3. A point Williams himself makes. See ibid.

besides. Exploring how this is so, and how resources are found within Williams's thought to repair this situation, are also part of the journey to be undertaken in this work.

It is a journey that begins, in Chapter 1, with an exploration (in multiple voices) of divine difference in Williams's thought. God, in the adopted idiom of Nicholas of Cusa, is *non aliud*, 'not-other'. In a derived double neologism that is not Williams's, but faithfully represents his intuitions, God is thereby not '*an*-other' (not any thing or cause within creation that can be itemized), but also God is '*not*-other' (generatively and maximally present to all things and causes). This construal of divine difference is seen to be shot through even the Trinitarian life. It both complicates, and makes possible, Christological mediation. In Chapter 2, we move on to explore Williams's positive Christological presentation. Jesus of Nazareth is understood to be the perfect performance of God's life in the medium of time and humanity. It is an, at times, self-consciously orthodox presentation. It draws upon the lineaments of the Alexandrian and post-Chalcedonian traditions. It is also, in ways that will impact discussions to come, a vision that returns one to history to transform it. Chapter 3 moves towards the oblique Christology found, particularly, in Williams's work on Dostoevsky. Centrally, Williams understands Prince Myshkin, the protagonist of *The Idiot*, to be a parody of Christ. But Myshkin also provides a counterpoint of failure by which to comprehend Jesus's significance. Myshkin's is a privative humanity. In its insufficiency, it foregrounds the necessity for a Christ fully embedded in the tragic complexities of time and human agency. The oblique Christology that Williams undertakes through Myshkin, thus, like Williams's positive Christological presentation found in the previous chapter, returns one to history. That history, however, is now understood to be haunted by tragic exigencies.

Chapter 4 explores the extent to which exposure to these exigencies complicates Williams's Christology, bringing into it a sense of suspension and potential failure. Insofar as Christ's human agency is, like ours, hemmed in by the constraints of the history that we know, its unfallenness and innocence are a difficult pronouncement. Thus, what is put at risk in this exposure is the perfection of Jesus's human performance of the divine life. The possibilities of Christological mediation become open to question. Chapter 5 moves on to explore the more general dynamics of mediation's operations in Williams's work. What is thereby discerned are two tensioned mediatorial logics at play in Williams's thought, visible in his Christology and elsewhere. One is the pacific logic of a God generatively present to the whole of what is. The other is a logic of dialectical crisis, or '*syncrisis*'. At times, the latter logic threatens to overcome the former, and to effectively undo mediation's possibilities. It appears that, in a history paralysed by exigencies that can only be called tragic, God might only appear as an ambiguous and disruptive interruption, or even only as a silence or a wound.

Chapters 6 and 7, drawing upon resources implicit within Williams's work, begin a reparative operation to make mediation more thinkable, if never less than complex. Chapter 6 looks at the place of the tragic in Williams's thought, especially drawing upon the influence of one of his teachers at Cambridge, Donald

MacKinnon. But it also traces two dialogues that potentially ameliorate that influence, and begin a healing of the tragic by setting it against an eschatological horizon. In both Augustinian and Hegelian thought, Williams finds ways to talk about creation as a process, or drama, that is subtly shifted away from the tragic. The cause of this shift is the appearance in time of Christ's perfect performance. By mediating the divine end of creation, Christ constellates it anew. It is now a manifold growing less allergic to mediation's possibilities because it is less enflamed with tragedy. Chapter 7 draws out further the eschatology, often implicit and rarely emphasized, that frames this shift in Williams's thought. It is proleptically established in the resurrection of Christ. It is, in various ways, instantiated in the ecclesial community which that resurrection creates. It is an eschatology that proposes an 'endless end', or *epektasis* (a continual movement forward) of all things in relation to God. For Williams, creation is drawn in Christ's wake into an endless vivifying movement. This is what it ultimately means for Christ to be creation's 'last word'. Jesus does not so much finish the drama, as perpetually reopen it to further depths of significance and meaning. The *dénouement* of the entire created order in its relation to God is endless, a polyphony of voices caught up in a life-giving conversation in which there is always 'something else' to be spoken.

One final note on methodology: the preponderance of this book will focus on Williams's writings up to, and including, 2008 (the publication year of *Dostoevsky*). In part, this is to make a project on a living, and still very active, subject feasible. It is also governed by the theological significance that I have found in *Dostoevsky*. However, some later works, such as *The Edge of Words* (2014), are referenced insofar as they buttress the intuitions that arise from extensive reading of the pre-2008 material. Ultimately, it has been a comfort to find, in reading Williams's most recent output (and even, at the time of finishing this manuscript, attending a series of lectures on Christology given by him at the Cambridge Faculty of Divinity), that while sometimes interlocutors change, and vocabulary and emphases shift, the fundamental forms of Williams's thinking remain intact. The polyphony of his work has been added to in the last few years, but without any discernible dissonance with what has come before.

Chapter 1

The Difference of God

Introduction

A young girl once wrote a letter to God, enquiring: 'How did you get invented?' Rowan Williams, becoming aware of the letter, wrote to the girl in turn, imagining the following as part of God's potential reply: 'But there was nothing and nobody around before me to invent me. Rather like somebody who writes a story in a book, I started making up the story of the world and eventually invented human beings like you who could ask me awkward questions!'[1] There is a good deal of theology implicit in this apparently simple response to a child. In recent years, the analogy of God as an author has become something of a motif in Williams's thought. This chapter begins there as a way into exploring a wider question – what is the nature of God's difference from the created world and created agents? This is a key exploration in a book on Christology because one of Christology's key questions is this: 'How is God present in Jesus' humanity?' In answering that question, the nature of the difference of God from that humanity becomes a pivotal enquiry. This chapter will explore that difference through a constellation of interlocking discussions in Williams's work, which weave together to give voice to a distinctive grammar of divine difference. It is one in which God is maximally different from any created thing or agent, and one in which God can never be enumerated or mapped as if God were an agent or cause within the world. Yet, it is also a grammar in which God is paradoxically maximally and generatively present to *all* things or agents as their very possibility to be what they are. As I will show, this grammar is refracted through, and intensified by, the doctrine of the Trinity as Williams understands it. It is also a grammar that complicates, and yet makes possible, Christology itself.

The Analogy of Authorship

Authoring fictional characters, who seem to take on a life of their own in being written, is perhaps one of the closest analogies open to us in thinking through

---

1. Reported by Damien Thompson in *The Telegraph*, 22 April 2011. Available at http://blogs.telegraph.co.uk/news/damianthompson/100084843/a-six-year-old-girl-writes-a-letter-to-god-and-the-archbishop-of-canterbury-answers/. Cited in Benjamin Myers, *Christ the Stranger: The Theology of Rowan Williams* (London: T&T Clark, 2012), 3.

God's creation of sentient agents. But fiction writers, and their various fictions, are a rather diverse set of creatures. If, as I will argue, Williams thinks through divine difference by likening God to an author, the question is: What sort? One, perhaps, a little like the cantankerous and often disturbing Flannery O'Connor, a point Williams gestures towards in his work *Grace and Necessity* (2005). A Catholic living in the twentieth-century American South, O'Connor's fictions often resorted to the grotesque and the extreme. Yet, to Williams, her authorial method was still marked by a certain species of ascetic self-effacement and restraint – evidenced by the retreat of the narrator's, and thus (in any simple sense) the author's, voice. It is not the narrator's task to speak as a cypher for the author, or to frame the plot; it is rather the characters and action, in the integrity of the plot, that speak for themselves. Thus Williams notes that what meaning and coherence there is in O'Connor's fictions emerges immanently in and through the narrative, and not through god-like and determining authorial interjections in the guise of a narrator's commentary.[2]

Something like this authorial restraint, and even asceticism, is gestured towards by Williams in his work on a very different Catholic and American writer in a 1998 essay on Thomas Merton. Commenting on Merton's reflections on poetry, Williams suggests that good poetic practice involves a certain reticence by the poet to impose, too quickly, meaning into his or her work. A poem's meaning, rather, emerges through the writer's attentiveness to his work's subject matter. Williams casts this reticence as analogous to a religious practice that will 'allow truth, allow God'. It is even, in the renunciation of the poet's ego, an attunement to God's 'pure act'.[3] So, if the difference of God is somewhat – to Williams – like that of an author or poet's difference from his or her creations, then God might be a little like an author who does not hastily intrude upon his fictions to impose their meaning. Rather, a divine poetics is one that patiently creates a space wherein creatures find their own coherence and voice. This is a restrained 'writing' in which, to speak with a degree of theological daring, the divine ego is left behind.

This analogy of authorship is re-presented by Williams in *Dostoevsky* (2008), if with a different nuance and a debt to the Russian philosopher and literary scholar Mikhail Bakhtin. For Bakhtin, Dostoevsky's genius lay in the 'Copernican

---

2. Rowan Williams, *Grace and Necessity: Reflections on Art and Love* (London: Continuum, 2005), 95–7. See also Flannery O'Connor, *Mystery and Manners: Occasional Prose* (New York: Noonday, 1970), 74–6. O'Connor herself casts this approach as a form of asceticism: 'Art is a virtue of the practical intellect, and the practice of any virtue demands a certain asceticism and a very definite leaving-behind of the niggardly part of the ego.' See *Mystery and Manners*, 81–2.

3. Rowan Williams, *A Silent Action: Engagements with Thomas Merton* (Louisville: Fons Vitae, 2011), 47–8. For another account of poetry as contemplative practice, see Williams's essay 'Suspending the Ethical: R. S. Thomas and Kierkegaard', in *Echoes of the Amen: Essays after R.S. Thomas*, ed. D. W. Davies (Cardiff: University of Wales Press, 2009), 217–8.

revolution' he wrought in terms of the author's position towards his fictions. He even credited Dostoevsky with the generation of a new art form – the polyphonic novel.[4] Emphasizing this repositioning seen by Bakhtin, Williams notes that in Dostoevsky the author is now 'alongside' his creations, *in* but not *over* the action and characterization of the text. The author's voice is heard in the text, but not as a godlike intervention that imposes itself upon the characters and plot. Rather, his voice is an active dialogical presence within a polyphony of voices. It is a presence that prompts other voices within the plot to 'life and definition'. What especially intrigues Williams is Bakhtin's use of 'theological models and idioms'. While Bakhtin's own religious agenda is a matter of continued discussion, a 'theologically minded reader' can follow the traces of his work in order

> to see the otherness that exists between author and character in the Dostoevskian world as giving a clue to the otherness of God and the human creation. It is an 'alongside' relation that is at the same time very different from the mere occupying of the same space. The author does not *contend* with his or her characters, and so does not appear as *a* character in any simple sense.[5]

A more contentious authorial presence might infringe upon the integrity of the fiction and perhaps constitute, on another level, the sort of intrusion O'Connor, in her authorial restraint, sought to avoid.

For O'Connor, the author – as narrator – must seek to not be a controlling or determining voice in his or her narrative, thus the need for restraint. This is an authorship that, in its restraint, connotes something like the maximal difference of God from creation. This author does not appear as a discernible voice within his or her creation; his or her voice is not enumerable as one among others in the unfolding plot. Dostoevsky, however, seems at first sight to lack such restraint. His authorship comes to be *alongside* his creations, and yet, there is a species of restraint here as well. This author, as Williams notes, does not become another character 'in any simple sense'. He does not jostle his creations for space, nor does he finalize them. Rather, in addressing them within the polyphony of the plot and its voices, he prompts them to life and definition. The analogical hint provided here towards thinking through the difference of God is one that connotes a sort of maximal generative presence *within* difference. This author unfolds a world with its own integrity by providing time, space and, above all, a dialogue that vivifies his or her creations without determining them.[6] This is, to Bakhtin, 'the activity of God in His relation to man',[7] and this hints at the complexity behind the response

---

4. Mikhail Bakhtin, *Problems of Dostoevsky's Poetic*, trans. C. Emerson (Minneapolis: University of Minnesota Press, 1984), 7, 49, 57–8, 285–6.

5. Rowan Williams, *Dostoevsky: Language, Faith and Fiction* (London: Continuum, 2008), 137–8. See also Bakhtin, *Problems*, 67–8.

6. See Williams, *Dostoevsky*, 149.

7. Bakhtin, *Problems*, 285–6. This passage is cited by Williams (*Dostoevsky*, 137).

to a young girl's letter. God is like a writer who allows voices to emerge other than his own, voices that can ask 'awkward questions'.

An Interfaith Divine Grammar

There is another, less literary, discussion wherein the contours of this divine difference emerge, and that is in a shared grammar Williams comes to discern across multiple religious traditions. This can be seen in a 2004 address to the Christian and Muslim *Building Bridges* seminar, where Williams identifies a negative moment replicated across multiple faiths, both Asian and Abrahamic. In that address, he notes that there is an aspect of *unbelief* inherent in thoughtful belief itself; it is an unbelief that appears in the refusal to identify spiritual enlightenment or the divine with any immanently available conceptual form or object. The divine, as a conceivable sort of thing for finite minds, is *disbelieved* in. In the Abrahamic traditions, Islamic, Jewish and Christian, this is instantiated by the denial of any possibility of a positive definition for God *qua* God. Williams cites in support of this contention such thinkers as Ibn-Sina, Maimonides and Nicholas of Cusa.[8] Elsewhere, he even suggests that this shared negative moment is 'the common sense of all reflective religion'.[9]

An important text in this discussion of an interfaith grammar of divine difference is Williams's succinctly titled essay 'God' (2005). It opens with an exploration of a shared Abrahamic 'treatise *de deo uno*',[10] and a key interlocutor is David Burrell, who argues that 'the received doctrine of God in the West was already an intercultural, interfaith achievement', the work of Ibn-Sina and Maimonides, flowing into Aquinas.[11] For Burrell, this interfaith achievement entailed a grammar emphasizing God's difference as pronounceable only in negations,[12] a contention that looks quite like what Williams would term a species of reflective religious 'unbelief'. And, like Burrell, Williams sees emerging from a medieval interfaith exchange a degree of substantive agreement on just such a

---

8. Rowan Williams, 'Analysing Atheism: Unbelief and the World of Faiths', in *Bearing the Word: Prophesy in Biblical and Qur'ānic Perspctive*, ed. M. Ipgrave (London: Church House Publishing, 2005), 4–5.

9. Rowan Williams, 'The Deflections of Desire: Negative Theology in Trinitarian Disclosure', in *Silence and the Word: Negative Theology and Incarnation*, eds O. Davies and D. Turner (Cambridge: Cambridge University Press, 2002), 116.

10. This is not a prescriptive statement about where theology should begin, but a tactical move to facilitate the conversation Williams wishes to have. See Rowan Williams, 'God', in *Fields of Faith: Theology and Religious Studies for the Twenty-First Century*, eds D. F. Ford, B. Quash and J. Martin Soskice (Cambridge: Cambridge University Press, 2005), 75.

11. David B. Burrell, *Knowing the Unknowable God: Ibn-Sina, Maimonides, Aquinas* (Notre Dame: Notre Dame Press, 1986), 109.

12. Ibid., 2.

grammar.[13] In his essay, he defends that grammar's lineaments and contends that, for all its negativity, it coheres with that generative agency already spoken of under the analogy of authorship.

Williams acknowledges that what might be termed the classical grammar of God, such as that proposed by Aquinas, is open to question. There is scepticism towards this construction from a robust Trinitarianism that finds any beginning with a treatise *de deo uno* unpalatable, and from those who believe that traditional negations, such as immutability and impassibility, distort God into one who can neither suffer nor empathize with suffering.[14] Yet Williams gives short shrift to the idea of a God who suffers or changes as anything other than 'a rhetorical moment, a conscious deployment of myth'. Taken literally, such language implies for him that creatures are agents 'strictly external' to God, but with the capacity to impinge upon God. God is thereby pulled into the same logical space as creatures, and into potential competition with them. If Williams's analogy of authorship suggests that God is alongside creatures, while not contentiously occupying their space, what this Abrahamic grammar establishes is a *disbelief* in God as something that *can* occupy that space in any simple way. A simply present God who shares our space, being not different enough, would constitute a bad authorship. It could only establish its authorial providence by domineering those whose space it shares. This is a deity that is in need of reflective religion's unbelief. What the interfaith achievement of the traditional grammar of God accomplishes, for Williams, is a difference 'different from all differences'. God, as Nicholas of Cusa puts it, is *non aliud*, literally 'not other'. God is therefore not *an*-other agent among agencies. Only this can protect the integrity of creaturely agencies, allowing them to persist in a non-competitive relationship with God.[15]

The Concept of Non Aliud

Nicholas of Cusa, the fifteenth-century theologian and polymath, is cited both in 'God' and in the *Building Bridges* address. The term Cusa coined, *non aliud* ('not other'), is

13. See Rowan Williams, 'God and Risk (2)', in *The Divine Risk*, ed. R. Holloway (London: Darton, Longman and Todd, 1990), 14–5; Williams's interview in Rupert Shortt, *God's Advocates: Christian Thinkers in Conversation* (London: Darton, Longman and Todd, 2005), 20–1; and Rowan Williams, 'Christians and Muslims before the One God: An Address Given at Al-Azhar Al-Sharīf, Cairo on 11 September 2004', *Islam and Christian-Muslim Relations* 16, no.2 (2005): 187–9. In the latter two pieces, Williams identifies Ibn-Sina, Maimonides and Aquinas as important in this agreement, reflecting Burrell. Cusa has lost the place he had in *Building Bridges*.

14. Williams, 'God', 75–6.

15. Ibid., 83–7.

deployed at multiple points in Williams's work.[16] For him, it 'crystallizes' the intuitions of the earlier medievals,[17] and is a legitimate extrapolation of the grammar defended in 'God'. It is also, for Williams, another idiom in which divine difference finds a voice. The concept of *non aliud* emerges in Cusa's text *De Li Non Aliud*. It is not so much a proper name for God *per se*, but a grammatical conception for thinking about divine difference and presence.[18] Cusa understands it to be consonant with a Dionysian affirmation that God is nothing nameable or patient of conception, not in any way a 'thing'.[19] This negative affirmation, another instance of reflective religion's necessary negative moment, is, in fact, Williams's primary usage of the term – to denote the maximal difference of God from creatures and creaturely agents. He employs it to mark that God is not '*an* other, an item enumerable in a list along with the contents of the universe'.[20] This touches on one of Williams's most fundamental instincts:

> The more carefully you examine the grammar of 'God' in its traditional uses (God as creator, as 'last end' of creation, as Trinity, as source of unconstrained grace and mercy), the more it should be clear that we are not talking about an item in any possible list of objects, but about what is other than the world as such.[21]

However, it is also unfair to Cusa to read *non aliud* as a simple negation.[22] As a concept, it entails a number of (not always easily held-together) things, both

16. See for instance: Rowan Williams, 'Language, Reality and Desire in Augustine's *De Doctrina*', *Journal of Literature and Theology* 3, no.2 (1989): 139–40; 'Deflections of Desire', 121–4; 'Balthasar and the Trinity', in *The Cambridge Companion to Hans Urs von Balthasar*, eds E. T. Oakes and D. Moss (Cambridge: Cambridge University Press, 2004), 44; *Wrestling with Angels: Conversations in Modern Theology* (Cambridge: Eerdmans, 2007), 40, 80.

17. Williams, *Wrestling with Angels*, 51, n.14.

18. Nicholas of Cusa, *Nicholas of Cusa on God as Not-Other: A Translation and Appraisal of De Li Non Aliud*, trans. J. Hopkins (Minneapolis: University of Minneapolis Press, 1979), 2:7, 35.

19. Ibid., 1:5, 33; 17:81–2, 109; 20:94, 121. For the Dionysian flavour of Cusa's thinking, see Peter Casarella, 'Cusanus on Dionysius: The Turn to Speculative Theology', in *Re-Thinking Dionysius the Areopagite*, eds S. Coakley and C. M. Stang (Oxford: Wiley-Blackwell, 2009), 141–6.

20. Williams, *Wrestling with Angels*, 80.

21. Ibid., 212. This quote emerges in an, at times critical, essay on Simone Weil (pp. 203–27). For Williams, her truest instinct is her emphasis on the difference of God from all imaginations, another salutary form of unbelief.

22. This is a point made by von Balthasar, in a volume that Williams helped to translate. For him *non aliud* implies a negation so powerful it transposes itself into an affirmation of presence. See Hans Urs von Balthasar, *The Glory of the Lord: A Theological Aesthetics, Vol. 5: The Realm of Metaphysics in the Modern Age*, trans. O. Davies, et al. (Edinburgh: T&T Clark, 1991), 226–8. See also von Balthasar's *Cosmic Liturgy: The Universe According to Maximus the Confessor*, trans. Brian Daley (San Francisco: Ignatius Press, 2003), 83, for an understanding of Pseudo-Dionysius as a thinker who prefigures Cusa's understanding of divine difference as entailing radical presence. Denys Turner has also argued that Cusa's

positive and negative. It *is* a way of saying that God cannot be construed under the rubric of any comprehended difference, for 'when [Not-other] is sought as an other, it is not at all considered as it is'.[23] This is very much in line with Williams's negative point; God is not just another type of difference in the same category set as creaturely differences. But for Cusa, *non aliud* also denotes that everything has its being and definition from God.[24] Even more, his is a grammatical conception that proposes God as a radical presence to creation, if a presence that cannot be identified with any determinate point *in* creation.[25] Thus, God is not anything in the world (and, to play with the language of *non aliud*, can therefore be spoken of as not *an*-other – connoting maximal difference), but God is also vivifyingly present to everything created (and thus, again to play with the language of *non aliud*, is not-other to anything in the world – connoting maximal presence in divine difference).

If Williams most overtly deploys *non aliud* to make the negative point – that God is not *an*-other within creation – its positive connotations are still entailed in his theological vision.[26] They are implied in the analogy of authorship, where the author is emphatically *not*-other to his or her creations. Characters and narratives have their own integrity, but only through the writer's active presence. They are entirely what the author is doing as an author, but they are *not* the author. The author remains present to all, but different from any, different from any differences *within* the narrative. These positive aspects of *non aliud* are also congruent, as I will make clear in coming discussions of creation and causality, with the interfaith achievement of a divine grammar. It is a grammar in which God, as the generative cause of all things, is intimately present to them, even in absolute distinction from them. This, to Williams, is a fundamental theological instinct in line with the tradition exemplified in Christianity by Aquinas – that 'God is more deeply involved with any creature than we can imagine'.[27]

Things, Signs and Icons

Before exploring this deep divine involvement within creation, another discussion where Williams articulates divine difference needs investigating – his exploration of

grammar of divine difference is 'Dionysian', and passes beyond any creaturely concept of similarity and difference. See his article 'Dionysius and Some Late Medieval Mystical Theologians of Northern Europe', *Modern Theology*, 24:4, 662–4.

23. Cusa, *De Li Non Aliud*, 3:10, 39; see also 20:94, 121.

24. 'Since everything that exists is not other than itself, it does not have this fact from any other. Therefore it has it from Not-other.' Ibid., 3:10, 39.

25. Ibid., 6:20–1, 49–51; See also 22:103, 129–31.

26. In an essay on Balthasar, Williams notes that *non aliud* as a principle implies inexhaustible difference, but also that creation 'is not an independent subject alongside the divine life'. See *Wrestling with Angels*, 80–1.

27. Shortt, *God's Advocates*, 7. Williams cites Herbert McCabe as the inspiration behind this quote. He also sees this Thomist instinct as replicated in Augustinian and Eastern Orthodox thought. See also Burrell, *Knowing the Unknowable God*, 94–5.

the distinction between the concepts of *res* and *signum* in Book I of Augustine's *De Doctrina Christiana*. In a 1989 essay, one of a number of engagements undertaken with Augustine, Williams explores the difference between a *res* as a thing 'not determined by the function of meaning something else', and a *signum* as a thing that has become part of a system of representation. God is 'supremely *res*', 'determined by nothing else, confined by no function, requiring no context or interpretation'. What God is not is *signum*; God is not a term in something else's definition, and does not signify meanings beyond God. As 'supremely *res*', God is everything's context, and nothing is God's. But, paradoxically, God is also, in another sense, not *res* at all. In Williams's reading of Augustine, God is not a thing in a series of things, and is, therefore, '*non aliud* as later theological tradition would put it'.[28]

Augustine's grammar of the divine is thus, in Williams's mind, explicitly linked with Cusa's, emphasizing the negative point of maximal difference, that God is not *an*-other thing.[29] Augustine is thus read as in tune with that religious sensibility which disbelieves in a truthful construal of the divine that can be positively articulated. God is 'beyond all naming', and Williams deems it a legitimate extrapolation of Augustine to say that 'no *signum* is adequate to his being'.[30] Yet, there are also intimations in Williams's reading of Augustine of that positive immanence *non aliud* connotes. God is still every other thing's context; and there is also what Williams reads Augustine as going on to say in relation to the incarnation – that 'God is *res*, and, in respect of him, all else is *signum*'. First of all, the Incarnate Word, a *res* within history, is God's authorized *signum* that 'manifests the essential quality of the world itself as "sign" or trace of its maker'. But in the light of the incarnation, the entire manifold of creation then comes to open out into what Williams calls 'restless fluidities of meaning', so that 'no *res* is left alone. It can be used, and so become a sign; it can mean what it is not'.[31] Arguably, a world where no *thing* is left alone, and where everything points beyond itself, becoming (quite literally) *significant* of God, is one marked by a certain species of immanence.

An illustrative way of thinking through this grammar of *res* and *signum* is through parallels to be found in Williams's discussions of icons. Noting the oddity, considering biblical prohibitions in such matters, of the development of a tradition of Christian sacred imagery, Williams points to iconography's Christological warrant. It was to God circumscribed in humanity that defenders of icons looked for their legitimation.[32] This Christological authorization can be mapped within

28. Williams, 'Language, Reality and Desire', 138–40.

29. See also ibid., 147.

30. Ibid., 139–40. Augustine rules out even the negative affirmation that God is 'inexpressible' as saying too much. See Augustine, *Teaching Christianity (De Doctrina Christiana)*, trans. E. Hill (New York: New City Press, 1996), I.6, 108.

31. Williams, 'Language, Reality and Desire', 140–1.

32. Rowan Williams, *The Dwelling of the Light: Praying with the Icons of Christ* (Norwich: Canterbury Press, 2003), xiii–xvi. See also 'A History of Faith in Jesus', in *The Cambridge Companion to Jesus*, ed. M. Bockmuehl (Cambridge: Cambridge University Press, 2001), 224–5.

the same conceptual field as the authorization found in Augustine for rendering the whole manifold of existents as *signa*. The incarnation summons things in the world towards restless fluidity, to point beyond themselves; icons are an especially pointed instance of this signification.

Williams strikingly implies that, in their fluidity, icons are (at least in a certain sense) not objects. They are surfaces to look *through,* opening out towards an excess beyond themselves.[33] They do not 'occupy a space *alongside*' the viewer; nor, in a way, do they share the same dimensional world.[34] What Williams comes close to saying is that icons are things slipping the bounds of their quality as *res*, by virtue of the fact that they are consummately significant. They are arguably physical parables of the divine *non aliud*, of maximal difference and presence co-inhering – becoming not *an*-other object in the world, while continuing to be *not*-other to the world. They invite a turn to the physical parable of the incarnation that authorizes them. Thus, discussions of Cusa, Augustine's *res-signum* distinction, and icons all share a family resemblance. They reflect a grammar of divine difference in which God is not an entity within the world, and yet is the context of all. Everything comes to signify the One who is truly *res* without being a *res*.

A 'Postmodern' Diversion – Différance *and de Certeau*

In his essay on *De doctrina*, Williams points to affinities between his reading of Augustine and the insights of 'postmodern' literary criticism. His Augustine might even agree that there is no 'absolute knowledge', only 'an interminable web of texts': 'In the sense that no worldly *res* is securely settled as a fixed object "meaning" itself, or tied to a fixed designation, that no worldly state of affairs can be allowed to terminate human desire, that all that is present to us in and as language is potentially *signum* in respect of the unrepresentable God.'[35] This 'postmodern' Augustine is commented upon by Jeffrey McCurry. He sees in Williams an inscription of Derrida's *différance* into Augustine that enables the saint to say more than he could have intended. While not Augustine's *ipsissima verba*, the result is a genuinely Augustinian performance, part of a Christian tradition of reperforming

---

33. See Williams, *Dwelling of the Light*, xvii-xviii; *Grace and Necessity,* 69; *Dostoevsky,* 206–7. An early intimation of this may be found in Williams's article 'Christian Art and Cultural Pluralism: Reflections on *L'art De L'icone*, by Paul Evdokimov', *Eastern Churches Review* 8, no. 1 (1976), 39.

34. Rowan Williams, *Lost Icons: Reflections on Cultural Bereavement* (Edinburgh: T&T Clark, 2000), 186. A negative counterpoint to this non-objectivity of icons may be found in statues, generally disapproved of in Eastern Orthodox tradition. Far from being surfaces, they are definite three-dimensional objects. See Williams, *Dwelling of the Light,* xviii.

35. Williams, 'Language, Reality and Desire', 145.

canonical texts in new contexts.[36] McCurry cites a personal conversation with Williams as authority for Derrida's importance,[37] but nowhere in the 1989 essay is Derrida actually mentioned.[38] However, when Williams revisits the theme of *res* and *signum* in a later essay, another twentieth-century French thinker is – Michel de Certeau.[39] And, in the previously mentioned essay 'God', de Certeau is used to voice divine difference in yet another register, making a Cusan point in a contemporary idiom.[40]

For Williams, 'more than any other recent analyst of religious language', de Certeau opens a way into making fresh sense of the classical conception of God.[41] He describes a contemporary trauma for Christianity, in that the church no longer instantiates a robust ecclesial body to support its own discourse. As this body experiences dissolution, so does the power of its speech.[42] As this occurs, notes

---

36. Jeffrey McCurry, 'Towards a Poetics of Theological Creativity: Rowan Williams Reads Augustine's *De Doctrina* after Derrida', *Modern Theology* 23, no. 3 (2007), 418–9. McCurry's intuition is consonant with Williams's view of the relation between theological innovation and tradition. Williams has never been a mere theological conservationist. For him, axiomatic theological intuitions and canonical texts must be reperformed in new contexts, answering new questions, to maintain theology's vitality. The first part of his theological postscript to the monograph on Arius offers an eloquent explication of this understanding (see *Arius: Heresy and Tradition*, 2nd ed. [London: SCM, 2001] 233–9). However, James Andrews has argued that Williams, at least in this reading of Augustine, is in danger of turning the Bishop of Hippo into 'a twentieth- and twenty-first-century philosopher dressed in a toga' and effacing the challenge of Augustine's voice when heard on its own historical terms. See James Andrews, 'Relevant Augustine: What *De Doctrina Christiana* Says Today' in *Studia Patristica*, vol. 50, ed. A. Brent and M. Vinzent (Leuven: Peeters, 2011), 309–20, and *Hermeneutics and the Church: In Dialogue with Augustine* (Notre Dame: Notre Dame University Press, 2012), 45–6, 88–9.

37. McCurry, 'Towards a Poetics of Theological Creativity', 432, n. 28.

38. Elsewhere Williams is quite critical of Derrida. See, especially, his essay 'Hegel and the gods of postmodernity', in *Wrestling with Angels*, 25–34.

39. 'Augustine's Christology: Its Spirituality and Rhetoric', in *In the Shadow of the Incarnation: Essays on Jesus Christ in the Early Church in Honor of Brian E. Daley, S.J.*, ed. P. W. Martens (Notre Dame: University of Notre Dame Press, 2007), 178–9. de Certeau has been an important dialogue partner for Williams. See his coy comments in his essay 'Theology in the Twentieth Century', in *A Century of Theological and Religious Studies in Britain*, ed. E. Nicholson (Oxford: Oxford University Press, 2003), 250.

40. De Certeau has written on Cusa. See 'The Gaze: Nicholas of Cusa', *Diacritics* 17, no. 3 (1987), 2–38.

41. Williams, 'God', 83.

42. Michel de Certeau, 'The Weakness of Believing: From the Body to Writing, a Christian Transit', in *The Certeau Reader*, ed. G. Ward (Oxford: Blackwell, 2000), 215–8. F. C. Bauerschmidt has queried what he reads as de Certeau's overwrought language of the dissolution of the ecclesial body. See his article 'The Abrahamic Voyage: Michel De Certeau and Theology', *Modern Theology* 12, no. 1 (1996), 20. This criticism is noted by Williams in 'God', 82.

Williams, the explanations of religious phenomena become colonized by other discourses – social, psychological and scientific. With its weakened explanatory power, religious speech becomes equivocal in relation to them. Yet, reality cannot be exhaustively described by these secular discourses:

> No discourse can offer a systematic way of relating the regions of thought to each other. Thus the 'real' is, says de Certeau, always receding, always 'lacking' … the lack which is marked in scientific discourse is not a gap capable of being filled, because the 'un-said', the not-yet-thought, is something quite other than a specific problem within the system.

Thus there is an evasive 'un-said' behind all speech, and the job of theological speech is 'to understand its own difference' from secular discourses and point to that 'un-said', an otherness every discourse confronts but cannot encompass. What theology must not do is bring 'hidden things to light' by trying to make that un-said sayable within the world's processes. To transpose this into idioms already discussed – there is some 'thing', or *res,* un-said and unsayable, which is signified by the things of the world, and perhaps even *not*-other to them. Secular discourses, because they deal in worldly things as the sum total of the sayable, are thus destabilized. Whatever their intention, they signify beyond themselves towards 'an otherness that is always being assimilated and always escaping and repositioning itself'.[43] To try and bring the un-said into the domain of sayable things is to mistakenly attempt to render that which is *non aliud* as *an*-other in a series.

Difference in Creation and Causality

There is one more discussion to be pursued as a locus for that maximal difference of God from creation, which is also a maximal presence to creation. Burrell has marked how deeply God's difference, as conceived in Aquinas's synthesis and explored in the discussions of an interfaith grammar, is bound up with the doctrine of creation. As God alone is self-subsistent *esse* or existence – and, thus, in unqualified difference from creation – God alone is the possibility of every other's existence. And, in giving each creature its existence, God is intimately present to it as its generative cause.[44] This is a form of creaturely participation in God's 'inexhaustible act of existing', in which there is an 'inherent link' between all creatures and their creator.[45] Thus, as mentioned earlier, this Thomist vision is

43. Williams, 80–1. Indented block quote from p. 81, where Williams is citing de Certeau's *La faiblesse de criore* (Paris: Seuil, 1987), 198.

44. Burrell, *Knowing the Unknowable God,* 94–5, 108.

45. David Burrell, *Towards a Jewish-Christian-Muslim Theology* (Oxford: Wiley-Blackwell, 2014), 21–2.

one wherein 'God is more deeply involved with any creature than we can imagine'. A very distinct concept of the difference of God is implied in this doctrine of creation. This God is both not *an*-other to creatures in unqualified difference, and yet still *not*-other to everything created. Both directions of intimation within the concept of *non aliud*, of difference and deep presence, are entailed.

This distinct concept of difference is reflected in Williams's own understanding of the doctrine of creation *ex nihilo*. It is a doctrine he defends, in the essay 'On Being Creatures' (1989), from criticisms that it portrays a God whose difference to creation is *un*-generative because it implies distance and hierarchy.[46] *Pace* such criticisms, creation cannot be an exercise in hierarchical domination because, without it, there is nothing to dominate. Rather, 'Creation affirms that to be here at all, to be part of this natural order and be the sort of thing capable of being named – or of having a role – is "of God"; it *is* because God wants it so'.[47] But for Williams, the real error of such criticism is that, for all its concern about difference coded as distance and domination, it fails to see that a God who dominates *is not different enough*. This is an intuition Williams affirms in an essay on Augustine's doctrine of creation. Hierarchy is an *intra*-systemic problem, but a God who is not *an*-other in the same frame of reference cannot jostle for dominance with creatures. Rather, 'the creative power of God is not exercised unilaterally over some other force, but is itself the ground of all power and all agency within creation'.[48] There are, as implied in the discussions of 'God', no 'strictly external' agencies that can sensibly be in competition with a God internal to every agent as its possibility to be.

This different frame God inhabits in relation to creatures can be understood as a different mode of causality. This emerges in a 1996 essay, where Williams critiques Marilyn McCord Adams's construal of divine agency; it is to him insufficiently different. To Williams, her vision of divine action in creation is reactive and episodic, consisting of multiple interventions determined by contexts other than God. God is, thereby, drawn into the causal give and take of contingency, *an*-other cause in a series. He contrasts this with Aquinas's identification of God's act and being. Their co-inherence implies that God *is* an eternal singularity of

---

46. Williams, *On Christian Theology* (Oxford: Blackwell, 2000), 64–7. Williams mentions the critiques of Ruether and MacFague, both of whom read traditional accounts of creation as implying too extrinsic a relation between God and the world, a relation like that of an artisan to the object of his or her making. Creation is thus understood under the rubric of the projection of 'cultural power', a mindset in part responsible for our ecological crisis. Williams questions this reading of the artist–creation relation (66), and the idea of authorship already traced in this chapter would itself seem to undermine that particular form of artistry as an external projection of power. For a parallel engagement with MacFague, see ' "Good for Nothing?" Augustine on Creation', in *Doctrinal Diversity: Varieties of Early Christianity*, ed. Everett Ferguson, *Recent Studies in Early Christianity* (New York: Garland, 1999), 32–3, 39–43.

47. Williams, *On Christian Theology*, 68–9.

48. Williams, 'Good for Nothing?', 41.

active existence, generatively grounding all creaturely agencies but modified by none. God is, therefore, not found in the field of action and passion as *an*-other cause, even an especially potent or prescient one, but is the possibility of that field's dependent existence.[49] The God whose act and being are coterminous, the same God who is self-subsistent *esse*, does not share creaturely space, nor dwell in coordinates within any mappable causal manifold. Thus God's is a difference *beyond* distance, for distance still implies a shared spatial field. But this difference beyond distance passes over into a presence to creaturely space. God is *not*-other to it as its possibility for being. It is the absoluteness of that difference which enables its relation with creation to be generative. Maximal difference is what makes possible a non-invasive and non-competitive maximal presence.[50]

The God who creates *ex nihilo* is the one for whom, as Williams said in his letter to a child, 'there was nothing and nobody around before me to invent me'. This God is different, present and no impingement; for the God who creates out of nothing is the 'God who does not want to be Everything'.[51] Creation has an integrity secured by divine difference. But it is an integrity to which the eternal act of being God is *not*-other – and this returns us to the authorial analogy, where God is likened to an authorship alongside, but not competing with, his characters. A good writer does not wish to be 'Everything'. He or she does not impose himself or herself upon the text, but is a 'patient presence'.[52] Good authors allow the artefacts of imagination to emerge. Williams goes as far as to imply that the divine Author is not an interventionist in creation, if what that means is being an agent responding piecemeal to creaturely actions and sharing their 'logical space'.[53] Like O'Connor, God does not interrupt his narrative to interject meaning. But this begs a Christological question, for the interjection of meaning into the narrative of creation, in a life dense with the Author's presence, is implied in the incarnation. Also implied is a certain sort of becoming *an*-other in the manifold of creaturely causality, a sharing of our space. The one who, in *Dostoevsky*, 'does not appear as a character in any simple sense', has become one with unique intensity. What I will suggest by the end of this chapter is that the grammar of difference laid out so far is one that both complicates and makes possible this Christological becoming in

---

49. Williams, *Wrestling with Angels*, 266–8. Williams here draws on another work by Burrell, *Aquinas: God and Action* (London: Routledge & Keegan Paul, 1979).

50. This seems to be the force of Kathryn Tanner's argument in *God and Creation in Christian Theology: Tyranny or Empowerment?* (Oxford: Blackwell, 1988). In her vision of the 'non-contrastive transcendence' encoded into the logic of Christian theology, there is a need 'to radicalize claims about both God's transcendence and involvement with the world if the two are to work for rather than against one another' (46).

51. Williams, *On Christian Theology*, 74–5; see also 105. Williams is quoting J.Pohier, and cites *God in Fragments*, (London: SCM, 1985), 266ff.

52. Williams, *Dostoevsky*, 138.

53. Williams, *Wrestling with Angels*, 269. See also *Writing in the Dust: After September 11* (Grand Rapids, MI: Eerdmans, 2002), 8.

an-other human life – a life to which God is consummately *not*-other. However, before exploring this, we will examine the refraction and intensification of divine difference that occurs for Williams within the doctrine of the Trinity.

De Deo Trino

If the exploration of an intra-Abrahamic grammar found agreement around a treatise *de deo uno*, Williams also offers an important Christian and Trinitarian reworking of that grammar. The *Trinitarian* God is *non aliud* – not *an*-other to, and yet *not*-other to, maximally present to, and yet maximally different from even God-self. Divine difference does not persist simply in relation to creation. It is internally encoded for Williams into the life of God conceived of as Father, Son and Holy Spirit. Two essays are pivotal to this discussion: 'The Deflections of Desire: Negative Theology and Trinitarian Disclosure' (2002),[54] and 'What Does Love Know? St Thomas on the Trinity' (2001).[55] Both essays begin with a problem, a perceived potential failure by important figures within the Christian tradition to maintain a proper and rigorous Trinitarianism.

In 'Deflections of Desire', Williams argues that by the fourth and fifth centuries, the negative moment in Christian theology, that unbelief elsewhere inherent in reflective religion, had come to focus on 'the idea that the divine essence constituted the mysterious heartland of the Godhead'. This was especially, argues Williams, the case in Cappadocian thought. A potential implication from this development *could* be that an ineffable *ousia* or divine essence comes to be seen as the incommunicable un-said *behind* the persons. This could fracture Trinitarian discourse off into a secondary level of speech, separate from talk of God *proper*.[56] A breach would

54. First given as a lecture in Birmingham in 1999.

55. Myers (*Christ the Stranger*, 85) mentions both of these essays as part of an exegesis of the Trinity he calls Williams's 'most important scholarly contribution throughout his years as Archbishop of Canterbury'. However, the essays were written *before* Williams came to Canterbury.

56. Williams, 'Deflections of Desire', 115–7. Williams, in fact, argues that the Cappadocians forestalled this danger. For a rather sympathetic reading of Nazianzen on the unknowability of God, see Williams's ' "Is It the Same God?" Reflections on Continuity and Identity in Religious Language', in *The Possibilities of Sense*, ed. J. H. Whittaker (Basingstoke: Palgrave, 2002), 206–8. However, to Williams, the later Palamite tradition had not been so careful. The detachment of a prior divine interiority from the Trinitarian economy, ontologically privileging the former, is diagnosed by him within Palamism. Palamas is read as the victim of a Neo-Platonic tendency to ontologically prioritize inparticipatable essence, whereas the post-Nicene tradition was inflected by a corrective Aristotelianism. See the early essay by Williams, 'The Philosophical Structures of Palamism', *Eastern Churches Review* IX:1–2 (1977), 32–9. Its argument is foreshadowed in Williams's doctoral thesis ('The Theology of Vladimir Nikolaievich Lossky: An Exposition and Critique' [Doctoral Thesis, University

thus open up between talk of God in God-self, and God as God is known through the persons in the economy of salvation. A similar potential loss of Trinitarian perspective is also pointed to in the opening of 'What does love know?' Williams there cites the charge that Aquinas unduly separates theological knowledge of the one creator God from the knowledge of God as Trinity.[57] Thus, both essays begin with the suspicion of a disjunction between God's essential oneness and Trinitarian discourse. Williams, however, seeks to dispel these suspicions, defending Thomas and, in 'Deflections', arguing that theological negativity cannot be confined to the divine essence, but pertains to the persons.[58] Both essays voice a theology of the Trinity that intensifies and re-nuances the grammar of God's difference.

The Spirit as a 'Second Difference'

In 'Deflections', Williams inscribes the difference of God into the entirety of the Trinitarian life by going through that most negative of Christian mystics, John of the Cross.[59] The pivot point of Williams's argument is what he calls, in a turn of phrase borrowed from John Milbank, the 'second difference' of the Spirit.[60] The Spirit is cast in the essay as the 'excess' of love and mutual desire between the Father and the Son, an excess which itself constitutes a third presence in the divine life. It is the Spirit, as a second moment of difference, subsequent to but co-eternal

of Oxford, 1975], Chapter 6 *passim*. There the critique includes Lossky's usage of Palamas (for more on Lossky and Palamas, see Vladimir Lossky, *The Mystical Theology of the Eastern Church*, trans. Fellowship of St Alban and St Sergius [London: James Clarke, 1957], 76–89). The problematic tendency towards primordial oneness in Neo-Platonism also plays a role in Williams's critique of Arius's theology (*Arius*, 242–3), and is an element in Williams's softer critique of Pseudo-Dionysius (see *The Wound of Knowledge: Christian Spirituality from the New Testament to St John of the Cross*, 2nd Rev. edn. [London: Darton, Longman and Todd, 1990] 121–2).

57. Williams, 'What Does Love Know? St Thomas on the Trinity', *New Blackfriars* 82:964 (2001) 260–1. Williams cites Catharine Mowry LaCugna as an example of this tendency.

58. Williams, 'Deflections of Desire', 117.

59. Williams begins with John's versified meditations in the *Romanzas*. For other discussions of these poems, see his *Open to Judgement: Sermons and Addresses* (London: Darton, Longman and Todd, 1994), 274–9 and *Choose Life: Christmas and Easter Sermons in Canterbury Cathedral* (London: Bloomsbury, 2013), 50–2. Elsewhere he notes that the 'controlling theme' of John's writing is that 'God is not the same as anything else' (*The Wound of Knowledge*, 165–6). John is also mentioned in *Arius* (242–3), along with the Cappadocians, Maximus the Confessor and Aquinas, as one who practised an apophaticism that avoided focusing on the primordial essence of God.

60. Williams ('Deflections of Desire', 118, n.6) borrows the phrase from Milbank's essay 'The Second Difference', in *The Word Made Strange: Theology, Language and Culture* (Oxford: Blackwell, 1997), 171–93.

with the first difference between the Father and the Son, who keeps the divine life from imploding into a 'mutual reinforcement of identity' between the Father and Son. The Trinity is, thus, not a 'closed mutuality' between a dyadic pair, but always opens out into a 'further otherness' in which love and desire are constantly 'deflected' between the persons.[61] This is a movement where intra-divine desire never finds a terminus, and the persons never become, in a certain sense, *objects* to one another: 'In the life of God, love is always deflected from the "object" that would close or satisfy, that would simply be the absent other imagined as the goal of desire; the other is always engaged beyond, engaged with another otherness.'[62]

This language of slipping objectivity, and opening out into a further otherness marked as excess, recalls the earlier discussion of icons. Considering the reality icons attempt to render, this is not accidental. Nor is it accidental that a visual portrayal of what Williams is articulating is found, for him, in Rublev's icon of the three angels at the Oaks of Mamre, usually taken as a representation of the Trinity. The observant viewer is drawn in that icon into an endless interplay of glances between these figures. There is no cessation of that movement, and no figure is ever fixed as an object, as none of the three (partially averted) faces can be gazed upon in full. Rather, each gazes onwards to the next, retaining an elusiveness even as they are beheld. Importantly, this icon is also a depiction of hospitality, wherein the viewer is invited to sit at the table and be caught up in this continuous interplay. The implication is that the Trinity is a movement of deflected desire to be participated in.[63]

However, returning to John of the Cross, when this interplay is inscribed through participation into the life of a contemplative, its mode is that of a 'dark night' whose prototype is found in Jesus's loss of the Father in the dereliction. As the self seeks God, who is 'no determinate object', it becomes bereft of anything tangible that might reinforce its sense of self. For Williams, this loss of consolation in discernible objects, even in God, 'is how the *non aliud* of God's difference is concretely encountered *because* this is the *non aliud* of the presence of the

---

61. Williams, 'Deflections of Desire', 118f. See also Milbank ('The Second Difference', 188), where the Spirit is the 'reflective interval' that prevents the Father–Son dyad from collapsing into a problematic sameness. For both Williams and Milbank, the Spirit sustains difference in the Trinity and, as Myers (*Christ the Stranger*, 85–6) puts it, 'rescues God from narcissistic collapse'. This is a point Williams has also made in relation to Bulgakov in his *A Margin of Silence: The Holy Spirit in Russian Orthodox Theology/Une Marge De Silence: L'esprit Saint Dans La Théologie Orthodoxe Russe* (Québec: Éditions du Lys Vert, 2008), 22–3, and (inchoately) in his doctoral work ('The Theology of Vladimir Nikolaievich Lossky', 185–8). Sarah Coakley has recently expressed a similar intuition, but with a corrective caution against seeing the Spirit as a subordinate function of a prior dyad. See *God, Sexuality, and the Self: An Essay 'on the Trinity'* (Cambridge: Cambridge University Press, 2013), 55–8, 330–4.

62. Williams, 'Deflections of Desire', 121–2.

63. Ibid., 128–9. See the parallel discussion in Williams, *Dwelling of the Light*, 45–63.

Trinitarian persons to each other'.[64] And this is the crux – the non-objectivity of the Trinitarian persons to one another, divine desire's unceasing deflection, is how God is *non aliud* to God-self, not *an*-other object even to God.[65] There is an eternal movement and interplay of difference *within* God prior to any divine difference in relation to creation, and not dependent on any account of a pre-Trinitarian essence. Elsewhere, in the context of another discussion of Rublev's icon, the possibility of such an essence is, in fact, discounted: 'There is no static and detached "divine nature" somewhere beyond the active love that is God. God is threefold relationship, God is the love that welcomes us, and there is, in one all-important sense, nothing more we need to know of God.'[66] To say that God is *non aliud* is more than a statement that God is not one of a series of objects to be conceptualized or located in the world. It is a claim that an unending difference, and therefore, in some sense, a maximal difference inheres in God.

Love and Knowledge

In 'What does love know?' Williams recapitulates aspects of the argument in 'Deflections', and, again, the pivot point is a pneumatological second difference. In Williams's reading of Aquinas, the two processions of the Trinity, Word and Spirit, are analogous to an inseparable double procession of intellect and love in human knowing. The intellectual procession involves the repetition of the object known, as *verbum* or image, within the knowing subject. The object of knowledge is, thereby, present to the subject in a form of intellectual participation. In the analogous procession of the Word – the *verbum* or image of the Father – God becomes present to, and reflexively knowing of, God-self. The Father, in the generation of the Son, comprehends 'what is involved in the divine life, generating in himself that participatory image of otherness that is the effect of the act of understanding'.[67]

But this dynamic of participatory presence is not simply repeated in the second procession of knowing, the procession of the will or love. No equivalent *verbum* is established in the subject. Rather, what is produced is an inclination in which the object persists in the subject only as a provocation to desire. If intellectual knowledge is marked by the continuity of a participatory presence, love or will has to do with evocative discontinuity, the knowledge that the object is inclined towards but not possessed. The Spirit, understood analogously to this second procession, thus signifies that God has a more oblique and elusive self-presence in a second mode. This is the excess of the first self-presence, an accompanying longing

64. Williams, 'Deflections of Desire', 121.

65. This point is also alluded to in the essay 'Trinity and Ontology' (1989): 'God is "other to himself" or "himself in the other" in the differences of the persons' (Williams, *On Christian Theology*, 165). Notably, Milbank's 'second difference' is again cited.

66. Williams, *Dwelling of the Light*, 73.

67. Williams, 'What Does Love Know?' 262–4.

within God.[68] Perfect participation within the divine life then persists alongside an endless 'invitation' and 'stimulus of difference', as if God were both utterly known and utterly strange to God-self.[69] In this reading of Thomas, the Spirit is again a second difference, which introduces deflection into the self-knowing of God, an eternal inclination towards that which is both present and evasive.

The Non Aliud *of the Trinity*

In 'Deflections', Williams works out a Trinitarian grammar that refracts the negative moment throughout the Trinity's life, as opposed to locating it in some primal essence. God is not *an*-other object, even to God; God is potentially maximally different from God and within God. In 'What Does Love Know?', however, the more positive connotations of the grammar of *non aliud* are incipiently encompassed. God is *not*-other, in the Word, to God-self, present as image or *verbum* in the Father's self-knowing. Yet, lest that positive '*not*-other' implode into sameness, the Spirit again introduces an elusive non-objectivity. God is thus, to God, both participatory object and desired non-object, present and yet allusive.

This refraction through the Trinity intensifies the difference of God, but it also modulates it. If a pre-relational essence remained the locus of negativity, then what is potentially posited out of such an understanding is a God who is a simple self-identity behind the modal mask of the persons. Such a God could be not *an*-other to creatures, maximally different from them, but the divine interiority itself would arguably collapse into self-sameness. Williams's reading forestalls this possibility, and a mystery of negativity permeates the *intra*-divine life. Mystery goes all the way down, but so too does intimacy. The Word is *not*-other to the Father, a non-identical repetition of identity that also authorizes a known-ness to creation. In Williams's reading of Aquinas, the generation of the Word encompasses the generation of all possible relations with what is not God.[70] As noted in the discussions of Augustine and icons, the Word becomes an object, even a *res*, within creation that is so consummately significant that it invites all of creation to be caught up in signification. This is a becoming that would be impossible for God coded as a self-identical yet unknowable hinterland *behind* the persons[71] – and this leads our discussions into the questions of Christology.

The Possibility of Christ

We began with a discussion of Williams's conception of divine difference under the analogy of authorship. Christologically speaking, this 'Author' has become

---

68. Ibid., 264–5.
69. Ibid., 271.
70. Williams, 'What Does Love Know?', 263–4.
71. This is, in part, the burden of Williams's critique of Arius. See *Arius*, 243–4.

a character in the narrative with a unique intensity. But, *prima facie*, becoming *an*-other character seems inconsistent with the grammar of God as *non aliud* – and, in *Dostoevsky*, Williams seems to preclude this Author becoming a character in any 'simple sense'. This is a problem. God being *an*-other within the field of action and passion, *not*-other to a particular human life, is what is implied in the incarnation. The concluding part of this chapter will argue that, for Williams, it is counter-intuitively his conception of the difference of God that makes a sensible Christology possible, even while complicating that possibility.

To return to the discussion of creation and causality, and the critical dialogue with McCord Adams, Williams asserts there that 'God is never going to be an element, a square centimetre, in any picture, not because God's agency is incalculably greater but because it simply cannot be fitted into the same space'. But this assertion has a Christological supplement, an intuition 'that the presence of the Word as incarnate in Jesus should in no sense be conceived as "competing" with the full created subjectivity or identity-as-subject of Jesus'.[72] Just as God does not, in general, jostle with creatures for space, so the Word and Jesus's human subjectivity do not competitively occupy 'a square centimetre' of the same ground, even while being present in the same person. This is a point made from a different angle in the closing section of Williams's book, *Lost Icons*. The presence of the divine agency 'without qualification within the material identity of one historical agent (Jesus Christ)' is a presence that is not 'in *any* way like that of one other subject in the system'.[73] It is the absolute difference of God, as not *an*-other 'subject in the system' that enables God to be *not*-other to Jesus – to be in that fully human life, and yet not competitively in the same space as that humanity. This intuition can also be traced in two essays written decades apart: ' "Person" and "Personality" in Christology' (1976), and 'Augustine's Christology: Its Spirituality and Rhetoric' (2007).

Person and Personality

In ' "Person" and "Personality" ', a younger Williams endeavours to defend the tradition of Christology stemming from Chalcedon from a criticism by Anthony Hanson that it denies Jesus a properly human personality. In affirming that Jesus's *hypostasis*, or 'person', is that of the Word, this tradition comes to construe his human nature as consequently, in some sense, *anhypostatic*, as persisting without its own *hypostasis*.[74] Hanson understands this to imply that Jesus's humanity is

---

72. Williams, *Wrestling with Angels*, 270.

73. Williams, *Lost Icons*, 182.

74. Some caution should be reserved about the use of '*anhypostatic*' to characterize the Chalcedonian tradition. In John of Damascus, the more positive *enhypostatos* – implying a humanity with no *hypostasis* of its own, but positively subsisting in the *hypostasis* of the Word – is preferred (See U. M. Lang, 'Anhypostatos-Enhypostatos: Church Fathers, Protestant Orthodoxy and Karl Barth', *Journal of Theological Studies* 49:2 [1998], 648–57).

thus 'impersonal'. Williams concedes that this would be a serious problem; it could imply no recognizable 'internal history' or human psychology in Jesus, something (properly) incredible to our contemporary ears. However, he crucially argues that Hanson makes an error in equating the lack of a human *hypostasis* with the lack of a human 'personality'.[75]

For Williams, the concept of a *hypostasis* should be understood as something akin to Aristotle's primary substance. More obscure than an individual thing as it is known, the primary substance of an entity is its 'unique ground', its 'terminus' of predication, but something itself beyond all predication.[76] Read in this light, *hypostasis* or 'personhood' implies something like a mysterious 'unitary form of subjectivity' or 'ultimate ground of continuous identity'. It is conceptually distinct from 'personality', understood as the ensemble of truths about a person's mental life. A personality is not the ultimate ground of individuation; that is the *hypostasis*. Personality is predicable to a person, but personhood is *more* than personality; it is the ground that makes personality possible.[77]

To say, for Williams, that the *hypostasis* of Jesus is that of the Word is thus *not* to say that Jesus had no recognizably human personality. It is, rather, to deny that his humanity, including its personality, has an existence separable from the Word as its ultimate ground. The Word, as the 'person' of Jesus, is the effective possibility of his full human agency – its potential to be. Although this is not claimed in the essay, in one sense the incarnation is then an acute example of how Williams elsewhere envisions God's generative relation to creatures. God is intimately present and internal to every creature as its possibility; there *are* no agencies strictly external to God. In Jesus, this general reality is hyperbolically and exceptionally so, in a 'confrontation with a whole existence somehow permeated with "difference" despite the ordinariness of its details'.[78]

Daley argues that *anhypostatic* as a term does not come into its own until the sixteenth century, and that the ascription *anhypostatos* was taken by the late Patristics as potentially implying the *non*-existence of Jesus's humanity (see 'Anhypostasy', in *Encyclopaedia of Christian Theology*, ed. Jean-Yves Lacoste [London: Routledge, 2005], 40–1). For John of Damascus, Christ's humanity does not 'lack subsistence' (*oude anhupostatos estin*), even if it is only had in the Word. See *Exposition of the Orthodox Faith*, in *Nicene and Post-Nicene Fathers Series Two, Volume IX*, eds P Schaff and H. Wace (Grand Rapids: Eerdmanns, 1988–91), 3.9, 668. Greek transliterated from Lang's (650) citation.

75. Rowan Williams, ' "Person" and "Personality" in Christology', *The Downside Review*, 94 (1976) 253–5. Williams criticizes Lossky for a similar error in 'The Theology of Vladimir Nikolaievich Lossky', 106–10.

76. Williams, ' "Person' and "Personality" ', 255. Williams acknowledges his debt here to Donald MacKinnon's 'Aristotle's Conception of Substance', in *New Essays on Plato and Aristotle*, ed. R. Bambrough (London: Routledge & Kegan Paul, 1965), 97–119.

77. Williams, ' "Person "and "Personality" ', 255–7.

78. Ibid., 257–8.

Augustine's Christology

The term *anhypostatic,* which Williams defends in ' "Person" and "Personality" ', is deployed by him elsewhere in the context of arguing that 'God is what is constitutive of the particular identity of Jesus', and that *outside* of that constitution, his humanity is an 'impersonal' abstraction.[79] In the essay 'Augustine's Christology', Williams undertakes a parallel exploration of what could be termed an Alexandrian vision, but paradoxically through the most famously Latin of theologians.[80] In doing so, he comes to replicate much of the logic found in the earlier ' "Person" and "Personality" '.

Williams reads book IV of Augustine's *De trinitate* as:

> in effect an anticipation of the scholastic notion that the humanity of Christ is distinct not because of an extra element alongside the human soul and body (as if the incarnate Word were part of a threefold complex of equipollent parts) but because the soul-body compound is in this case completely animated and individuated by a single divine agency.[81]

This is consonant with the *anhypostatic* understanding of Williams's earlier work; a humanity 'completely animated and individuated' by the Word is a psychosomatic unity whose generative ground is the second person of the Trinity. Without that ground, what is left is an inanimate and un-individuated abstraction, something with no *hypostasis,* no subsistence of its own.

When Williams turns to Augustine's use of *persona,* the Latin equivalent of *hypostasis,* further echoes emerge. *Persona* in Augustine, he argues, is a 'flexible' and 'analogically complex term', employed to identify the speaking agent. Deployed in terms of Christology, it can have multiple meanings. Jesus's vocalizations of distress in the Gospels are 'spoken in the *persona* of a fully vulnerable member of the human race', a particular human subject in history. In the Psalms, for Augustine, Christ himself also speaks in the *persona* of the general human condition, even in its distressing alienation from God. But crucially, 'the entire phenomenon that is the Word incarnate invariably speaks for the *persona* of divine Wisdom, since it is the action of divine Wisdom that creates the divine-human grammatical subject

---

79. See Williams, *On Christian Theology,* 156–7, 188. MacKinnon's 'Prolegomena to Christology' is cited as an exposition of this view that approaches 'classical status'. The term *anhypostatic* does not appear in that essay, but what is affirmed is that God is the subject of the incarnation, and the humanity assumed 'is constituted by an openness to the divine so uniquely thoroughgoing … that it is rendered in itself impersonal' (*Themes in Theology: The Three-Fold Cord* [Edinburgh: T&T Clark, 1987], 172–3, 178).

80. Williams (in 'Augustine's Christology', 177, 188) claims that Augustine's theology has a 'Cyrilline' structure.

81. Ibid., 180.

we hear speaking in Christ'.[82] Thus Wisdom, by which Augustine understands the second person of the Trinity, is the foundational identity, or *persona*, of the human being Jesus, a way of speaking that recalls the Word constituting his *hypostasis*. The answer to the question 'Who is speaking?' when directed at Jesus, is Wisdom. But this 'does not entail a divine speaker which can be identified alongside a human one'.[83] The *persona* speaking is the grounding possibility of the humanity it instantiates, of a particular human voice in history. It is an agency that is *non aliud* in being not *an*-other 'alongside' that humanity, even while being *not*-other to it.

No Drama

For Williams, there is in Augustine's schema no equivalent to the Antiochene anxiety to attribute different sayings or actions to Jesus *qua* his human or divine nature. The Word makes possible any word from Jesus, and is not a separable speaker alongside him: 'There is, one could say, no "drama", no dialogue of resistance and engagement and submission, between Jesus and the Word, as between the Word and other human beings.'[84] This lack of 'drama' is also reflected in the essay 'God'. There Williams reads the New Testament vision of the divine act in Jesus as precisely *not* one of interaction between two agents:

> God is not 'in' Jesus as an element in his biography, but as what the entire biography expresses, transcribes or communicates. The divine life which is eternally realized in the Logos is not an overwhelmingly important dimension of Jesus' life, but the deepest source of that life's meaning in all the actuality of its historical and narrative detail.

Thus, Jesus's 'action and passion' are a coherent phenomenon held together by a divine act that 'is not an element or moment alongside' his narrative. This is, for

---

82. Ibid., 183. For an exposition of Augustine's Christological reading of the Psalms, see Rowan Williams, 'Augustine and the Psalms', *Interpretation* 58:1 (2004), 17–27.

83. Williams, 'Augustine's Christology', 184.

84. Ibid., 185–6. This intuition has a precursor in Williams, ' "Person" and "Personality" ', where a patristic tendency to ascribe Jesus's actions to different natures is decried as 'a piece of confused mythologizing' (258). Elsewhere, Williams characterizes the Antiochene approach as one that 'struggles to preserve the essential integrity and transcendence of the holy; it is present on earth only in a relationship that is in some sense dialogical or dramatic in respect of created agency'. See Rowan Williams, 'Troubled Breasts: The Holy Body in Hagiography', in *Portraits of Spiritual Authority: Religious Power in Early Christianity, Byzantium and the Christian Orient*, eds J. W. Drijvers and J. W. Watt (Leiden: Brill, 1999), 73.

Williams, the import of what is being worked out in classical Christology.[85] In the language of *Tokens of Trust* (2007), to be explored in the next chapter, Jesus's human identity, as a whole, performs the music of God's life.[86] In the language of Augustine, it is God who speaks in that whole life. This is an *anhypostatic* Christology where the Word is the *persona* of Jesus, and yet generatively grounds a real human personality.

The similarity between God's generative relation to creatures and, in an amplified and different sense, to the humanity of Jesus has already been marked. What is intriguing is the way that the 'dramatic' construal of the divine action in Christ, which Williams rejects – God is not just an element in Jesus's biography, or a dialogue partner 'alongside' him – corresponds to the reactive and episodic account of divine agency in creation that Williams rejects in McCord Adams. God does not episodically intervene in Jesus's life, any more than in creation. God is not conditioned by creaturely agents, because no agent – hyperbolically so Jesus – is strictly external to God. God is maximally present (*not*-other) to them, but is also maximally different, not *an*-other in their causal space. Both a 'dramatic' Christological grammar and a grammar of reactive intervention in creation are bad grammars. They erode the difference of God by uncomplexly dragging God into creaturely space, into the causal systems operant in contingency. To return to the register of divine authorship, they make God a clumsy and intrusive writer who tussles with and speaks over his characters. For Williams, it is divine difference, in its un-eroded form, that makes possible a divine presence that is generative and non-competitive. That difference enables the authoring of both a coherent creation, and that particular and coherent human life that is Jesus's. That divine difference that allows for intimate presence is the precondition for a Christology that does not dissolve into nonsense.

Conclusion: Non Aliud *and Christology*

In the first part of this chapter, through multiple discussions, a grammar of divine difference was discerned. In the second, it was shown that this grammar was refracted through, and intensified by, Williams's Trinitarian theology. But this was not the intensification of a pure negativity; *non aliud*, as one expression of that grammar of difference, was never meant to connote pure negation. The Word is *not*-other to God even as, in the continual deflection elicited by a pneumatological 'second difference', God is not *an*-other to God. In the Word being *not*-other is the possibility for God to be *not*-other to creation. In Christ, it enables the becoming of a *res* so consummately a *signum* it draws the world into signification. In *Dostoevsky*, Williams – in a turn of phrase that will become increasingly important in this

85. Williams, 'God', 79–80.
86. Rowan Williams, *Tokens of Trust: An Introduction to Christian Belief* (Norwich: Canterbury Press, 2007), 68–9.

book – terms this the presence of the 'last word', the transcription into a human life of an authorial 'patient presence' in relation to which all 'may discover an exchange that is steadily and unfailingly life giving and free of anxiety'.[87] Somehow, the one who is not *an*-other, but who generatively is *not*-other to creation, becomes *an*-other within it. As will be seen in the next chapter, he does so in a manner so surefooted that his generativity is maintained, while the not-so-latent potential of any human *an*-other to provoke anxious competition is not. And if this is pushing at the doors of paradox, it is because the difference of God is, for Williams, that which makes possible *and* complicates Christology.

87. Williams, *Dostoevsky*, 138–9.

Chapter 2

A Christological Presentation

Introduction

If the incarnation entails God becoming *an*-other in creaturely space, it seems that God, who 'is never going to be an element, a square centimetre, in any picture', must work against the divine grammar – and yet, the positive connotation of maximal and life-giving presence (*not*-other), which Williams's concept of divine difference entails, seems to open up what negation shuts down. If this Author does not become a character in any 'simple sense', in Jesus they are densely *not*-other to a human life. The Author's generative presence is mediated in that life, a 'last word' in interaction with whom is found a vivifying and uniquely non-anxious possibility. It is, as will emerge in this chapter, as if instilled in that life is the generativity of God's presence as *not*-other to his creation, while the possibility of anxious conflict inherent within any *an*-other is brought into a unique abeyance. This chapter will explore this Christological vision across a range of Williams's writings, and faithfully reproduce its lineaments. It will then discuss the importance for Williams of the historical particularity of Jesus as a human *an*-other, and the way this importance interacts with a theological vision that has a form of historicism at its heart.

What will also emerge is something already implicit in the last chapter's discussions: Williams's Christology is self-consciously related to the mainstream of Orthodoxy. Belied by the range of idioms employed is a concern 'to hold on to a very Alexandrian Christology with a full account of Jesus' human choices'.[1] That is to say, Williams's Christology is Chalcedonian in character – taking seriously humanity and divinity as non-competitive realities within one coherent life. Note that Williams assumes a fundamental continuity between Cyrilline Alexandrianism, the council of Chalcedon and the tradition that arose in its wake.[2]

---

1. Personal correspondence with the author, 10 May 2011.

2. While this is not an uncontested view, Williams is not alone in this assumption. See John McGuckin, *Saint Cyril of Alexandria and the Christological Controversy: Its History, Theology and Texts* (Crestwood, NY: St Vladimir's Seminary Press, 2004), 233–42; Demetrios Bathrellos, *The Byzantine Christ: Person, Nature, and Will in the Christology of Saint Maximus the Confessor* (Oxford: Oxford University Press, 2004), Chapter 1 *passim*; Thomas G. Weinandy, 'Cyril and the Mystery of the Incarnation', in *The Theology of Cyril of Alexandria: A Critical Appreciation*, eds T. G. Weinandy and D. A. Keating (London: T&T Clark, 2003), 43–6. It is not accidental to this that Williams's early career included an immersion in the Cyrilline-influenced Eastern tradition through his studies of Lossky.

His 'Alexandrian' instincts – most fundamentally his understanding that the Word constitutes the 'person' of the human agent – were broached in the last chapter. Much of this chapter will turn on describing the ways in which that human agent is expressive of the divinity that grounds it, and on the importance of that divinity being the source of a particular human life that is *an*-other in history. If the last chapter was concerned with charting the Christological possibilities and problems inherent in Williams's account of divine difference, this one turns from those possibilities to Williams's positive Christological presentation.

Part 1 A Performance in Time

A Musical Analogy

In *Tokens of Trust* (2007), Williams describes Jesus in the following way: 'Here is a human life so shot through with the purposes of God, so transparent to the action of God, that people speak of it as God's life "translated" into another medium.'[3] This life is both the 'human narrative' of a 'skilled artisan', and the narrative of 'God's work among us'.[4] In it is found, echoing Chalcedon's language of two natures in one *hypostasis*, 'two sorts of life, one of them unconditionally powerful, one utterly vulnerable, but lived inseparably in one person'. Williams deploys an analogy he has found helpful over the years to describe this phenomenon – that of a musical performance. A superb performance is one wherein a work is realized by a 'human being at the limit of their skill and concentration'. They remain fully and intensely themselves, yet allow the vision of another to find fruition in them and 'saturate' their being. Jesus's life can be understood under this analogy as a whole humanity given up to a virtuoso performance: 'He is performing God's love, God's purpose, without a break, without a false note, without a stumble; yet he is never other than himself, with all that makes him distinctly human taken up with this creative work.'[5]

This analogy is deployed by Williams at several points to describe the mode in which God is *not*-other to Jesus's humanity. In a 1998 *Church Times* article, he says that Jesus embodies the Word 'as totally as (more totally than) the musician in performance embodies the work performed'.[6] In *The Dwelling of the Light* (2003), Williams describes how, in Orthodox icons of the Transfiguration, Christ emerges

---

3. Rowan Williams, *Tokens of Trust: An Introduction to Christian Belief* (Norwich: Canterbury Press, 2007), 57.

4. Ibid., 68–9.

5. Ibid., 72–5. A very similar sentiment, if not expressed using a specifically musical analogy, can be found earlier in Rowan Williams, *The Truce of God* (London: Fount, 1983), 75–6.

6. Rowan Williams, ' "No Life Here – No Joy, Terror, or Tears" a Response to Bishop Spong', http://anglicanecumenicalsociety.wordpress.com/2010/06/10/bishop-spong-and-archbishop-williamss-response.

from a dark background, evocative of the depths of divinity undergirding his humanity. In that book, he deems a musical performance a 'small and inadequate analogy' for what is communicated pictorially in this emergence. A 'great current of music' becomes present, but inseparably from the performative humanity foregrounded in the icon.[7]

What is striking, considering the implicit emphasis this analogy lays on Jesus's human agency as the locus of a performance, is just how congruent Williams finds it with an *anhypostatic* Christology.[8] In *Tokens of Trust,* it is emphasized that this is a performance in which there is one flow of action and a singular agent, the Word. Yet, Jesus's humanity is 'most full and real' in this flow. It retains its integrity without interruption or supplement by divinity.[9] Turning to *The Dwelling of the Light*, the divine depths from which Christ emerges are an 'infinite "hinterland" that is the background, the inner dimension, of Jesus's human life'. This language of 'inner dimension' and 'hinterland' recalls, in a different modality, the intuition that the Word is the *hypostasis* of Jesus's humanity, its 'ultimate ground of continuous identity'.[10] *Tokens of Trust* and *The Dwelling of the Light* are more popular works, but these intuitions run deep in Williams. For him, 'the entire human identity of Jesus is a divine gift',[11] and the Word is the singular possibility, person, hinterland and *hypostasis* of the fully human subject Jesus. This is Williams's basic Christological instinct, one consonant with Cyrilline Alexandrianism.[12]

Yet, such an 'Alexandrianism' is congruent, for Williams, with the Chalcedonian concerns already present in *Tokens of Trust*'s paraphrasing of the council's language of the hypostatic union. The Word is 'translated', in that book's idiom, into a medium meaningful for creatures in being translated into a human narrative. That

7. Rowan Williams, *The Dwelling of the Light: Praying with the Icons of Christ* (Norwich: Canterbury Press, 2003), 4–7.

8. Andrew Moody cites Williams's usage of the musical analogy in the context of accusing him of a presentation of the incarnation, at times, 'so de-mythologized as to approximate adoptionism'. See Moody, 'The Hidden Center: Trinity and Incarnation in the Negative (and Positive) Theology of Rowan Williams, in *On Rowan Williams: Critical Essays*, ed. Matheson Russell (Eugene: Cascade, 2009), 45. The argument of this section will be that the analogy is part of a general Christological presentation that works in quite the opposite direction, in support of an *anhypostatic* Christology irreconcilable with adoptionism.

9. Williams, *Tokens of Trust,* 74–5.

10. Williams, *The Dwelling of the Light,* 17.

11. Rowan Williams, *On Christian Theology* (Oxford: Blackwell, 2000), 91–2.

12. This is obliquely referenced in Rowan Williams, 'Augustine's Christology: Its Spirituality and Rhetoric', in *In the Shadow of the Incarnation: Essays on Jesus Christ in the Early Church in Honor of Brian E. Daley, S.J.*, ed. P. W. Martens (Notre Dame: University of Notre Dame Press, 2007), 188. For Cyril, the Logos is the singular subject of the incarnation; Jesus has a human nature and soul, but apart from the Logos, that nature has no distinct agency and that soul is not a locus of personhood. See McGuckin, *Saint Cyril of Alexandria and the Christological Controversy,* Chapter 3 *passim.*

narrative *is* the performance, and the musical analogy entails attention to it; the divine music is only had in attending to its human recital. Thus, a high theology of the incarnation returns one to history and humanity, the human life whose underlying truth is a divine hinterland. Ultimately, for Williams, the 'Alexandrian' intuition that the Logos is the *hypostasis* of the incarnation is also the animating principle of Chalcedonian Christology and its affirmation of the integrity of that humanity. What Chalcedon established was that

> the eternal Word becomes the animating, defining principle of an individual human life, in such a way that you cannot separate the reality of this human life in any way or in any moment from the underlying active life of the Word. There is one *hypostasis* involved, that is, one actively existing principle, eternally real in the life of the Trinity, becoming real in our world at the point of Jesus' conception. But this does not mean that the Word turns into something less than God, or that the individual human Jesus becomes other than human: the lesser reality is activated and transfigured by the greater, but not changed in essence.[13]

If implied in Williams's musical analogy is the importance of a human agency and its performance, even if its *hypostasis* is the Word, also implied is a second level of agency, even if it is *not*-other to Jesus's humanity and not a second agent alongside him. There are, one might say, *two* wills at work and brought together into *one* agential flow, the performer's will and the will performed. This language echoes that of a late patristic theologian whose work treated a number of continuing questions arising from Chalcedon: Maximus the Confessor. To Maximus, there persists in the one agent Jesus both a divine and human will, corresponding to the continuing integrity of the divine and human natures.[14] Yet, these wills are not competitive. The human will is deified in its agreement with the divine, 'eternally moved and shaped' and 'in accordance' with it.[15] This dynamic is present, archetypally for Maximus, in Gethsemane's 'not my will but yours' (Luke 22:42). There is, Maximus notes, a shrinkage from death in that garden, but it is an epiphenomenon of the human nature's proper aversion to life's cessation. Christ's humanity, as well as its will, is deified in the hypostatic union, but it does not cease to be human, 'for nothing at all changes its nature by becoming deified'.[16]

---

13. Rowan Williams, *Why Study the Past? The Quest for the Historical Church* (London: Darton, Longman and Todd, 2005), 45. Not coincidently, Cyril is cited in making this point (119, n.19). See also Williams, *On Christian Theology*, 26, n. 20.

14. 'We make no diminution at all in the natural wills, or energies, just as we make no diminution in the natures themselves, in the case of the one and same God the Word Incarnate.' See *Opusc.* 7.80 B. Translation from Andrew Louth, *Maximus the Confessor* (London: Routledge, 1996), 185.

15. *Opusc.* 7.80 C-D. Ibid., 185–6. For the importance of the Gethsemane narrative in the Monothelite controversy, see Bathrellos, *The Byzantine Christ*, 141–7.

16. *Opusc.* 7.81 C-D. Louth, *Maximus*, 187.

Williams is familiar with Maximus, but does not cite him in discussing the musical analogy.[17] As will emerge later, he departs from Maximus in that he regards the human struggle in Gethsemane as something more than an epiphenomenon. Yet, Maximus's Christology is strikingly congruent with much of what Williams is trying to say. If Jesus's human life is the flow of a single, virtuoso, performance, it is one wherein he can never be in competition with the composer's will. Without a false note, he willingly submits to the score. In this, his humanity does not merely remain, but it operates to the full extent of its volitional powers. Yet, in its willing submission, it is saturated with the deity performed. This is not far off from a humanity, as well as a human will, that remains itself but is 'deified'. It is a life, to recall earlier words by Williams about Chalcedon, wherein 'the lesser reality is activated and transfigured by the greater, but not changed in essence'. It might not be too much to say that the theology displayed in the musical analogy is conceptually underwritten by a Maximian sensibility.[18] It is certainly evident, from the discussions above, that Williams's Christology operates with a debt to the mainstream of patristic thought.

The Nature of the Performance – Judgement and Creation

If a musical performance is an apt analogy for the mode in which God is *not*-other to the human Jesus, there are questions to be pursued as to the content of that performance. It is a human narrative entangled within a historical-cultural context. It is distinctly Jewish and of its time. Yet, for Williams, it is not a predictable outcome of its time. It injects a disruptive novelty that is transformative, ultimately, of all contexts and times.[19] In being both historical, and 'gratuitous and unpredictable', it evidences 'the basic Christological duality behind the classical formula of Chalcedon'.[20] It is the

---

17. Maximus, a major interlocutor for Lossky, appears at multiple points in Williams's doctoral thesis. See 'The Theology of Vladimir Nikolaievich Lossky: An Exposition and Critique' (Doctoral Thesis, University of Oxford, 1975), 21–4, 96–8, 157–8, 171–6. Other discussions of Maximus include *The Wound of Knowledge: Christian Spirituality from the New Testament to St John of the Cross*, 2nd Revised ed. (London: Darton, Longman and Todd, 1990), 122–3, and *The Dwelling of the Light*, 30–41.

18. Looking back to last chapter's discussions, a further correspondence between Williams and Maximus is their shared understanding of the fundamentally non-competitive relation of the divine and human wills, based on a grammar of divine difference. For Maximus, the natural divine energies of the Word, and its human energies, are not the same sort of *things* in a shared field that can compete. Nor can the divine be thought to dominate, by asymmetrical preponderance, the human – 'for that which dominates belongs itself to those who suffer'. See Bathrellos, *The Byzantine Christ*, 101. The quote is from Maximus, *Opusc.* 5, 64 A-B as cited by Bathrellos.

19. Jesus's story is 'the climax of Israel's story, yet it is not in the order of nature, not a predictable part of the world's process'. See Rowan Williams, *Open to Judgement: Sermons and Addresses* (London: Darton, Longman and Todd, 1994) 25–6.

20. Williams, *On Christian Theology*, 58.

advent within history of a divine freedom inseparable from a particular historical subject that performs that freedom. It is, for Williams, such an advent because it accomplishes two things that the narratives of Israel had taught attentive listeners to be the works of God – *judgement* and *creation*. In enacting, as a creaturely *an*-other, a life wherein the threat of anxious conflict is brought into unique abeyance, Jesus poses a questioning *judgement* on the conflictual ways of humanity. Yet, he also mediates God's generative presence as *not*-other, *creating* a new set of possibilities.

This trope of judgement and creation can be mapped alongside a determinative pattern of crucifixion and resurrection; together they form a twin polarity that structures much in Williams's Christological presentation. Jesus's life is a judgement (*krisis* in Greek), in that he is a crisis for his context. He is God's response to Israel's particular hopes, but one that those in power 'found unrecognizable' and 'profoundly menacing'.[21] Thus, he dies, misrecognized, at the hands of his community's arbiters of truth, a crisis for those who hold Israel's story to be truth-bearing. But, this crisis is followed by a resurrection that retroactively endues Jesus's crucifixion with meaning. It becomes, *recognizably*, God's action, and the pattern of death and resurrection becomes determinative for a community that will arise from this history.[22]

That this pattern of crucifixion and resurrection coheres with Jesus's human performance as both judging and creating can be seen acutely in an essay concerned with the genesis of Christological dogma, 'Beginning with the Incarnation' (1989). There Williams proposes that Christology has its inception in human encounters with the story of Jesus. It is a story that mediates a 'primitive' sense of a 'truth being told about us as human beings implicated in a network of violence and denial'. The primary locus of this intuition is the debacle of the cross, a narrative that implicates its hearers in a judgement upon their human religious possibilities. But then comes a second moment, resurrection. It creates ('*ex nihilo*') a possibility beyond the frontiers of human failure. Williams's use of creational language is deliberate in identifying the resurrection as a moment that does not emerge from dynamics immanent within Jesus's human narrative, but comes as a divine gift from beyond it. Jesus's story, while remaining ineradicably historical, thus displays possibilities unforeseeable within history. Those who encounter it find themselves judged, but also converted in the hope of a new, creative possibility.[23]

Judgement in Christ

If Christ's judgement involves a 'truth being told' about our 'violence and denial', this intuition rests in a broader construal by Williams of the nature of justice. In a sermon, aptly enough given to a judicial circuit, he suggests that administering

---

21. Ibid., 95.
22. See Williams, *The Wound of Knowledge*, 3–5.
23. Williams, *On Christian Theology*, 81–3.

justice begins in responding 'to the *reality* of another', reflecting back 'the truth of what they are'. Thus, justice is not primarily a function of retribution, but of attentive truth-telling. Its prerequisite possibility is a willingness to endure the 'costly and careful' attention of God, which 'opens our eyes to what we would rather not face in ourselves'.[24] This discussion of human justice, placed against a divine horizon, is indicative of Williams's understanding of God's justice. It, too, is an attentive truth-telling, a crisis wherein we discover who we are before God, and it is enacted in Jesus's performance of God's life. For instance, in John's Gospel, Williams notes how judgement takes place in encounters with Jesus wherein the occluded dispositions of his interlocutors are revealed, their truth reflected back to them, and a choice for or against that truth demanded.[25]

For Williams, the most telling truth reflected to us as human beings is that of our violence. Human life is engulfed in an endemic process of mutual diminishment and competition, a process that precedes even our consciousness of it. In the book *Resurrection,* this is characterized as an '"already" which theology (sometimes rather unhelpfully) refers to as original sin'.[26] Original sin is also invoked in *Tokens of Trust* to speak of how, ineradicably, in the process of our maturation we are inducted into a world of mimetic competition, learning what to desire in the presence of others, but also learning to compete against those others in order to achieve those desires.[27] Jesus's performance forces this violent and rivalrous reality to our attention precisely by performing, as *an*-other within our turbulent human history, the life of the *non aliud* God; he 'mediates historically the meaning of a non-negotiable and therefore non-competitive presence'.[28]

If God is the generative ground of all, creatively *not*-other to all that is but not a locatable *an*-other in the creaturely field, another way to put this is to say that God is unconditioned by creaturely negotiation and is 'what he is quite independently of what the world is and what the world thinks'.[29] God is, therefore, uniquely

24. Williams, *Open to Judgement*, 243–4.

25. Williams, *On Christian Theology*, 32.

26. Rowan Williams, *Resurrection: Interpreting the Easter Gospel*, 2nd Revised ed. (London: Darton, Longman and Todd, 2002), 18.

27. See Williams, *Tokens of Trust*, 82–3. 'We learn how to be human only as we learn also the habits of self-absorption. We learn what we want, as some contemporary thinkers have stressed, by watching someone else wanting it and competing with them for it' (82). Although Girard is not explicitly mentioned as one of these 'contemporary thinkers', his theory of mimetic desire is in view here, and his work is in the background of many of this section's considerations. For Williams's treatment of Girard, see *Wrestling with Angels: Conversations in Modern Theology* (Cambridge: Eerdmans, 2007), Chapter 9 *passim*, especially 172–3.

28. Williams, *On Christian Theology*, 247.

29. Rowan Williams, 'Christians and Muslims before the One God: An Address Given at Al-Azhar Al-Sharif, Cairo on 11 September 2004', *Islam and Christian-Muslim Relations* 16, no. 2 (2005), 190.

non-competitive, and there is a corresponding divine freedom from anxious self-assertion. The performance in humanity of that freedom is the quintessence of Jesus's disruption to his context. He mediates a generative discontinuity to history's violent continuities. Only a human intervention within history can heal it; only divine freedom, free from mimetic competition, can enact this intervention. This is the soteriological importance of Jesus's humanity *and* divinity; he 'is the human event that reverses the flow of human self-absorption because it is unconditionally open to divine freedom'.[30] This is part of the essential content of his being the 'last word', in which is found a vivifying and non-anxious possibility. As one to whom God is intensely *not*-other, the competitive threat that attends any human *an*-other is brought, in Jesus, into a unique recession.

To trace this further, in *Resurrection* Williams speaks of Jesus being a judge inasmuch as he is also, to use a phrase that resonates with the thought of René Girard, a 'pure victim'. When victimized, Jesus does not reciprocate in kind, but embodies 'an unconditional and universal acceptance'. Offering no resistance, he is, in Johannine parlance, 'lifted up' in sacrifice. Judgement then becomes the Son's prerogative precisely because of his concrete and non-vindictive involvement in the historical processes of violent exclusion. His justice comes not as a vertical intervention, but from within the broken field of human relations, from *an*-other whose conviction of the world is by the mediation of a peaceable presence.[31] A similar theme is picked up when discussing the Lukan trial narrative in *Christ on Trial*.[32] There it is Jesus's peaceable eschewal of worldly power that draws his interrogators' violence. He refuses the 'mimetic trap' (echoes of Girard again) of the desire for power, and thereby calls the world of competition into question. He even unites those previously mired in enmity, Pilate and Herod, in friendship against him. Their judgement is their uncomprehending and violent reaction to their victim.[33]

For those, like Pilate and Herod, who are mired in history, the performance of the divine freedom from competition is a crisis and a judgement. It pushes the truth of their violence into the unwelcomed light. Jesus as the 'last word', precisely in opening up the possibility of freedom from anxiety, paradoxically induces it and provokes enmity. To continue the Girardian theme, this word becomes a scapegoat whom others, previously at odds, unite to destroy. This is Jesus's story; it speaks this judgement: 'This is what your untruth means: you have been offered unconditional mercy and you turn from it in loathing. You have come to the place where you cannot recognize life itself for what it is. You don't know the difference

---

30. Williams, *Tokens of Trust*, 83.

31. Williams, *Resurrection*, 7–8.

32. Williams characterizes Luke as a Gospel concerned with the 'intelligence of the victim', a phrase borrowed from James Allison, himself much influenced by Girard. See Rowan Williams, *Christ on Trial: How the Gospel Unsettles Our Judgment* (Grand Rapids: Zondervan, 2000), 50.

33. Ibid., 69.

between life and death. The reality in you is dead.'[34] The judgement of the world is that Jesus is killed *because* he mediates God's non-negotiable life.

It is a judgement particularly pronounced against the world of human systems of manufacturing meaning and, above all, against religiosity. Religion does not escape the conditions of its production in a manifold of competitive sectional interests. Williams's theology is one chastened by the knowledge of religion's darker potentials, that it is 'very nearly true' that integrity in religious speech is unrealizable.[35] Such speech often slips into an ideological 'phenomenon of power, the sign of the dominance of an interest group',[36] and 'can be a tool to reinforce diseased perceptions of reality'.[37] The specifically *divine* nature of the judgement enacted in Jesus is, in part, glimpsed in the way his story functions as a universal crisis for religious constructions, and the way it creates a community of reflexive self-criticism.

In the essay 'The Finality of Christ' (1990), Williams argues that Jesus's life has universal import as a 'universally crucial question rather than a comprehensive ontological schema'. As already alluded to, the content of the incarnation is a human narrative that provokes a crisis for a particular community, Second Temple Judaism.[38] As a 'historical unity determined by particular systems of power', it found itself unable to be true to its origin because of the distortions imposed by those systems. Religion became enmeshed with ideology 'in the malign sense of that word'.[39] This particular crisis becomes universal when the (inherently contestable) claim is made that 'the Jewish story with its interruption and repristination in Jesus' is also God's history, manifesting a divine freedom from ideologically determined religion. It generates a renunciation of God as bolstering sectional interests, and points towards a potentially universal community. The narrative of Jesus, ensconced in Israel's story, is then that of 'a religious tradition generating its own near-negation', and thus of a divine discontinuity within human history that generates a possibility beyond all sectional interests.[40] This does not guarantee Christianity's innocence – it, too, can become a 'large-scale tribalism' – but when a Christologically mediated divine judgement on religion persists within it, as 'a charter for the task of Christian self-criticism', this possibility is, at least in part, forestalled.[41]

---

34. Williams, *Tokens of Trust,* 84–6. See also *Open to Judgement,* 241. For Girard, it is in uniting around the sacrifice of an outsider that those locked in mimetic desire can, like Herod and Pilate, find unity. See, again, Williams, *Wrestling with Angels,* Chapter 9 *passim.*

35. Williams, *On Christian Theology,* 5–6.

36. Rowan Williams, 'What Is Catholic Orthodoxy?', in *Essays Catholic and Radical,* eds R. Williams and K. Leech, (London: Bowerdean Press, 1983), 13.

37. Rowan Williams, *Writing in the Dust: After September 11* (Grand Rapids, MI: Eerdmans, 2002), 5.

38. Williams, *On Christian Theology,* 94.

39. Ibid., 97–9.

40. Ibid., 104.

41. Williams, *On Christian Theology,* 99–100. For more on the restless self-critical nature of Christianity, see Williams, *Tokens of Trust,* 179 and 'To Stand Where Christ Stands', in *An Introduction to Christian Spirituality,* eds R. Waller and B. Ward (London: SPCK, 1999), 9.

To Williams, the modes of this judgement's persistence include scripture, preaching and sacrament. Judgement is re-presented to the church in the reading of scripture. For Williams, to be a 'biblical person', as opposed to a religious one, is to put oneself in the way of judgement, of being interpreted and questioned by scripture.[42] To read a text like Matthew, for instance, is to encounter a story wherein the appointed guardians of God's wisdom meet Wisdom incarnate, and connive in its destruction. To read it well is to learn to question claims to religious fluency, even one's own[43] – and insofar as preaching reflects on scripture, it, too, re-presents this judgement. At points in Williams's preaching, Jesus is cast as a strikingly non-religious, and even secular, figure. He is unconcerned with the 'cottage industry' of religiosity around the temple.[44] Crucified, he is the 'ray of darkness' that disrupts 'our religious fantasy'.[45]

But judgement persists in perhaps its most concentrated form in the eucharist. Focused intensely as it is on the locus of the passion, the sacrament is an eating and drinking of judgement upon religious pretensions. Its reworking of the Passover portrays, *in nuce*, the disruptive juxtaposition of Jesus's continuity and discontinuity with Israel.[46] What is rehearsed is a narrative that occurs 'on the night he was betrayed', ensnaring the communicants in that betrayal. They are identified with an apostolic band dissolving in cowardice,[47] and reminded that this narrative is not just where Jesus's possibilities end, but where the religious aspirations of his friends crumble as well.[48] Furthermore, Williams argues that the eucharist is a curiously *secularizing* ritual. Just as it calls to mind Jesus's scapegoating by the religious, it echoes the secularity of Jesus over and against the religiosity of his context. Following (again) Girard, the eucharist is 'a demystifying mystery, an anti-sacrificial sacrifice', which foregrounds the violent capacities of human constructions of the sacred.[49]

If the judgement on human violence comes from its contrast with the transcription of the non-competitive difference of God into the conditions of humanity, then the judgement against religiosity is also a function of this same transcribed difference. If God is not *an*-other creaturely reality, then creaturely language cannot pronounce God. As suggested in the last chapter, 'reflective religion' – non-ideological religion insofar as such a thing is possible – cultivates an unbelief in God as an element in the world, preserving a negative moment in its operations. The generative negative moment of Christianity is the dissolution

---

42. Rowan Williams, 'Being Biblical Persons', in *William Stringfellow in Anglo-American Perspective*, ed. A. Dancer (Aldershot: Ashgate, 2005), 184–5.

43. Williams, *Christ on Trial*, Chapter 2 *passim*.

44. Williams, *Open to Judgement*, 54.

45. Ibid., 122.

46. Williams, *On Christian Theology*, 203; *Tokens of Trust*, 114–5.

47. Williams, *Resurrection*, 34; *On Christian Theology*, 10, 204.

48. Williams, *On Christian Theology*, 83.

49. Williams, *Wrestling with Angels*, 179–83.

of human religiosity in Jesus's narrative. As Williams puts it in a sermon to ordinands, we encounter Jesus as 'a kind of annihilating judgement on all we say'.[50] Given that this negativity has its primary locus in the events around the crucifixion, what Williams proposes is something similar to a Lutheran *theologia crucis*, in which 'God himself is the great "negative theologian"', who shatters all our images by addressing us in the cross of Jesus'.[51] To move to Williams's essay on *De doctrina*, the cross persists as an 'anti-representation' signifying the distance between God and the world. Insofar as it is empty of worldly 'meaning and power', it, paradoxically, is supremely significant of God who is no term in the world. Jesus crucified thus becomes God's speech, the *signum* of the divine *res*, because he is a sign that is intrinsically destabilizing, ending our ability to remain content with any immanent fixity of meaning.[52]

This does raise the question of how belief in God is to be positively manifested: Is it more than endlessly generative of self-criticism? In *Dostoevsky*, Williams intriguingly pursues this question through the narrative of the Grand Inquisitor from *The Brothers Karamazov*, a passage he has repeatedly mined in his writings for its potential theological content.[53] To Williams, the Inquisitor, with his offer of 'miracle, mystery and authority', functions as an emblem of ideological religion, 'religious power as simply another face of the power that manages and secures the world'.[54] Christ's response in the narrative is a mute kiss, doubled by Alyosha's kiss for Ivan. Negative in its wordlessness, it is still to Williams a free and compassionate riposte that refuses the terms set. It elucidates the divine liberty of Christ, and gestures 'beyond the world of cause and effect'. It is a fictional representation of a moment where Jesus mediates divine discontinuity within history – and it more than negates the world's possibilities: it begins a new set of possibilities, expanding beyond Jesus to enable other agents, such as Alyosha, to act likewise. In *Dostoevsky*, Williams relates this to the Orthodox doctrine of *theosis*. In assuming a human nature, the Word communicates divine liberty to humanity.[55] The result is a transformation of human possibilities that goes beyond judgement and towards a positive existence of faith and action. This lays the ground for our next set of considerations, and a shift of focus from the judgement enacted by Christ's performance, tied conceptually to the crucifixion, to a creative expansion beyond judgement, tied to the resurrection.

50. Williams, *Open to Judgement*, 107.

51. Williams, *The Wound of Knowledge*, 149.

52. Rowan Williams, 'Language, Reality and Desire in Augustine's *De Doctrina*', *Journal of Literature and Theology* 3:2 (1989), 144.

53. See Williams, *The Wound of Knowledge*, 59–60; *A Silent Action: Engagements with Thomas Merton* (Louisville: Fons Vitae, 2011), 26–7; *Open to Judgement*, 178–9; *Wrestling with Angels*, 100–1; *Christ on Trial*, Chapter 6 *passim*.

54. Rowan Williams, *Dostoevsky: Language, Faith and Fiction* (London: Continuum, 2008), 26–8.

55. Ibid., 31–3.

Creation in Christ – the Resurrection

A community that rehearses the paschal narrative, that moves through betrayal, death and then on to resurrection, is one, for Williams, that has learnt that 'failure is both real and not final'. In reckoning with failure's reality, it can leave behind the fantasy of a 'decisively successful' religious performance. In reckoning with failure's *non*-finality, it can imagine a future beyond failure.[56] But that ability to imagine the future is not immanent to the community. For Williams, it is a creative gift from God, given *ex nihilo* in the resurrection. To quote from the theological postscript of *Arius*: 'The distinctiveness of Christian identity is bound up with the idea of "new creation", of an event that makes a radical, decisive and unforeseeable difference in the human world: something that is brought out of nothing, life from death.'[57]

What is thereby expressed is a hope that exceeds historical possibilities, yet one that creates a community *within* history. In the passage from death to life, the concentrated irritant of divine judgement expands to offer humanity a divine 'liberty to act, to heal and to create community'.[58] In the resurrection, God countermands ideological religion's verdict on Jesus. He is no longer vulnerable to history's violence, but is a living, transhistorical, presence. In this, his human life is validated as a divine performance.[59] Importantly, it is a performance that mediates God's creative presence as *not*-other to what he calls into being. In the last chapter's discussion of creation and the difference of God, it was established that God is an intimate, vivifying presence to creatures as their possibility to be. Now, in the resurrection, Jesus is established as the 'last word' in whose presence new possibilities for humanity come to be. He is God's generative presence as *not*-other to a community that instantiates those possibilities.

That the resurrection is linked to the creation of a community, for Williams, itself points to Jesus's performance as divine. Creation, and the creation of communities, are held as hallmarks of divine agency, what the narratives of Israel taught their listeners to understand as divine work. Williams notes the nascent emergence of the doctrine of creation *ex nihilo* in the post-exilic context, intertwined with an emerging view of God as the one who, in events such as the Exodus and exilic return, creates and recreates a people out of chaos and loss. How God forms creation, and how God creates a community, became inseparable grammars. Thus, for Jesus to create a community out of loss, in the passage from death to resurrection, is for him to do something that evokes the creative *élan* of Israel's God[60] – and it is also the character of the community created that provokes this intuition. Here, again,

56. Rowan Williams, 'Resurrection and Peace', *Theology* 92, no. 750 (1989), 488–9.

57. Rowan Williams, *Arius: Heresy and Tradition*, 2nd ed. (London: SCM, 2001), 240–1.

58. Williams, *On Christian Theology*, 104.

59. Ibid., 251. See also Williams, *The Wound of Knowledge*, 4–5; *Resurrection*, 55; *Open to Judgement*, 67–9.

60. Williams, *On Christian Theology*, 68–9, 139–40, 234. See also Rowan Williams, 'God', in *Fields of Faith: Theology and Religious Studies for the Twenty-First Century*, eds D. F. Ford, B. Quash, and J. Martin Soskice (Cambridge: Cambridge University Press, 2005), 77.

the language of *ex nihilo* comes to bear. In an essay on Augustine's doctrine of creation, Williams makes the point that the grammar of *ex nihilo*, with its implied stark difference between God and creation, also speaks of a divine love for creation that is '*not* based on kinship or similarity'. From this can be discerned 'a thread of connection between a repudiation of tribal or sectarian accounts of love and what has to be said about the gratuity of creation'.[61] In other words, a doctrine of creation steeped in the grammar of God's difference speaks of a love disinterested in sectional loyalties, one gratuitously *not*-other to the whole of what is. It is *this* love that is refracted through the community Jesus creates, and to whom he is *not*-other. In its best hopes for itself, it displays the agency of God as 'one who is beyond all partisanship, all self-interest, whose whole being is selflessness: that mystery which the doctrine of the Holy Trinity supremely reveals to us'.[62]

This possibility was, for Williams, implicit in the life of Israel, if occluded by those distortions judged in Jesus's confrontation with her arbiters of truth. In the resurrection, Israel is now reassembled around the one rejected by those arbiters. Implied is a new universalism of access; God is no longer a protected possession of religious power.[63] Thus, to the earliest Christians, the epithet Christ came 'to mark out the shape of the potential future for all human beings'. Jesus's existence is recognizably divine 'from first to last because it is recognized as having a potential for bringing together the whole of the world we know in a new unity and intelligibility'. Thus divine freedom, the difference of God communicated to humanity, creates a universal community – one that is not just *an*-other community in a world of sectional competition, but one that seeks to be *not*-other to the whole world. It is one made up of lives lived in analogy to Jesus, an 'ensemble of human stories' which is his 'body', and without which his meaning cannot be fully understood.[64] This is why, in a chapter on Williams's Christology, one will find oneself having to return to ecclesiology. If Christ is generatively *not*-other to his ecclesial body, that body becomes, in its own way, a set of Christological data.

If the lives lived in this community are analogous to Jesus's, by implication they share in his peaceable generativity. '(B)rought into being by Christ's resurrection' is a people where 'no one's welfare is to be pursued at the expense of someone else',[65] where if one is diminished, all are.[66] To paraphrase Anthony of Egypt, it is a

---

61. Rowan Williams, ' "Good for Nothing?" Augustine on Creation', in *Doctrinal Diversity: Varieties of Early Christianity*, ed. Everett Ferguson, *Recent Studies in Early Christianity* (New York: Garland, 1999), 41–2.

62. Rowan Williams, 'No-One Can Be Forgotten in God's Kingdom', *Anvil* 25:2 (2008), 123.

63. Williams, *On Christian Theology*, 98–9. See also Williams, 'God', 77–9 for a fuller expression of Israel's life as reflective of God's agency.

64. Williams, *On Christian Theology*, 171–3. See also Rowan Williams, *Faith in the Public Square* (Bloomsbury: London, 2012), 305–8.

65. Rowan Williams, 'Penance in the Penitentiary', *Theology* 95:764 (1992), 89.

66. Williams, 'No-One Can Be Forgotten in God's Kingdom', 122–3. See also *Faith in the Public Square*, 28–9.

community where 'our life and death is with our neighbour'.[67] In other words, self-interested mimetic competition is brought into a recession in this community in a way analogous to its abeyance in Christ's performance – and this is not merely an intra-communal trait; it also characterizes the community's external relations to a world it hopes, one day, will be internal to it. As the community of the one whose presence is made possible in all places by the resurrection, there is no need to create *a* place over and against others, no need for '*Lebensraum*'.[68] This is the *theosis* of human possibilities spoken of in *Dostoevsky*, communicated to individuals and to a community.

But it is an incomplete *theosis*. The Christian community is set under a binding irony, noted by Williams in an essay on Gillian Rose; it paradoxically represents the *interests* of a *disinterested* God. It is charged with the vocation 'of realising a corporate life whose political practice constantly challenges sectional interests and proprietary models of power or knowledge'. Yet, it does so within the social manifold where those interests and models function.[69] This binding irony is *also* that of the incarnation. The God who occupies no square centimetre paradoxically becomes *an*-other, even 'a term in a conflict' within the world, and the potentially universal community created by that particular history is, itself, unavoidably a term in history's conflicts, even while trying to live in divine discontinuity with them. It cannot pursue its transformative vocation without taking the risk of interaction.[70] Thus, it must enter, alongside Christ who is *not*-other to it, into a field where it risks being misinterpreted, and even misinterpreting itself, in ideological and sectional ways.

In entering this field, the church comes 'to stand where Christ stands'.[71] It functions as a community of 'place-holders' for the one who is *not*-other to it. This activity of place-holding is not reducible to indwelling one competing ideology or territory among others. It is, rather, indwelling Jesus's transformative perspective, his divine freedom. In living a divine discontinuity within a world of rivalrous territories, it becomes possible for this community 'to see, to say and to do certain things that aren't possible elsewhere'.[72] It becomes possible to refuse the world's terms, just as Alyosha did in kissing his brother. This is what indwelling Jesus's transformative perspective looks like, as is another

---

67. Ibid., 128. For a fuller exposition of what this means, see Rowan Williams, *Silence and Honey Cakes: The Wisdom of the Desert* (Oxford: Lion Hudson, 2003), Chapter 1 *passim*.

68. *Open to Judgement*, 257.

69. *Wrestling with Angels*, 72. See also *Faith in the Public Square*, 78, where the church is described by Williams as 'a community both alongside, and of a different order to, political society'.

70. Rowan Williams, 'God and Risk (2)', in *The Divine Risk*, ed. R. Holloway (London: Darton, Longman and Todd, 1990), 22–3.

71. Williams, 'To Stand Where Christ Stands', *passim*.

72. Williams, 'Christian Identity and Religious Plurality', *The Ecumenical Review* 58:1 (2006), 69–72 (quote from p. 71).

illuminating hint provided in Williams's exposition of the character Sonya from *Crime and Punishment*. She is a '*Platzhalter*' for Christ.[73] Her agency is marked by 'the acceptance of the painful cost of action that will alter the world for others'. She indwells a world of mutual diminishment, but in such a way as not to diminish, but to bolster, others. The place she holds is one where others find 'time and space for unforced human growth'.[74] Thus, her life is a transcription of the vivifying 'last word', an analogue of the risen Christ who is creatively *not-other* to her.

To sum up the previous discussions, the resurrection is a moment where the judgement of human possibilities in Christ's passion becomes more than an occasion for criticism. It creates a divine possibility beyond human acumen. Jesus is more than a universal crisis (although he is that as well). His perfect performance of God's life mediates a divine disruption of history's violent continuity, in order to create a peaceable and universal community. There has been a *theosis* of human possibilities, a change wrought in history. But, as already alluded to, it is only wrought in the process of God becoming *not-*other to a particular and historical *an-*other, a stretching of the divine grammar.

Part 2 Intractably An-*other*

The Catholic theologian Thomas Weinandy has described modern theology's renewed interest in Jesus's historical humanity as a movement of the Spirit, one that has re-engaged us with the intractable particularity of a first-century Jew.[75] As much as he could be characterized an 'Alexandrian' or 'Chalcedonian' theologian, Williams can be cast in this modern context as well. In a 1987 essay, co-authored with the New Testament scholar Richard Bauckham, they together note that the incarnation is sub-Christian when it means 'God became man', rather than 'God became *this* man'. Even the tradition's classic Christological formulae are deemed misleading when the 'intended reference to the particular man Jesus is forgotten'.[76] Two years later Williams asserts that, to avoid becoming 'a rather baroque formulation', Christology must be oriented to the 'whole historical identity of Jesus' (including the history of his reception).[77] As has been argued already, this focus on Jesus as *an-*other historical human life, but one to whom God is decidedly *not-*other, in fact constitutes the particularly Chalcedonian nature of Williams's

73. Williams, *Dostoevsky*, 152–3.

74. Ibid., 157.

75. Thomas Weinandy, *In the Likeness of Sinful Flesh: An Essay on the Humanity of Christ* (Edinburgh: T&T Clark, 1993), 3–6.

76. Rowan Williams and Richard Bauckham, 'Jesus – God with Us', in *Stepping Stones: Joint Essays on Anglican Catholic and Evangelical Unity*, ed. C. Baxter (London: Hodder & Stoughton, 1987), 28–9.

77. Williams, *On Christian Theology*, 82.

Christology. But it is worth probing further why Williams focuses on Jesus's historical particularity, and exploring the import history more generally carries in his thought.

Incarnational Historicism

A curious aspect of Williams's 1975 Oxford DPhil thesis, which focused on the work of the Russian Orthodox theologian Vladimir Lossky, is that its final pages are largely concerned with a different Russian theologian, Georges Florovsky. In part this was to place Lossky within a tradition he and Florovsky shared, one sceptical of philosophical idealism and its manifestation in Russian religious thought through the sophiology stemming from Solovyov.[78] Florovsky's opposition to this tendency was buttressed, notes Williams, by a countervailing metaphysics of radical indeterminacy, enmeshed with a form of historicism. The sheer scope of human freedom within history entails an epistemology wherein knowledge is 'inexhaustible and provisional'. Knowledge only emerges *in* history, but that historically gained knowledge is of other persons in their indeterminacy, and cannot be bound up in definitive interpretations. The Christian historian, however, has a unique acumen for navigating this indeterminacy, one sourced in the incarnation. For Florovsky, the incarnation is the *eschaton* in history's midst, granting history a certain positive significance and sense. As 'the key and centre of the whole series', it catches history's underdetermined particulars up into a valid, but not deterministic, story.[79] I will argue that Williams essentially shares with Florovsky something formally similar to the latter's Christologically nuanced historicism.[80]

One of the works that Williams draws upon in his doctoral thesis is Florovsky's essay 'The Predicament of the Christian Historian'.[81] It is a text that is important for understanding Florovsky's historicism, and one in which he argues that Christianity – as '*essentially historical*' – injected a new concept of history into the ancient milieu. Antique history, oriented towards an eternal return of the same, was submerged into a 'general morphology of being'; only the 'typical' and 'patterned' were granted significance.[82] What Christianity's affirmation of the incarnation wrought was a qualitative transformation in this historical consciousness. It proposed a centre in time that was both historical and eschatological – the

---

78. For a later discussion of Florovsky on these matters, see Rowan Williams, 'Eastern Orthodox Theology', in *The Modern Theologians: An Introduction to Christian Theology in the Twentieth Century*, ed. D. F. Ford (Oxford: Blackwell, 1997), 508–10.

79. Williams, 'The Theology of Vladimir Nikolaievich Lossky', 271–4.

80. Although Williams becomes less enamoured of an emphasis on freedom, which can run in unhelpfully volunteerist directions. See his 'Eastern Orthodox Theology', 510.

81. In *Religion and Culture: Essays in Honour of Paul Tillich*, ed. Walter Leibrecht (New York: Harper & Brothers, 1959), 140–66.

82. Ibid., 158–61.

appearance of time's *telos* in time's midst. That which preceded the incarnation was now ordered and retrospectively validated in relation to it. That which follows is now oriented towards that end which the incarnation proleptically establishes. In this transformation, Christianity introduced a linear conception of time, if one 'bent' at its incarnational centre. Time is now graced with a potential for novelty and progression it did not previously have. As all events and particulars hold a singular place within this progression, they all become significant in relation to time's Christological centre. It would not be too much to say that, for Florovsky, the incarnation makes *meaningful* history possible.[83]

A consideration of Florovsky on history ends Williams's doctoral thesis, but he reappears near the beginning of another early work, a series of lectures on T. S. Eliot's *The Four Quartets* first given by Williams at New York's General Theological Seminary in 1974. Perhaps not accidently, it was during this trip to America that Williams took the opportunity to meet Florovsky in person.[84] In his lectures, Williams takes the Russian as an exemplar of the 'traditional Christian view' of the relation of the incarnation to history. Speaking of the particular human history of Jesus, he states:

> The human context of the Incarnation, its 'before Easter' is not devalued, but supremely *validated* by this pivotal event, an event in a series, only *itself* as occurring in a series, yet containing in itself, in its particularity, the fulfilment of the past and the anticipation of the future. It cannot be generalized into a 'meaning' which is separable from its historical detail: the detail of the history of Jesus *is* the meaning, and so the detail of all human history is, finally, included in this.[85]

Following Florovsky, Williams is arguing that the incarnation only has 'meaning' as a historical complexity of particular happenings bound up in a larger manifold. This singular complexity is also the meaning, and supreme validation, of that manifold. It is as if the point Williams later makes in relation to the *res–signum* distinction is foreshadowed here, in the idiom of history. Just as the incarnation is a *res* among *res*, but renders by its consummate significance all creatures *signa*, so here it is one historical particular in an underdetermined swathe of particulars. Yet, in relation to the incarnation, all particulars, and the swathe itself, become significant. History has meaning that can be attended to because one eventful life within it has rendered it consummately meaningful – and, vitally, that life cannot be abstracted (as a general meaning or truth) from its complex historical

---

83. Ibid., 161–3.

84. See Rupert Shortt, *Rowan's Rule: The Biography of the Archbishop* (London: Hodder & Stoughton, 2008), 89.

85. Rowan Williams, 'The Four Quartets', (1975) Lecture 1, 6. I am grateful to Ben Myers for sharing the unpublished typescript of a 1975 version of these lectures, given to the sisters at Fairacres.

particularity without also becoming a sub-Christian formulation. Williams here, in his own way, is as much a historicist as Florovsky, although perhaps the better term is an *incarnational historicist*. It is only as *an*-other within history, as one part of the manifold, that Jesus can be a transforming presence to the whole of it.[86]

Florovsky ceases to be more than an occasional interlocutor in Williams's mature writings, but another presence exerting a similar pull maintains itself for longer – Williams's undergraduate teacher Donald MacKinnon. Notable is what may be an unacknowledged citation of MacKinnon's essay 'Philosophy and Christology' (1956) in Williams's *Why Study the Past?* (2005). In a discussion of the importance of historiography, Williams notes: 'All serious study, *it has been said*, is a kind of dispossession; difficulty is a moral matter, something that refuses us the comfort we crave.'[87] MacKinnon's 'Philosophy and Christology' makes a remarkably similar point, that like philosophical *ascesis*, or a mystical dark night, historical study initiates an agony of questioning, an interrogation theology must expose itself to,[88] and for Christological reasons: 'No theology whose axiom is the sovereignty of Christology can escape the problems of *history*.' What theology *cannot* do for MacKinnon, echoing Florovsky's hesitancy about idealism, is escape history by recourse to 'an idealist philosophy of religion.'[89] Thus, two of Williams's earliest influences – one of whom, as will become apparent, has had a continuing impact upon his theology – push in the direction of entangling Christianity with history, and with one historical *an*-other, for precisely Christological reasons.

This entanglement is evident throughout Williams's writings, beginning with his lectures on Eliot which trace a theological journey running through the cycle of the *Quartets*. 'Burnt Norton', the first poem, is cast by Williams as a liminal work that leaves readers caught, unsatisfactorily, between a history without meaning and a flight into timeless ecstasy. It is to this impasse that Williams brings Florovsky to offer the way forward of a Christologically underwritten return to history. Eliot is then read as reaching for this possibility in the remainder of the cycle.[90] In 'East Coker', with its reference to Christ as the 'wounded surgeon', and the cross as the

---

86. Williams elsewhere notes a more general trend towards historicism among the Abrahamic traditions, insofar as they are united in the conviction that 'it pleased God to work by words and acts and events that need to be received, interpreted, thought through; it pleased God to touch this historical world by setting up chains of historical relationship'. See Rowan Williams, 'Islam, Christianity and Pluralism: The Zaki Badawi Memorial Lecture, Lambeth Palace, London 26 April 2007', *Islam and Christian-Muslim Relations* 19, no. 3 (2008), 346–7.

87. Williams, *Why Study the Past?*, 112. Emphasis mine.

88. Donald MacKinnon, *Borderlands of Theology and Other Essays* (London: Lutterworth Press, 1968), 77–81.

89. Ibid., 75–6.

90. Williams, 'The Four Quartets', Lecture 1, 6–9. For a brief reiteration of what Williams outlines in these lectures, see his sermon 'Lazarus – In Memory of T.S. Eliot' in *Open to Judgement*, 214–18.

'axial tree', a 'tentative "definition" of salvation is offered'. It is a 'commitment to the historical process to which God has decisively committed Himself in a particular historical life'.[91] By 'Little Gidding', Christ is the '"midwinter spring" which illuminates the whole bleak landscape of time'.[92] He is, again, what Florovsky would term time's bent centre, *an*-other, in time, who transfigures it.

In its own way, Williams's first book, *The Wound of Knowledge*, recapitulates the return to time found in the early Eliot lectures. One of its themes is that Christian spiritual practice is a summons to the temporal and particular underwritten by the incarnation. Programmatically, 'if the heart of "meaning" is a human story, a story of growth, conflict and death, every human story, with all its oddity and ambivalence, becomes open to interpretation in terms of God's saving work'.[93] Within its milieu, argues Williams, this insight gave antique Christianity a unique concern with history, struggle and maturation.[94] Thus a basic form evident in Florovsky's historicism is replicated here: a Christological centre of history graces other histories with meaning, and graces Christianity with an acumen for locating it.

Turning to Williams's substantial early study on Arius – not coincidently a piece of difficult historiography focused on Christological debates – some of the above themes are met again. Williams cites MacKinnon's intuition that the Nicene settlement secured 'a certain seriousness about the conditions of human history'. By denying a mythological history of transactions *within* God – an absolute monad generating the Son as the first principle of creation's multiplicity – it focused attention, instead, 'on the history of God with us in the world', in Israel, the incarnation and all that flows from it.[95] This movement from mythology to temporality is an oblique echo of Florovsky's view that the incarnation moved historical consciousness from a concept of history submerged into an account of being, towards meaning's emergence in time. What this account also gives is a reason to distrust de-historicized renderings of the incarnation. They mythologize into timeless principle the relation of humanity and God, instead of looking for that relation's locus in history. Ultimately, part of the importance of Nicene theology's establishment of Jesus's divinity was that it also functioned as a

> stimulation to clarification of the *verus homo* in the century and a half after the council: the Word of God is the condition of there being a human identity which

91. Williams, 'The Four Quartets', Lecture 2, 4–5.

92. Ibid., Lecture 3, 7–8.

93. Rowan Williams, *The Wound of Knowledge: Christian Spirituality from the New Testament to St John of the Cross*, 2nd Revised ed. (London: Darton, Longman and Todd, 1990) 2.

94. Ibid., 22–3.

95. Rowan Williams, *Arius: Heresy and Tradition*, 2nd ed. (London: SCM, 2001), 243–4. Williams cites Donald MacKinnon's 'The Relation of the Doctrines of the Incarnation and the Trinity' in *Creation, Christ and Culture: Essays in Honour of T.F. Torrance*, ed. R. McKinney (Edinburgh: T&T Clark, 1976), 104.

is the ministering, crucified and risen saviour, Jesus Christ; but the existence of Jesus is not an episode in the biography of the Word. It remains obstinately – and crucially – a fact of our world and our world's limits.[96]

The Word being 'the condition of there being a human identity' recalls the last chapter's discussion of *anhypostatic* Christology, even if such terminology only developed long after Nicaea. But, in Williams's reading, the precursors of a full-blown Alexandrian-inflected Chalcedonianism are already present in the council's conclusions. They necessitate a return to history and humanity, as a high theology of Jesus's divinity passes into the need to take seriously the human *an*-other to whom divinity is predicated.[97]

To move to the more recent, and already cited, *Why Study the Past?*, history is again rendered central to a Christian theological sensibility, and for precisely Christological reasons. The book's primary focus is, however, not on that singular *an*-other Jesus, but upon the import he communicates to numerous, especially Christian, *an*-others. In a discussion that recalls what was previously said about Christians as 'place-holders', Williams argues that a Christian historical vision is refracted through the doctrine of the ecclesial body of Christ. Insofar as the incarnation is the 'one divine action that sustains the Church', the ecclesial body is the continuing locus of Christ's activity. He is, as was said earlier, *not*-other to it. An orientation to Jesus's story therefore entails an orientation to multiple ecclesial lives and communities, present and past, as the placeholders where his agency persists.[98] In this light, Williams's interest in the history of spirituality, in works such as *The Wound of Knowledge*, is revealed to be something more than esoteric. It is attention to that 'one divine action' in the incarnation as it is re-embodied within multiple historical *an*-others. This, in turn, makes sense of the point made earlier, that attention to the historical particularity of Jesus includes attentiveness to the history of responses to him, to a 'new historical humanity formed in confrontation with the story of Jesus'.[99] The divine activity that is the incarnation is not just manifested in the bent centre of history that is Jesus's life, but in the historical members of a body that stems from that life, histories drawn into significance by his consummately significant history. It is in

---

96. Williams, *Arius*, 244.

97. For an argument that Nicaea implies the full humanity of Christ, see Williams's article 'Athanasius and the Arian Crisis', in *The First Christian Theologians: An Introduction to Theology in the Early Church*, ed. G. R. Evans (Oxford: Blackwell, 2004), 166–7. However, Williams admits elsewhere that a high theology of Jesus's divinity *can* distract from the mediatorial nature of his humanity. See his 'The Nicene Heritage', in *The Christian Understanding of God Today*, ed. J. M. Byrne (Dublin: The Columba Press, 1993), 47.

98. Williams, *Why Study the Past?* 91–6. This discussion includes an unusual late citation (n. 3, p. 123) from Florovsky ('The Work of the Holy Spirit in Revelation', *The Christian East* 13.2 [1932], 49–64).

99. Williams, *On Christian Theology*, 82.

attention to this multiplicity constellated around Christ that the full import of his life is apprehended.

Thus, just as the ecclesial body is a Christological datum, ecclesial historiography is a species of Christological investigation. To quote a 1989 essay: 'Who Jesus is must be (and can only be) grasped in the light of what Christian humanity is.'[100] But this intuition is reciprocally underwritten by Christological commitments. To return to *Why Study the Past?*: 'The *conviction of Christ's status as divine* allows us to see the possibility of identifying his presence in an unlimited variety of human lives associated with his by faith; and the continuing activity of so "reading" human lives and finding Christ fills out practically the belief in his identity as more than an historical individual in the past.'[101] A high theology of the incarnation not only opens the doors to taking seriously the human history of Jesus, but it also opens the doors to the significance of multiple other histories as *loci* of divine action. These histories gain meaning as they are constellated around their singular Christological centre. Williams is an incarnational historicist in that the incarnation drives him to see history as the arena of meaning's emergence. In return, the meaning that emerges fills out the content of belief in the incarnation. This is the positive theological import of Williams's focus on the historical. It begins in that stretching of the divine grammar to insist that God, who is *non aliud*, in a particular history comes among us as *an*-other. In doing so, history itself is transfigured.

Conclusions

To unite this last section's discussions with the previous ones, it is worth returning to how this constellating of history into meaning occurs. If Florovsky describes history prior to its Christological inflection as an eternal return of the same, moribund in terms of progress, Williams comes in his mature theology to cast this as a continuity of violence. The eternal return is that of mimetic competition, that always preceding human mis-desiring and the consequent history of violent diminishment. As I showed in the first section, it is this violent sameness that is foregrounded and judged in Jesus's human performance. What he mediates, though, is not just judgement, but a divine discontinuity to this sameness. If progress and change are now possible in history, it is because of the *theosis* of human possibilities in the place-holding lives constellated around Jesus's history. They hold the place of a universal hope, an eschatological prospect within history's midst, which renders it meaningful. Williams inhabits the basic grammar, incarnational and historicist, which Florovsky sketched; but he comes to do so in his own distinct manner.

100. Ibid., 25. See also 171–3 & Rowan Williams, 'Looking for Jesus and Finding Christ', in *Biblical Concepts and Our World*, ed. D. Z. Phillips and M. von der Ruhr (Basingstoke: Palgrave MacMillan, 2004), 151.

101. *Why Study the Past?* 104. Emphasis mine.

It is ultimately, for Williams, a set of possibilities created by the resurrection that allows us to move beyond the impasse represented in 'Burnt Norton'.[102] We no longer have to choose between escape from, or surrender to, a meaningless and vicious history. Its eternal return has been transfigured by a perfect human performance of God, a disruptive and creative axial moment that endues history with consummate significance. In Christ, God is *not*-other to a human life in whom competition and threat have been brought into a unique abeyance, and who uniquely mediates God's creative presence. That life becomes *not*-other to a community that holds its place in history. In this way, Christ is, again, history's eschatological 'last word', a presence 'with whom ultimately every speaker may discover an exchange that is steadily and unfailingly life giving and free of anxiety'.[103]

Postscript

All this occurs because of a stretching of the divine grammar – to be *not*-other to *an*-other – that is not without consequence. In a 1990 essay, Williams makes the point that living as *an*-other in time commits one to interaction and converse. It consequently foreswears the possibility (however mythological) of pure self-definition. Conversation entails the risk of admitting others' interpretations into the equation of the self. To refuse this is to flee from time itself, an unsatisfactory choice tellingly related to the unsatisfactory possibilities laid out in 'Burnt Norton'.[104] For Williams, the risk God undertakes in the incarnation is this inherently perilous commitment to interaction. God, in a certain sense, surrenders the possibility of divine self-definition by becoming *not*-other to a historical agent. Therein, God commits to an openness of interpretation, to being a *signum* that can be misidentified by creatures in even idolatrous ways.[105] In a turn of phrase from Gillian Rose that will become crucial in this book, this divine venture into history can be termed an entry into a '*drama of misrecognition*'.[106]

---

102. Arguably one of the weaknesses of the Eliot lectures, corrected by Williams's later theology, is that they propose a *theologia crucis* insufficiently tempered by a doctrine of the resurrection. The accent is on the 'axial tree', while the resurrection is an ambiguous sign (Williams, 'The Four Quartets', lecture 3, 8). If anything, the incarnation 'validates history' by *condemning* it 'to unresolved tensions, to the clash of apparent absolutes, to puzzlement and darkness, failure, death, all seen as the only mode of created existence possible, and to the only vehicle of salvation possible' (lecture 3, 5). This rhetoric points to the judgement on human possibilities in Christ's crucifixion, but does not allow much space for the expansion of those possibilities, however tentative, in the resurrection.

103. Williams, *Dostoevsky*, 139.

104. Williams, 'God and Risk (2)', 12–14.

105. Ibid., 15–6.

106. See Gillian Rose, *Mourning Becomes the Law: Philosophy and Representation* (Cambridge: Cambridge University Press, 1996), 72.

It is only by venturing this risk that God transforms history. If the grammar of *non aliud* is what makes possible and complicates Christological mediation, here is where complexity begins to bite. Becoming *an*-other not only stretches God's grammar, it also permits others to garble it. It allows for interpretations that call into question the generative nature of God's being *not*-other. In the chapters to come, this complexity will be explored.

Chapter 3

Parodies

Introduction

If the last chapter explored Williams's positive Christological presentation, this one focuses on a more oblique Christological approach carried out in a dialogue with literature, and with particular attention to the role of parody. This more oblique approach arguably constitutes an inchoate negative Christology, persisting alongside Williams's positive approach. It supports, and yet persists in some tension with, that approach. The trail of this literary negative Christology is first picked up in Williams's essay 'Making it Strange: Theology in Other(s') Words' (2002).[1] It continues through into an interrogation of Prince Myshkin, the protagonist of *The Idiot*, in Williams's writings on Dostoevsky. In following this trail, what emerges further is the positive importance of Christ becoming *an*-other in what Gillian Rose would call a '*drama of misrecognition*'. Yet, what also emerges is what was hinted at towards the end of the last chapter – the tension and complexity the entry into this drama brings to Williams's Christology. This second point will emerge more fully in Chapter 4.

Part 1 A Parodic Christology

Parthenogenesis

The essay 'Making it Strange' comes out of Williams's cooperation with the poet Michael Symmons Roberts and the composer James MacMillan in the production of a piece of musical theatre entitled *Parthenogenesis* for the *Sounding the Depths* festival in Cambridge. Premised on an urban myth from the Second World War, it tells the story of a young German woman who spontaneously conceives in the trauma of an Allied bombing raid – a shock-induced, and scientifically improbable, act of human parthenogenesis. The resultant girl child is, necessarily, a genetic clone of her mother. Symmons Roberts, as a poet, describes the work as portraying a 'negative-print' of the incarnation, a virgin birth in which violence, not God, is

---

1. In *Sounding the Depths: Theology through the Arts*, ed. J. Begbie (London: SCM, 2002), 19–38.

the instigator.[2] Williams, as a theologian, speculates that such a 'negative-print' might itself constitute a fruitful object for theological investigation. He proposes the possibility of a particularly modern mode of negative theology, through the interrogation of a certain sort of parody. Insofar as *Parthenogenesis* projects the story of the incarnation into a graceless 'world of absences', it transposes faith's half-remembered echoes into the registers of secular modernity. But, in this parodic transposition, Williams intuits that what is half-forgotten may be recalled, and the questioning force of the original narrative can re-emerge with a new energy.[3]

What Williams sketches is a negative theological method to be pursued in an artistic mode. Its object of enquiry is the interval of difference between the original account and its parodic transposition, as we 'imagine the translation of a religious narrative into the framework of secularity; then prompt the question of what has changed'.[4] The intuitions behind this method are that straight descriptions of God are never adequate, and that theology 'needs excursions into the mirror world of what it is *not* saying in order to find out what it *is* about'. Insofar as these intuitions also lie behind the apophatic tradition in Christian theology, this venture through parody is, for Williams, a legitimate manifestation of that tradition within modernity, and one especially suited to a religiously reticent age.[5]

In 'Making it Strange', Williams intriguingly names several *Christian* poets as transposers of the sacred into a world of absences, and, therefore, as potential exponents of this oblique theological way. Included in that list are two priest-poets, R. S. Thomas and (the not so modern) George Herbert.[6] The latter might seem an unlikely candidate for this accolade, yet in a series of published lectures Williams notes how, set against the 'paradisal' Platonism of the likes of Spencer or Traherne, Herbert sounds the dissonant key. He probes what might be the case if the world is experienced as proffering frustrating absences instead of a beneficent divine presence.[7] In the same lectures, R. S. Thomas's poem 'Via Negativa' is cited. There God 'is that great absence' who 'keeps the interstices/In our knowledge, the darkness/Between stars'.[8] For Williams, any sense of presence mediated in

---

2. From 'Introduction', in ibid., 18.

3. Williams, 'Making It Strange', in ibid., 30–2.

4. Ibid., 25.

5. Ibid., 30–2. Elsewhere, in an essay published in the same year as 'Making it Strange', Williams notes how 'the extremity of some sorts of art, verbal and visual' (presumably including the parodic) can be useful for contemporary theology in finding 'an appropriately difficult, distancing register'. See Rowan Williams, '"Is It the Same God?" Reflections on Continuity and Identity in Religious Language', in *The Possibilities of Sense*, ed. J. H. Whittaker (Basingstoke: Palgrave, 2002), 211–2.

6. Williams, 'Making It Strange', 30.

7. Rowan Williams, *Christian Imagination in Poetry and Polity: Some Anglican Voices from Temple to Herbert* (Oxford: SLG Press, 2004), 32.

8. Ibid., 37–8.

Thomas's poetry is 'only literally on the edge of silence'.[9] Both poets, in proposing that grace should not be read too easily upon the surfaces of a creation marked by absence and quandary, take at least a first step along an oblique theological way.

Yet, in 'Making it Strange', it is left to the Catholic lay writer Flannery O'Connor – some of whose contributions to Williams's thought have already been explored in our first chapter – to push this transposition into absence into its fully parodic mode. Her 'often grotesque' fictions reveal for Williams that, in a world without God, 'there is nowhere for some parts of the human constitution to go ... except into violence and madness'.[10] As D. Z. Phillips has separately noted, she is a writer who traces the exilic distances between where humanity empirically is, and its intended presence to God[11]; she, therefore, arguably traces something like that interval which Williams's theology through parody is looking for. In her world, as Williams notes in *Dostoevsky*, 'the variegated absences of grace – or sometimes the apes of grace – almost force the question'.[12] Parodically, and yet also theologically, the unacceptable is pursued 'in the ironic faith that the pursuit will vindicate God'.[13] It is a project informed by that distinctly apophatic intuition that 'the infinite cannot be *directly* apprehended',[14] that is, that straight theological description is never adequate.

Thus, for Williams, O'Connor, Herbert and Thomas each touch upon the absences in a world where God is no object of straightforward encounter. If God is *non aliud*, not *an*-other, God *can* ultimately be no such object. To recall the discussion of 'Deflections of Desire' and Williams's use of John of the Cross in Chapter 1, the inscription of divine difference into human experience can even come as the 'dark night' of an ego-annihilating absence. O'Connor is the writer who overtly exploits parody in her endeavours to probe a world of absence. But, when it comes to Williams's reflections on *Parthenogenesis*, what is not approached directly as an object, but as a transposed parody, is the incarnation. What is in play is not just a negative theology, but a negative Christology accomplished through parody. That female clone-child born out of a night of fearful destruction would,

9. Rowan Williams, '"Adult Geometry": Dangerous Thoughts in R. S. Thomas', in *The Page's Drift: R.S. Thomas at Eighty*, ed. M. Wynn Thomas (Bridgend: Seren, 1993), 94–5. For a parallel discussion, see Rowan Williams, 'Suspending the Ethical: R. S. Thomas and Kierkegaard', in *Echoes of the Amen: Essays after R.S. Thomas*, ed. D. W. Davies (Cardiff: University of Wales Press, 2009), 206–19.

10. Williams, 'Making It Strange', 26.

11. D. Z. Phillips, 'A Realism of Distances (Flannery O'Connor)', in *From Fantasy to Faith: The Philosophy of Religion and Twentieth-Century Literature* (Basingstoke: Macmillan, 1991), 213.

12. Rowan Williams, *Dostoevsky: Language, Faith and Fiction* (London: Continuum, 2008), 6.

13. Rowan Williams, *Grace and Necessity: Reflections on Art and Love* (London: Continuum, 2005), 100–1.

14. Ibid., 103.

to Williams, 'have been "messianic" in a pretty literal sense', her genetic sameness 'an extraordinary symbol' of National Socialism's obsession with the pure self-replication of racial integrity. Yet, this potential dark messianism is also, notes Williams, immediately subverted. Over and against the Nazi cult of masculine heroism, parthenogenesis as a process can only result in female offspring. This is racial purity accomplished at the expense of sexual difference; it is ultimately sterile and futureless – and, notably, the birth of this pseudo-messiah is through an assault of enemy aggression. To quote Williams directly: 'It is as if the cost of purity is both rape and castration.'[15]

Accompanying this parodic Christology is a parodic mariology. The child's mother, 'lacks the usual accoutrements: a lily or rose, a book of devotions'.[16] But, in her interval from this parodic double, Mary herself emerges from secular forgetfulness. As the agent of her baby's conception is no enemy, Mary's consent is integral to the Gospel narrative. The birth of her *male* child, by definition, rules out genetic identity; this is a new creation, not a repetition.[17] Therefore, though the conception is virginal, absent is an insistence on purity coded as sameness, an insistence indicative to Williams of a fear of history. History can only proceed, to him, through the generation of otherness, and the risky encounter with what is other than oneself. Thus the clone-child, as the genetic repetition of her mother, is a symbolic nullification of otherness, and an end to meaningful historical movement;[18] this is a parodic Christology and mariology that passes over into a parodic eschatology. As noted at the very end of the last chapter, being *an*-other in history is an entry into self-risking converse, even a '*drama of misrecognition*'. Thus, an insistence on pure sameness is a species of attempting to avoid the drama that God himself embraces in the incarnation. This is part of the parodic nature of the clone-child's messianism. The negative Christology presented in Williams's essay on *Parthenogenesis*, learnt through an excursion into a 'mirror world' of absences, thus flags up a set of cautions Williams has around any 'purity' that might avoid drama. It is potentially sterile and anti-historical, violent and darkly eschatological. These cautions reappear when investigating another parodic Christology, one Williams finds in the protagonist of *The Idiot*.

Dostoevsky and Christ Figures

In his 2008 book on Dostoevsky, Williams notes the author's use of literary Christ figures, but judges none of them to be an ultimate success. The reason for this is not artistic failure, but, rather, theological impossibility: 'To the extent that fiction cannot reproduce the gratuity of the once and for all particular existence

---

15. Williams, 'Making It Strange', 22.

16. Michael Symmons Roberts, 'Libretto for *Parthenogenesis*', in *Sounding the Depths*, 42.

17. Williams, 'Making It Strange', 23–4.

18. Ibid., 29.

of Jesus, any "Christ figure" is bound to be ambiguous."[19] Recalling the previous chapter's considerations, for Williams, Christ is a particular historical *an*-other whose transformative power is *through* his rendering of a singular performance of God's life enmeshed within a particular human and historical context. That virtuoso performance is, in and of itself, unrepeatable. Nothing, for Williams, can be 'contemporary with the alteration' it works on what can be said about God and humanity.[20] Thus, to try and figure Christ through another story is to figure someone *other* than Christ. Whatever the literary quality of the attempt, it entails some degree of theological failure.[21] Any attempt at a repetition of that divine performance pushes, intentionally or not, in the direction of parody.[22]

For Williams, Dostoevsky was enough of an artist and religious thinker to be ruefully aware of this dynamic, even as he struggled against it. He also argues that the only truly successful Christological performances in Dostoevsky's fiction – and fiction in general – are oblique. They picture Christ 'in those who are moving toward him'.[23] In other words, what is possible, in a non-parodic manner, is the image of a Christian disciple.[24] As alluded to in the last chapter, Alyosha and Sonya, 'placeholders' for Christ in Dostoevsky's fiction, in different ways constitute such an image. But more direct attempts, such as the character of Prince Myshkin, succumb to parody. Myshkin is a failure, but an instructive one. In his intervals of difference from Jesus, he provides the occasion for just that sort of negative Christology delineated in relation to *Parthenogenesis*. He does so not only because he is, as a Christ figure, the flawed outcome of a theologically mistaken endeavour, but also because he is a figure transposed into a world of secular absence. This transposition can, in itself, be read as a deliberate negative theological move by Dostoevsky.

19. Williams, *Dostoevsky*, 47.

20. Ibid., 107–8.

21. Hans Frei makes a similar point, noting also that such theological failure can be instructive; its distance from the original can draw us back to what is unique about Christ. In other words, it presents an instructive interval of difference. See Hans Frei, *The Identity of Jesus Christ: The Hermeneutical Basis of Dogmatic Theology* (Philadelphia: Fortress Press, 1975), 65, 82–4.

22. This is not a phenomenon confined to modernity. Williams has, for instance, noted the 'hilariously awful' apocryphal stories of Jesus's childhood created by early Christians (Rowan Williams, *Ponder These Things: Praying with Icons of the Virgin* [Norwich: Canterbury Press, 2002], 59–60). To him, 'they portray a superbrat combining unrestrained childish whimsy with unrestrained childish malevolence' (see Rowan Williams, 'Imagining Christ in Literature', in *The Oxford Handbook of Christology*, eds F. A. Murphey and T. A. Stefano [Oxford: Oxford University Press, 2015], 490).

23. Williams, *Dostoevsky*, 10.

24. Hans Frei notes that even the portrayal of a flawed disciple, such as the priest of *The Power and The Glory*, is more Christologically successful than a direct attempt. See his *The Identity of Jesus Christ*, 80–1.

René Girard has argued, in language that recalls some of Williams's moves in 'Making it Strange', that Dostoevsky does not offer us ' "religious" art in the ideological sense'. His is, instead, an art of 'extreme negation', suited to a religiously sceptical age where 'direct assertion and affirmation' are ineffective.[25] Williams would largely concur with this reading of Dostoevsky. For all that author's concerns with Christianity, Williams understands the Russian as consummately a writer of secular modernity. Like O'Connor et al., Dostoevsky, to him, explores a world of absences, attempting to show faith's ambiguities within it.[26] This exploration demonstrates 'what realism without grace looks like', a narration that terminates (ultimately like Myshkin) in collapse.[27] Dostoevsky's genius was to pursue his religious affirmations, at least at points, through negation. It is the contention of this chapter that Myshkin, although in aspects of his imaginative inception an attempt at a straightforward Christ figure, becomes such a negation. He is a parodic image of Christ cast within secularity. This, at least, is how Williams comes to read him and, in that reading, Williams himself engages in an oblique but instructive Christological investigation.

A Failed Icon

This investigation begins in the book *Grace and Necessity* (2005). Williams is intrigued in that work by the developmental journey the character of Myshkin takes in the multiple iterations of *The Idiot*'s plan. What begins as an attempt by Dostoevsky to write a figure violent in his moral extremism, morphs into what that author sees, at least at one stage, as a representative of the ideal of Christian love. Yet, the end result is ambiguous – Christ-like, yet close, for Williams, 'to a Nietzschean critique of Christianity'.[28] It is this flawed attempt at a 'positively good', or even 'positively beautiful' man (importantly, for the discussions ahead, both translations are possible), that Dostoevsky discusses in a letter to his niece.

25. René Girard, *Resurrection from the Underground: Feodor Dostoevsky*, trans. J. G. Williams (New York: Crossroad, 1997), 136–7.

26. Williams, *Dostoevsky*, introduction, *passim*. Diane Oenning Thompson, whom Williams draws on, notes how Dostoevsky transposes faith into the secular, where it is always subject to irony and 'double thoughts'. See her 'Problems of the Biblical Word in Dostoevsky's Poetics', in *Dostoevsky and the Christian Tradition*, eds George Pattison and Diane Oenning Thompson (Cambridge: Cambridge University Press, 2001), 69–70.

27. Williams, *Dostoevsky*, 74.

28. Williams, *Grace and Necessity*, 144–5. It is possible that Nietzsche had Myshkin in mind when writing *The Antichrist*. See P. Travis Kroeker and Bruce K. Ward, *Remembering the End: Dostoevsky as Prophet to Modernity* (London: SCM Press, 2001), 246–9. Steiner (cited in Williams, *Dostoevsky*, 144, n. 8), notes a similar trajectory to the one Williams traces. Myshkin is originally an 'ambiguous Byronic figure – a sketch for the Stavrogin of the *Possessed*'. Only in the seventh iteration of the novel's outline does he take the form of a Christ figure. See George Steiner, *Tolstoy or Dostoevsky: An Essay in the Old Criticism*, 2nd Edition, (New Haven: Yale, 1996), 151–2.

He admits, in language recalling the problematic around Christ figures, that the portrayal is impossible; there 'is only one positively good figure on earth and that is Christ'. His appearance is an 'endless miracle';[29] in the terms I have already set, it is an unrepeatable performance.

What, for Williams, is portrayed by Dostoevsky, even in a fairly literal sense, is a rather opaque icon of Christ. Physically, Myshkin bears a mischievous similarity to iconographic portrayals of Jesus, provoking a confused familiarity in some. Yet, he is 'deeply flawed by lack of self-knowledge, confused desire and passivity', flaws that render his iconic possibilities 'painfully enigmatic'.[30] To recall the discussions of *Parthenogenesis*, Myshkin thus persists as a parodic and half-remembered echo of faith in the modernity of nineteenth-century Russia. His iconic opacity, however, takes a darker turn for Williams in *Dostoevsky*. There Myshkin is taken for an 'anti-icon', whose superficial Christ-likeness belies his role as an 'unwitting force for destruction'. Williams marks as significant that a copy of the younger Holbein's painting of the dead Christ is a recurring motif in *The Idiot*, one that sheds a sinister light on the novel's protagonist. In a confessedly speculative move, he suggests that we see this painting as an 'anti-icon, a religious image which is a nonpresence or presence of the negative'. It is at odds with the iconographic traditions of Orthodoxy, not so much in its portrayal of Christ as dead, but as in profile. His is a dead and *averted* face that cannot be engaged with. Only, notes Williams, the demonic – or, at times, Judas – are so depicted. To the extent that it is associated with Myshkin, the painting implies that his figuring of Christ is not just questionable; it is potentially monstrous.[31] This half-remembered echo is, potentially, as darkly parodic as the clone-child of *Parthenogenesis*.

Williams's reading of Holbein's painting suggests that, at least in part, Myshkin's iconic failure is constituted by his opacity to engagement. He is associated with one whose face cannot be gazed upon, and who cannot return a gaze. He is also associated, in the novel, with the 'poor knight' of a Pushkin poem, whose face is obscured by a visor.[32] The anti-iconic force of this opacity to engagement becomes clear if we recall the discussion of Rublev's icon in our first chapter. The faces of Rublev's figures were averted, but only *partially* so, and only to initiate a journey for the beholder into the endless interplay of desire within the divine life. This is

---

29. Richard Peace, *Dostoyevsky: An Examination of the Major Novels* (Cambridge: Cambridge University Press, 1971), 59–63. Peace notes that 'positively good man' could be translated to 'positively *beautiful* man' (62–3). The letter, as cited by Peace, is in F. M. Dostoevsky, *Pis'ma*, ed. A. S. Dolinin (Leningrad/Moscow, 1928), vol. 2, 71.

30. Williams, *Grace and Necessity*, 144–6. For an example of the familiarity Myshkin provokes, see his first encounter with Natasya in Fyodor Dostoevsky, *The Idiot*, trans. David McDuff (London: Penguin, 2004), 123.

31. Williams, *Dostoevsky*, 53–4.

32. See ibid., 124–6 and Dostoevsky, *The Idiot*, 291–4. Like Myshkin, the poor knight ends in silence and madness.

an invitation that requires, first, an engagement, and then a travelling through that engagement to engage with another, and so on. An obliquely viewed corpse, however, cannot offer any invitation to engagement. Holbein's painting is thus, in the words of Julia Kristeva, an image 'without any prospect toward heaven'.[33] There is no movement on from it into the divine life. By implication, Myshkin offers no such heavenly prospect or impetus to movement either. Our gaze never really finds him, and thereby cannot move beyond him. Insofar as this is the case, both the painting and the prince are parodies, icons in and of a world of absence.

Yet, the painting itself, especially its nature as a profile upon which Williams places such weight, is never explicitly described in *The Idiot;* and others have read its significance quite differently. Irina Prinkhod'ko, in her review of *Dostoevsky*, questions Williams's use of it, and anecdotally recalls the impression made on a group of Russian academics when viewing Holbein's original. Noticeable, to them, was a (divine?) light suffusing Christ's corpse, perhaps foreshadowing a resurrection. To Prinkhod'ko, there is, in this perception, the suggestion of 'a totally different understanding of the novel and its principle character'.[34] Ben Quash, while not commenting on Williams's use of the painting, has questioned the stark reading of it offered by Kristeva. He sees Holbein's work as indicative of a 'newly interrogative attitude to death' in early modernity. It raises the stakes in its unflinching realism, but it does not rule out the hope of resurrection[35] – and, to a commentator like George Steiner, it is precisely in its interrogative realism towards death that the painting becomes, for Dostoevsky, iconic. It is a 'real form' of the original, forcing the question as to the presence of God in a life reduced to a corpse, as well as questioning a world 'in which a being such as He has been tortured to death'.[36]

To turn to Myshkin himself, Williams's stark reading of the prince is also not universally shared. Steiner acknowledges Myshkin's ambiguities, but sees him as a Christ figure 'rooted in Russian folk-lore and the hagiography of the Eastern Church'. He is 'the image of the wandering and persecuted Son of Man whom we may mistake for an idiot, of the holy prince recognized by the children, the holy beggars, and the epileptics'.[37] Here Myshkin is modelled on the figure of the Christ-like *yurodivy,* or 'holy fool' within Russian Orthodox tradition.[38] Travis

---

33. From Julia Kristeva, *Black Sun: Depression and Melancholia*, trans. L. S. Roudiez (New York, 1989), 112–5, as cited by Oenning Thompson, 'Problems of the Biblical Word', 74.

34. Irina Prinkhod'ko, 'Review Article: Rowan Williams. Dostoevsky: Language, Faith and Fiction', *Sobornost: The Journal of the Fellowship of St Alban and St Sergius* 32, no. 2 (2010), 78–9.

35. Ben Quash, *Found Theology: History, Imagination and the Holy Spirit* (London: Bloomsbury, 2013), 115–21.

36. Steiner, *Tolstoy or Dostoevsky*, 292.

37. Ibid., 292–3.

38. See the discussion, in a work translated by Williams himself, in Pierre Pascal, *The Religion of the Russian People*, trans. R. Williams (London: Mowbrays, 1976), 42–3.

Kroeker and Bruce Ward, in their co-authored work, make a similar contention. They note that such a figure, following Byzantine ascetic practices, 'adopted forms of behaviour – poverty, eccentricity and often feigned madness – that were exercises in self-humiliation and an indirect judgement of the "world" and its "common sense"'.[39] This trope of the *yurodivy* is almost certainly part of the imaginative hinterland informing Myshkin. But such a figure, as described above, enjoys a level of deliberative agency, and a grounding in a religious tradition, that I will argue Myshkin lacks. His idiocy is not, in the novel, feigned; and it should also be noted that the most overt example of such a 'fool' in Dostoevsky's fiction, Semyon Yakolevich, is himself a remarkably ambiguous figure.[40] Yet, even if construing Myshkin as something like a holy fool is problematic, it still remains the case that no less a theological influence upon Williams than Hans Urs von Balthasar – in a volume of the *Theological Aesthetics,* which Williams helped translate – and no less a reader of Dostoevsky than Mikhail Bakhtin – an important interlocutor in Williams's own readings – have separately offered more positive understandings of Myshkin.[41] Thus, Williams's darker reading is to be marked, and the following questions raised: Why does he see in Myshkin such a malignly parodic icon of Christ, and why does he find the painting of a corpse so negatively evocative? Perhaps because the figure Dostoevsky had in mind was, precisely, that of a *'beautiful'* man.

A 'Beautiful Soul'

To understand why this beauty is a problem, one first needs to talk about a friendship. The name of the Jewish philosopher Gillian Rose has already been mentioned. Williams first met her in 1991, and he came to regard her as among the foremost British thinkers of her generation. Their friendship lasted until her early death in 1995, and among the gifts she bequeathed Williams was a

---

39. Kroeker and Ward, *Remembering the End,* 249–50. Bonhoeffer, while not using the language of the holy fool, sees Myshkin as instantiating, in his eccentricity and self-humiliation, the judging and transformative question of 'Who?' that the Word provokes. See Dietrich Bonhoeffer, 'Lectures in Christology (Student Notes)' in *Dietrich Bonhoeffer Works, Volume 12: Berlin 1932–1933,* eds C. Nicolaisen and E. A. Scharffenorth, English edition L. L. Rasmussen, trans. I. Best and D. Higgins (Minneapolis: Fortress, 2009), 306–7.

40. See Fyodor Dostoevsky, *Devils,* trans. M. R. Katz (Oxford: Oxford University Press, 1992), 344–54. To Williams, in *Dostoevsky,* Yakolevich is 'parodic and grotesque' (191), and an 'icon reduced to a cartoon' (218).

41. See Hans Urs von Balthasar, *The Glory of the Lord: A Theological Aesthetics, Vol. 5: The Realm of Metaphysics in the Modern Age,* trans. O. Davies, et al. (Edinburgh: T&T Clark, 1991), 189–201, and Mikhail Bakhtin, *Problems of Dostoevsky's Poetics,* trans. C. Emerson (Minneapolis: University of Minnesota Press, 1984) 172–6, 241–2. Williams critiques Bakhtin's reading in *Dostoevsky,* 52–3.

new appreciation for the thought of Hegel.[42] Arguably, when considering the consternation Williams feels towards Myshkin, one should have in the back of one's mind Hegel's critique in the *Phenomenology* of a form of consciousness he labelled the 'beautiful soul', especially as this figure is mediated through Rose's writings.[43] For Hegel, the beautiful soul is a figure obsessed with its own purity. It 'lives in dread of besmirching the splendour of its own being by action and an existence'. In this self-defeating existential fastidiousness, 'it vanishes like a shapeless vapour that dissolves into thin air'.[44] In Rose's *The Broken Middle*, the beautiful soul is, therefore, 'impotent in the world'; its is 'an ethereal eros without form or contact'. To Rose it lacks, echoing Hegel's own words, 'actual existence', and is 'disordered to the point of madness'. Rose sums this existence up as '*beautiful*', but not 'holy'. It cannot give knowledge or love away, and cannot educate or form others, but denies life.[45] Another way to describe such a figure, in the terms of this book, would be to say that out of a desire for purity, it seeks to cease being *an*-other within the world.

To be clear from the outset, although Hegel is invoked in *Dostoevsky*,[46] and Rose appears in a couple of footnotes,[47] Williams does not deploy the language of

42. See Rowan Williams, *Wrestling with Angels: Conversations in Modern Theology*, ed. Mike Higton (Cambridge: Eerdmans, 2007), xiv and Shortt, *God's Advocates: Christian Thinkers in Conversation* (London: Darton, Longman and Todd, 2005), 16–7. The best extant secondary discussion of their relationship is probably in Ben Myers, *Christ the Stranger: The Theology of Rowan Williams* (London: T&T Clark, 2012) Chapter 6 *passim* (although Myers' contention that Rose 'radically' [52] altered Williams's appreciation for Hegel is arguably overstated). Williams's continuing regard for Rose is evidenced by his dedication to her of *Lost Icons*, and acknowledgement of her 'magisterial influence' in his *Faith in the Public Square* (London: Bloomsbury, 2012), 6. Most poignant of all is his poem cycle 'Winterreise', written in her memory. See *The Poems of Rowan Williams* (Oxford: Perpetua Press, 2002), 68–9.

43. Andrew Shanks, in a monograph that is a barely concealed apology for Williams, describes Rose's exegesis of the soul as a clarification of Hegel himself. See Andrew Shanks, *Against Innocence: Gillian Rose's Reception and Gift of Faith* (London: SCM Press, 2008), 132–9.

44. G. W. F. Hegel, *Phenomenology of Spirit*, trans. A. V. Miller (Oxford: Oxford University Press, 1977), § 658, 400. For the entirety of Hegel's discussion, see § 632–71, 383–409.

45. Gillian Rose, *The Broken Middle* (Oxford: Blackwell, 1992), 183, 236–7. Compare with Hegel, *Phenomenology*, 406–7. Rose's investigation of the soul is illumined and complexified by her interweaving it with the narratives of three Jewish women: Hannah Arendt, Rahel Varnhagen and Rosa Luxemburg. See Rose, *The Broken Middle*, Chapter 5 *passim* and Shanks, *Against Innocence*, 132–9.

46. Williams, *Dostoevsky*, 11, 19, 95, 174, 255, n. 32.

47. Ibid., 260–1, n. 15, 16.

the beautiful soul in connection with Myshkin[48] – and, in personal conversation, he has revealed that this connection was not one explicit in his own mind when writing about Myshkin.[49] Yet, if the soul's taxonomy is laid out alongside Williams's reading of the prince, the resemblances are striking. There is an interwoven changelessness, placelessness and timelessness to Myshkin that repeatedly resonates with the Hegelian figure. In his 'changelessness', he echoes the soul's inability to take action in time. He 'makes no adult choices', and this is part of the interval of his distance from Jesus. The latter makes definitional choices; in the desert, he refuses temptation, and in Gethsemane, he struggles to obey the Father. Myshkin evidences no such engaged agency.[50] He is also beset by a privation of context that renders him placeless and belies his actual existence in the world. He enters the narrative an orphan, with addled memories of his homeland and clothing comically ill-suited for the oncoming Russian winter.[51] He knows nothing about where he is going, or about what to do, and Williams reads his advent as recollecting the abrupt arrival of Jesus in Mark's Gospel, except that this parody 'has nothing to say or do when he arrives'.[52] Williams also notes Myshkin's lack of connection with the Orthodox faith; this Christ figure emerges from no ecclesial community or tradition.[53]

But more sinister than Myshkin's privation of context and agency is his timelessness. It is this that, to Williams, brings him closest to the diabolical.[54] In his illness, Myshkin is prone to ecstatic visions wherein 'time will be no more' (echoing Revelation 10:6). Belying the biblical allusion, this is for Williams a cryptically violent 'premature embrace of harmony'. It has 'no resources of memory and critical self-awareness to make it effective in the world of human relations'. Its outcome, in the novel's horrifying *dénouement,* is a parodic end of time in which the future, for Myshkin and others, is violently erased.[55] This timelessness echoes the impotence of the beautiful soul in time, but also recollects the implied ending of history in the clone-child of *Parthenogenesis.* Myshkin, too, presents a parodic eschatology. He is a parodic 'last word'; instead of vivifying dialogue, what is found through him is the silence of death and catatonic madness.

48. He does, in passing, use it of the Christ conjured in Ernest Renan's *Life of Jesus* (see Rowan Williams, 'A History of Faith in Jesus', in *The Cambridge Companion to Jesus*, ed. M. Bockmuehl [Cambridge: Cambridge University Press, 2001], 232). Dostoevsky was familiar with Renan's romanticized Christ, who appears to have been both an inspiration, and a foil, in his thinking. See Kroeker and Ward, *Remembering the End,* 243–6.

49. This issue was discussed in an interview between the author and Williams at Magdalene College, Cambridge, on the 29th of October, 2015.

50. Williams, *Dostoevsky,* 48.

51. See Dostoevsky, *The Idiot,* 6.

52. Williams, *Dostoevsky,* 48.

53. Ibid., 48, 189–90.

54. Ibid., 52.

55. Ibid., 49–50.

In considering this theme of diabolical timelessness, Williams cites two incidents in *The Idiot* where the allusion to Revelation, and time being no more, is invoked. The first is Myshkin's wandering in the euphoric preamble to a fit, and the second is Ippolit's speech before attempting suicide. The implication of these passages is that an 'ecstatic vision of harmony is bound up with *death*'.[56] Williams does not bring this out, but both incidents also have a violent coda – Rogozhin's attempt on Myshkin's life, and Ippolit's attempt to shoot himself – and both are connected with Holbein's painting. Myshkin's wandering is preceded (in the previous chapter) by the first foreboding encounter with that work, while Ippolit speaks of it in his speech. If a timeless harmony is 'bound up with *death*', it is also, in Dostoevsky's novel, attended by violence, and by the image of a dead Christ; an anti-icon of deathly silence travels with the parodic eschatology Myshkin proposes.

Privative Grace

In the previous chapter it was noted that Williams sees judgement, including that rendered by Christ, as a reflective telling of the truth about another that can be transformative. But Myshkin, in his privation of agency, place and timefulness, lacks the resources for such reflection and truth-telling. He cannot judge because, to Williams, he cannot 'listen to and *change* place' with another. He does not have the imaginative and analogical resources in himself that are needed for such a dialogue,[57] nor can he 'think in terms of actions that make a difference'.[58] To borrow language used by Rose, this beautiful soul has never undertaken the 'anxiety of beginning' or the 'agon of authorship'[59] within time. Thus, his eros is non-transformative, offering only 'ambivalent compassion'. This one, who has never authored a self, can only reproduce his own privation in others, in what Williams calls a 'diabolical authorship' that inscribes in them 'silence and death'.[60] To trace another interval of difference between Myshkin and Christ, and recalling the previous chapter's discussions, Christ is the one who enacts judgement *within* the broken field of human relations in order to transform it. As *an*-other in time, he mediates God's freedom. Myshkin inhabits neither the human field, nor his own agency properly. He, thereby, lacks the perceptual wherewithal to judge, to

---

56. Ibid., 49. Myshkin's wandering is in Dostoevsky, *The Idiot*, Book II, Chapter 5. For Ippolit's speech, see Book III, Chapters 5–7.

57. Williams, *Dostoevsky*, 53. In Hegel and Rose, the beautiful soul's reluctant purity is contrasted with the 'hard heart of judgement', and with the possibility of a reconciliation between these two poles. See Andrew Shanks, *Hegel's Political Theology* (Cambridge: Cambridge University Press, 1991), 36–41, *Against Innocence*, 132–9, and Rose, *The Broken Middle*, Chapter 5 *passim*.

58. Williams, *Dostoevsky*, 145.

59. See, for instance, Rose, *The Broken Middle*, 296.

60. Williams, *Dostoevsky*, 77–9.

tell adequately the truth of himself or others, and, therefore, he cannot transform. Rather, like the beautiful soul, he denies life, both his own and others.

Thus, Myshkin is an ape of grace who – to use language that Williams himself does not employ – offers a parodic soteriology. This is especially evident in his relations with the doomed Natasya. She pictures him in a vision as 'an absent minded Christ both blessing and ignoring the child leaning at his knee'. To Williams, this evokes Myshkin's dangerous timelessness, here revealed as the covert love of a prehistory before adult agency, the context in which his affection for children, evident in *The Idiot*, is embedded.[61] What Williams does not explicitly bring out is that Natasya's vision is also called a 'painting', a probable allusion to that other painting of Christ haunting the narrative. Like the latter, there is no transformative gaze in Natasya's vision. Face averted into a timeless totality, 'looking into the distance',[62] this Christ is as anti-iconic in his own way as the one whose face is averted in death. Through what Williams calls a 'timeless pity', this Christ-Myshkin inflicts damage upon the child, Natasya, infantilizing her agency. Having no history of maturation and choice of his own, Myshkin cannot penetrate the mechanisms of her behaviour. His ethereal eros cannot reflect back her truth, nor enable her transformation. Instead, he offers a static pity that drives her into Rogozhin's hands, and to the murder that her painting foreshadows. The dark grace communicated to Natasya is Myshkin's own privative helplessness.[63]

This dynamic is also visible in Myshkin's relations with Rogozhin, his double and nemesis within the novel. They – after the first encounter with Holbein's painting – exchange crosses. Yet, belying the cross as the locus of judgement, Myshkin offers *no* judgement of Rogozhin, and, therefore, no transformation. Williams offers a 'hard' reading of their exchange. He notes Myshkin's cross is tin, sold fraudulently by a soldier after drink. As 'the mark of a dead faith', it echoes the 'pseudo-icon of the dead Christ'. What is signified in this cruciform transaction that does not save is only a 'damaging' symbiosis.[64] In the end, Rogozhin and Myshkin are bound to the same fate, their agencies reduced to incoherence in the presence of Natasya's corpse – a trinity of agents reduced to silence or death in the house where the image of a dead Christ hangs.[65] It is as if they themselves have become a horrific parody of Rublev's icon.

Yet, if Myshkin diabolically authors silence, it is not because he is deliberately malign; there is a different demonology being offered here. The problem is that *deliberation* is missing in Myshkin. This beautiful soul is a privation of human agency, or what Williams calls a 'not quite human' absence who 'draws others into

61. Ibid., 76–7.
62. Dostoevsky, *The Idiot*, 530.
63. See Williams, *Dostoevsky*, 50–2, 77–9.
64. Ibid., 154–8. See also 54–5.
65. Dostoevsky, *The Idiot*, 714.

a void'.[66] He is, like that empty and swept house of Jesus's parable in Luke 11, a vacuum into which the demonic rushes, and Williams is enough of an Augustinian to understand that privation is the most apt description of evil's true nature.[67] Privative evil is, in the words of another scholar concerned with Augustinian accounts of evil, 'a literal absence of a lively and responsive presence with which we can engage in mutually creating and sustaining a human and public world'.[68] Inasmuch as the beautiful soul, in its concern for purity, exhibits this 'literal absence', it is fallen into evil – and, inasmuch as Myshkin is such a soul, he is a dark Christological parody. If Jesus is *an*-other in time who mediates God's creative presence, and in whom is brought into a unique abeyance the violent potential of any *an*-other, Myshkin apes this dynamic. His *an*-otherness is brought into a recession that renounces not just violence but its own agency. Paradoxically, the result *is* violence, and a demonic void that mediates no presence.

A Perverse Christ

In a discussion where *The Idiot* is referenced, but Myshkin not explicitly mentioned, Williams remarks that in Dostoevsky's fiction, 'the diabolical is implicitly characterized by sexual sterility'. This sterility is sourced in the 'impossibility of erotic responsibility for those who have already in various ways showed themselves unable to deal with real otherness'.[69] An inability to 'deal with real otherness' describes Williams's reading of Myshkin, but Williams does not capitalize on something *The Idiot* hints at – that Myshkin is sexually incapable.[70] Nor does he pay much attention to the motif of castration in the novel, which might recall the reference to castration in his discussion of *Parthenogenesis*.[71] The ethereality and impotence of this beautiful soul seems to have a literal aspect. Like

---

66. Williams, *Dostoevsky*, 124–5.

67. See Rowan Williams, 'Insubstantial Evil', in *Augustine and His Critics: Essays in Honour of Gerald Bonner*, eds R. Dodaro and G. Lawless (London: Routledge, 2000), 105–23.

68. Charles T. Mathewes, *Evil and the Augustinian Tradition* (Cambridge: Cambridge University Press, 2001), 168. This is said in the context of a discussion of Arendt's work on Eichmann. Mathewes reads Arendt as 'Augustinian' in her account of evil as a banal privation, and there are fascinating parallels between Myshkin and the Eichmann she portrays – in Mathewes' words, he is an 'automatically mendacious idiot' whose 'crimes were not rooted in a wicked character: he had no character to be wicked' (167).

69. Williams, *Dostoevsky*, 178–80. Williams suggests that the absence of happy couples in Dostoevsky's fiction and the subversion of the standard marriage plot, point to a 'negative theology' of the erotic wherein its significance 'is defined largely by the tracing of its absence or perversion'.

70. Myshkin tells Rogozhin that, because of his illness, he has no 'experience' with women (Dostoevsky, *The Idiot*, 17), and he cannot marry because of his health (ibid., 43).

71. Rogozhin is closely associated with the Castrates (see Williams, *Dostoevsky*, 155). His house, where the Holbein painting hangs, is inhabited by a member of that sect.

the clone-child, what Myshkin reproduces is a deadening sameness that brings histories to an end. As a parody of Christ, his communicative privation is even encoded in his sexuality, in a sterility with a tinge of perversity.

The intuition that a privative eros potentially passes over into perversity is part of the force of Williams's still controversial essay, 'The Body's Grace' (1989). Originally given as a lecture to the Lesbian and Gay Christian Movement, it established a frame for conceiving morality and perversity in sexual relationships. The 'moral question' is: 'How much do we want our sexuality to communicate?' How much is it part of a project of mutual sense making? Sexuality becomes 'sterile, undeveloped, or even corrupt' when disengaged from this project. Perverse relations are those that refuse the risk of a communicative and transformative encounter with another.[72] In 'Making it Strange', it is the sterile refusal to engage with otherness that stops history. In *Dostoevsky*, such a sterile lack of facility for otherness has moved from the ambit of perversity and into the patently diabolic, and Myshkin is implicated in this movement.

To return to Natasya's 'painting', there Myshkin's befuddled eros renders her a child. And it is in his relationship with children, embedded in his 'enthrallment to prehistory', that Myshkin's perversity is inchoately evident. For Williams, the attractive innocence of children is something that must be problematized. In the book *Resurrection*, discussing the motif of child abuse in *The Brothers Karamazov*, he makes the point that 'the "innocence" of the child is largely to do with the child's unformed capacity for responsible choice'.[73] In *Lost Icons*, this view is reinforced; Williams stresses that the latency of childhood must not be confused with '*adult* fantasies of innocence'.[74] With this in mind, the childlike aspect of Myshkin – a recurrent theme in the novel – is also problematized.[75] His 'innocence' becomes a latency inappropriate in an adult. His belief that children should teach adults,[76] *prima facie* an echo of Christ's teaching, becomes a suggestion that this latency should be taken on by others, of a piece with his tendency to reproduce his privative agency in others. In *Lost Icons*, Williams also notes the dangers present when the differences between adults and children are elided; their relationships become potentially rivalrous and abusive.[77] Myshkin, as a regressive adult, is prone to forgetting children's vulnerability, and collapses the difference between them and him. He believes 'one can tell a child everything'.[78] In his case, the abusive

---

72. Rowan Williams, 'The Body's Grace', in *Our Selves, Our Souls and Bodies: Sexuality and the Household of God*, ed. C. Hefling (Boston: Cowley, 1996), 61–2.

73. Rowan Williams, *Resurrection: Interpreting the Easter Gospel*, 2nd Rev. edn. (London: Darton, Longman and Todd, 2002), 7.

74. Rowan Williams, *Lost Icons: Reflections on Cultural Bereavement* (Edinburgh: T&T Clark, 2000), 14.

75. See, for instance, Dostoevsky, *The Idiot*, 89, 425.

76. Ibid., 80.

77. Williams, *Lost Icons*, 29. See also Rowan Williams, *Christ on Trial: How the Gospel Unsettles Our Judgment* (Grand Rapids: Zondervan, 2000), 62–3.

78. Dostoevsky, *The Idiot*, 79.

possibilities remain potential. In another Dostoevskian parodic Christ, they spill out into the open.

Williams's reading of Stavrogin, from *Devils*, presents a revealing counterpoint to Myshkin. He 'has about him a strong flavor of parodic Christology, not wholly unlike Myshkin'. He is both diabolical and Christological, his name recalling both the Russian for 'horns' (*rog*), and Church Slavonic's adaptation of the Greek *stauros* for 'cross'.[79] Like Myshkin, he is marked by the suspicion of impotency. He is also marked, in a different way, by a privation of agency. His is a parody of saintly *apatheia*; he has lost interest in choosing.[80] It is Stavrogin who, for all his implied impotence, apparently fulfils the abusive potential of one who has abnegated adult agency, seducing and abandoning to suicide a young girl.[81] Insofar as it is appropriate to read Myshkin in the light of this – explicitly darker – figure, it brings into relief the sinister ambiguities that surround him.

An Unfallen Christ

Yet, paradoxically, a part of Myshkin's ambiguity, even his perversity, is his apparent *unfallenness*. Williams reads Myshkin as 'something like a thought experiment', the imagining of a 'perfectly beautiful' character, an 'unfallen humanity' without the history of difficult choice and injury – given and received – that attends those who grow up in a historical manifold infected by 'systems of rivalrous desire'. He is innocent of that endemic relational violence that Williams associates elsewhere with original sin. Dostoevsky, in his novel, plunges this *naïf* into a world of rivalrous desire and watches. At first, there is a 'carnivalesque' liberation, an 'apparently miraculous renewal of vision that comes in the presence of someone without rivalry or pride'. It might for a moment resemble that divine freedom which Christ's discontinuity mediates in time. But the ultimate result demonstrates 'the disastrous effect of relationship with someone who has never "learned how to learn"'.[82] It is a relation with someone who, as Rose remarks of the beautiful soul, cannot help others to learn.

---

79. Williams, *Dostoevsky*, 106–7. Girard, in *Resurrection from the Underground* (81–3) describes the difference between Myshkin and Stavrogin as 'simultaneously immense and miniscule' (83), noting their common origin in Dostoevsky's notebooks.

80. Williams, *Dostoevsky*, 93, 99–100.

81. Ibid., 100–7. As Williams notes, the novel is vague about the veracity of Stavrogin's claim to have committed the crime.

82. Ibid., 55. For a parallel, see Frei's discussion of Melville's *Billy Budd* in his *The Identity of Jesus Christ*, 66–8. Budd is a figure of Adamic innocence, with striking similarities to Myshkin: 'He learns nothing and can neither develop nor shape events in which he is the chief ingredient' (68). Budd, however, retains an aspect of redeeming power in Melville's narrative.

To Williams, Myshkin belongs in an 'unfallen world',[83] but in *this* world, he is worse than useless. What Myshkin thus tests to destruction is the idea of a Christ figure without any 'tragic shadow'.[84] He is, as von Balthasar notes elsewhere, no sinner because he 'does not have the will to sin'.[85] Illness has degraded his acumen for deliberation, stripping away the volitional power to make decisive choices. But the world in which Myshkin persists is one marred by the tragic and, without the acumen for negotiating it through deliberation and volition, he compounds that tragedy. To shift registers, this unfallen parody of Christ – or, perhaps, parody of Christ's unfallenness – prematurely opts out of the hellish aspects of existence, and that hellishness returns with interest. This is to draw obliquely on Rose's autobiographical memoir *Love's Work*. Speaking of the blandishments encountered in the world of alternative healing, she notes that entailed within them was a more ubiquitous temptation – to 'dissolve the difficulty of living, of love, of self and other'. Such a dissolution is a *premature* flight to the non-tragic. It offers 'the counsel of despair which would keep the mind out of hell', rather than, in keeping with the book's epigraph, obeying the imperative to 'keep your mind in hell and despair not'. Myshkin is, in his parodic unfallenness, a premature dissolution of difficulty, a quack remedy that elides the difficult work of love in a fallen manifold. Thus, his ethereal eros exhibits what Rose calls 'edgeless love'. It

> effaces the risk of relation: the mix of exposure and reserve, of revelation and
> reticence. It commands the complete unveiling of the eyes, the transparency of
> the body. It denies that there is no love without power; that we are at the mercy

---

83. Williams compares him to the protagonist of Dostoevsky's short story 'The Dream of a Ridiculous Man' (*Dostoevsky*, 51). For the story itself, see Fyodor Dostoevsky, *The Best Short Stories of Fyodor Dostoevsky*, trans. D. Magarshack (New York: The Modern Library, 2001), 263–85. It presents as the narrative of a sinner's conversion, but proves more perplexing. The protagonist is, arguably, a parodic Christ figure who echoes both Myshkin and Stavrogin. He begins closer to the latter, afflicted to the point of suicide by a dark *apatheia*, and complicit through inaction in the sufferings of a young girl. In the dream upon which the story turns, he is brought to live in an unfallen world, and becomes the unwitting vector for sin's introduction. Filled with remorse, he can offer no healing atonement; he cannot even effect his own crucifixion (283). Upon awaking, he attempts to live in the light of the innocence he both saw and wrecked. In doing so, he becomes 'muddled', 'ridiculous' and rather more like Myshkin. His vision is literally untranslatable: 'I do not know how to establish heaven on earth, for I do not know how to put it into words' (284). He is unable to effect salvation in either world, dream or real. It seems that, for Dostoevsky, there is no way to live an unfallen life in the world as it is without some form of ambiguity, and even of parody.

84. Williams, *Dostoevsky*, 56.

85. von Balthasar, *The Glory of the Lord, Vol. 5*, 192.

of others and that we have others at our mercy. Existence is robbed of its weight, its gravity, when it is deprived of this agon.[86]

A Christ without this agon belies what Williams takes to be true, that 'the restoration of humanity is to do with "labor" ... including the labor of choice and self-definition'.[87] This labour of wise agency in fallen time is what Myshkin cannot undertake. His 'unfallenness' is a weightless privation that robs existence of its heft, denying others the agency he himself lacks. His edgeless love is both sterile and perversely reproductive.

Part 2 An Interval of Distance

In 'Theology in Other(s') Words', Williams offered the investigation of parody as a negative theological method. The next section, and in part the chapter that will follow, will use this method to discern what more is learnt about Christology in Williams's venture through the parodic mirror world of *The Idiot*. If Myshkin is 'anti-iconic', what more, in his interval of difference from Myshkin, can be said about Christ as an icon? If Myshkin is a beautiful soul, without an actual existence and agency, what is it for Jesus to be something different? And, although this will have to wait for the next chapter, if Myshkin is an 'unfallen' Christ, what does this imply about the unfallenness, or otherwise, of Jesus?

The Defaceable Icon

As has been shown, Myshkin is anti-iconic for Williams because he offers no prospect of engagement, and no movement beyond himself that can offer a prospect towards heaven. But this is a *Christological* failure, as well as an iconic one. Myshkin is, upon examination, found to be neither truly God, nor truly and sufficiently human in ways that matter. He, thus, arguably persists as something like a parody of Chalcedon's Christ. Recalling the previous chapter's discussions, the point, for Williams, of Chalcedon and the tradition that followed was to establish that the whole manifold of human action and passion that is Jesus was animated by the Word, his *hypostasis* and hinterland. But there is *no* divine hinterland to Myshkin. Just as Holbein's anti-iconic painting portrayed only the corpse 'of a man',[88] so Williams sees in Myshkin an icon 'with no God behind him'.[89] Movement

---

86. Gillian Rose, *Love's Work* (New York: New York Review Books, 1995), 105–6. Elsewhere, Williams cites from this section of *Love's Work*: 'A soul that is not bound is as mad as one with cemented boundaries' (105). See Rowan Williams, 'On Being a Human Body', *Sewanee Theological Review* 42:4 (1999), 413.

87. Williams, *Dostoevsky*, 56.

88. Dostoevsky, *The Idiot*, 475. This insight is put into Ippolit's mouth in the narrative.

89. Williams, *Dostoevsky*, 48.

thus stops with him, but not only because there is nothing divine to be found beyond Myshkin; there is also very little *to* him. In his privation – his lack of a solidified agency in time – he lacks a *human* hinterland as well.

To recall the discussions in Chapter 1, an icon – and consummately Christ's humanity – is an object, or *res*, in the world that has become so significant that it begins to slip the bonds of its quality as an object or *res*. But Myshkin parodies this dynamic. He slips the bonds of his human *an*-otherness not because he signifies anything, but because his humanity is an absence that cannot signify. There is little to him that offers traction for a sustained engagement, let alone an engagement that can prove redemptive. Christ's significance, on the other hand, is predicated on there being *something to him* that can offer itself as *signum*. This intuition is inherent in Williams's Christology, and will be developed more fully as we proceed – that the signifying power of Jesus entails a humanity that is precisely not privative. His iconic possibilities are tied not only to God being *not*-other to him, but also to the traction in time offered by his human *an*-otherness.

This is why, in *Dostoevsky*, Williams makes the point that an icon, including Christ as the 'primordial icon', is 'anchored in the actual world of decision and change'. Almost paradoxically, this non-privative anchoring does entail a *kenosis*. Icons repeat the 'authorial self-emptying' of the incarnation: 'The icon is in this sense a "powerless" image, in that it is not safe from what history may do to it; the crucifixion of the fully incarnate image of God lets us know that.'[90] And the ' "powerless" image', be it icon or Messiah, is committed in *kenosis* to 'a narrative of vulnerability accepted'.[91] In terms already used, it, thereby, enters a risky '*drama of misrecognition*'. But Myshkin's privation only parodies this *kenosis*. He is powerless, and ends badly, but only because he is an icon defaced before he begins. Or, rather, *he never actually begins*, never inhabits the 'world of decision and change'. He offers no 'narrative of vulnerability accepted', because such an acceptance requires the sort of sustained agency he does not have.

A Soul Holy or Beautiful?

To Williams, Jesus is emphatically *an*-other, an engaged human agent in a world of decision and change. This is Christ's interval of difference from Myshkin. Unlike Myshkin, he can judge and redeem, he can be iconic, because he authors a self in the broken field of human relations. As explored in the previous chapter, his timeful story of human maturation is therefore 'the heart of meaning'[92] that constellates time. What is ruled out by this emphasis of Williams's is any Christology that involves a premature evacuation from history, any ' "spirituality" without conflict',

---

90. Ibid., 207–8.

91. Ibid., 214.

92. See, again, Rowan Williams, *The Wound of Knowledge: Christian Spirituality from the New Testament to St John of the Cross*, 2nd Rev. edn. (London: Darton, Longman and Todd, 1990), 2.

and without reference to Christ's conflictual temporal life.[93] Williams's reading of Myshkin as a diabolical parody puts the accent upon this emphasis. The ecstatic escape that he read as sub-Christian in 'Burnt Norton' is what is critiqued – decades later – in Myshkin's hope that 'time will be no more'. Like Hegel's soul, this prince offers us beauty, but not the holiness crafted by a time-bound agent – and, *pace* Myshkin, such beauty will not save the world.[94] What is required, instead, is a holiness (with apologies to Rose) that keeps its mind in history and despairs not.

Thus, if Jesus is holy, as opposed to merely beautiful, it is because he realizes a certain sort of human agency in time. This is implied in Williams's deployment of the analogy of a musical performance. Such a performance can only be the product of an engaged agent, marking time and responding to the divine score's rigorous demands. It is also implied by Williams's Maximian attention to Jesus's human will. And, as already alluded to, Williams marks in *Dostoevsky* the contrast between a Christ who makes definitional choices in the wilderness and Gethsemane, and an anaemic Myshkin incapable of such choosing. The importance of choice is, in fact, encoded in the basic substructure of Williams's theological anthropology. Adult choosing is the gift and pathos that defines and limits the human self. It is both the expression, and curtailment, of human freedom.[95] This is argued in the chapter from *Lost Icons* previously cited in the discussion of Myshkin's childlike latency. The prince's lack of adult choosing is, again, part of what renders him an *un*defined self who can only offer an edgeless, or dangerously undefined, love. In contradistinction, for Williams, the content of Christ's humanity is the bounded and defined life of a fully engaged adult, one able to undertake the labour of the 'restoration of humanity … including the labor of choice and self-definition'.

The Christ actualized through choice in time is also the Christ who, again in contradistinction to Myshkin, decisively occupies a place. A theme that emerged in the previous chapter was the importance for Williams of Jesus's historical particularity. Christ is only able to re-constellate time insofar as he is a particular human *an*-other 'within a very specific context of ethnic, religious and political history'.[96] He emerges from that context, and interacts with it in appropriate, if challenging, ways to mediate a divine freedom transformative of all contexts. Such a performance requires a cultural acumen, and social acuity, that Myshkin lacks. Myshkin's placeless parodic idiocy obliquely draws our attention to this necessity,

---

93. Ibid., 11.

94. Myshkin's sentiment that beauty will save the world is already ironized by being mockingly reported on the lips of a feverish and suicidal Ippolit (see Dostoevsky, *The Idiot*, 446). Elsewhere Williams remarks that it is 'a bad candidate for the status of universal good news'. See Rowan Williams, *The Truce of God: Peacemaking in Troubled Times* (Norwich: Canterbury Press, 2005), 74.

95. Williams, *Lost Icons*, 32. See also Rowan Williams, *The Edge of Words: God and the Habits of Language* (London: Bloomsbury, 2014), 86–7; *Open to Judgement: Sermons and Addresses* (London: Darton, Longman and Todd, 1994) 178–84; *The Truce of God*, 120.

96. Williams, *On Christian Theology* (Oxford: Blackwell, 2000), 95.

as do, arguably, some comments made by Gillian Rose in an essay dealing with the French religious thinker Simone Weil, one of only two works by Rose cited in *Dostoevsky*.[97]

Quoting Gustave Thibon, Rose notes Weil's odd appearance and manner: 'Nor will I dwell on the ways she was outfitted and her incredible baggage – she had superb ignorance not only as to the canons of elegance but extending to the most elementary practices that enable a person to pass unnoticed.'[98] There is potentially an intriguing echo of Myshkin here. As already noted, he enters the first pages of *The Idiot* 'incredible' in his inappropriate clothing. He is also ignorant of social mores, with 'no decent gestures, no sense of proportion'.[99] His social antennae are consistently awry,[100] and he is, thus, un-*placed* in his cultural context, unable to navigate it, and consistently drawing the attention, and the mockery, of others.

Strikingly, Rose sees in Weil's social awkwardness something indicative of a spiritual failing, a social noisiness that amounts to an 'inability to pass unnoticed'. She contrasts this with, of all things, Agatha Christie's fictional detective, Miss Marple. That elderly sleuth is, precisely, who she appears to be, 'a proper, fussy, inquisitive old lady'. She inhabits her place, and can, thereby, pass unnoticed in society. But, she can also notice with acuity what occurs around her. She can see nuance and, therefore, effect justice.[101] If Weil is taken by Rose as something like a beautiful soul, ill-placed, like Myshkin, in her context, and – as Williams himself notes – unreconciled with 'time and the body',[102] perhaps we can see Christ as a little like Miss Marple. He is not always unnoticed, but he *is* able to navigate his context, and to effect justice. Or, maybe, Rose's Miss Marple is just a little like Christ.[103]

Importantly, for Williams, Simone Weil serves, fairly or not, as an example of something like that parodic *kenosis* seen in Myshkin – *kenosis* as a privation of the self, not as an engaged risking of the self in time and converse. He notes that for Weil, 'To say "I" ' became 'to lie'; the self as knowledgeable of its needs and desires

97. 'Angry Angels – Simone Weil and Emmanuel Levinas' in Gillian Rose, *Judaism and Modernity: Philosophical Essays* (Oxford: Blackwell, 1993), 211–23. Cited by Williams in *Dostoevsky*, 260–1, n. 16.

98. Rose, *Judaism and Modernity*, 222. Quote taken from Simone Pétrement, *Simone Weil: A Life*, trans. R. Rosthenthal (London: Mowbrays, 1976), 424.

99. Dostoevsky, *The Idiot*, 399.

100. See his inability to discern the sham courtesies at work during the Ypanchin's soirée. Ibid., 622–8.

101. Rose, *Judaism and Modernity*, 222–3. See also *Love's Work*, 144 for her desire to be a 'Miss Marple'.

102. Williams, *Wrestling with Angels*, xvi – xvii.

103. Rose obliquely hints at Marple's Christ-likeness in the coda to *Love's Work*: 'I aspire to Miss Marple's persona: to be exactly who I am, *decrepit nature yet supernature in one*' (144, italics mine).

must nullify itself for God to find space.[104] Spirituality, in this register, becomes a form of sought privation, and it is precisely in the context of a discussion of *kenosis* mistaken for self-nullification that Rose's essay on Weil is cited in *Dostoevsky*.[105] It is also in this context that Williams makes a 'Hegelian allusion' to elucidate a proper understanding of *kenosis*. It is 'a dialectical negation whose point is the *recognition* of the self in the other and in the ensemble of otherness that is the world's process'.[106] In other words, what is sought is not a privative self-nullification, but a decentring of the self to commit to a conversation, which entails, as any true conversation must, vulnerability. *Kenosis* is the risky staking of the self in a drama of misrecognition, which is, paradoxically, where one learns to recognize oneself. The contrary option is to refrain in almost aesthetic horror from one's own agency, the parodic *kenosis* of the beautiful soul. It seeks a 'beautiful' self-nullification, not a 'holy' vulnerability. In its fastidiousness, it vanishes 'like a shapeless vapour', and Weil's death, through self-starvation and tuberculosis, bears a tragic similarity to such a fate.[107]

In his own work on Weil, cited in *Dostoevsky* in conjunction with Rose's essay,[108] Williams brings out another potential echo of Myshkin's parody. He notes Weil's distrust of individual or particular loves, in favour of an unconditioned love for the whole.[109] Such a generalized love might be described by Rose as malignly 'edgeless', or might recall the love of Natasya's absentminded Christ, staring into infinity but forgetful of the *particular* child at his knee. Williams counters such an edgeless generalized love with the notion that 'love is a word we are taught to apply in certain sorts of relationship, fraught with all the ambiguities characteristic of human relationships as such, relationships vulnerable to time,

104. Williams, *Wrestling with Angels*, 209. The quotes are from Weil's *First and Last Notebooks* (London: Oxford University Press), 132, as cited by Williams.

105. Williams, *Dostoevsky*, 173–5. It is also the context in which the only other citation of Rose is made. See 260, n. 15.

106. Ibid., 174. Ben Quash, in *Theology and the Drama of History* (Cambridge: Cambridge University Press, 2005), 56–60, points to how, in Hegel, there is a necessary 'self-sacrifice' to realize one's self in the concrete freedom of an ethical community. This seems to be the Hegelian brand of *kenosis* Williams is talking about. See also Nicholas Adams, *Eclipse of Grace: Divine and Human Action in Hegel* (Oxford: Wiley-Blackwell, 2013), 40.

107. Hegel's inspiration for the soul came from the character of a consumptive aristocratic woman in Goethe's *Wilhem Meister's Apprenticeship*. See Rose, *Judaism and Modernity*, 178–9 and *The Broken Middle*, 188–92.

108. Williams, *Dostoevsky*, 261, n. 16. The essay is 'Simone Weil and the Necessary Non-Existence of God' in Williams, *Wrestling with Angels*, 203–27.

109. Williams, *Wrestling with Angels*, 215. See also Williams's review of Winch's *Simone Weil: The Just Balance* in *Philosophical Investigations* 14, no. 2 (1991): 162–6, and Adrian Poole, 'Simone Weil: Force, Tragedy, and Grace in Homer's *Iliad*', in *Christian Theology and Tragedy: Theologians, Tragic Literature and Tragic Theory*, eds Kevin Taylor and Giles Waller (Farnham: Ashgate, 2011), 120–1.

chance, forgetfulness and corruption'. Love, in other words, is an acumen learnt in that history which the beautiful soul would escape, 'learned from the constant and critical re-appropriation of the history of my relationships'. Its purification is found not in the evacuation of particularity, but in the renunciation of the tendency to elide the particularity of others. Its practice requires an imaginative 'analogical' skill – the ability to read the other 'through the medium of the possibilities of which my own contingent history has made me aware'.[110]

Such analogical skill is what Myshkin lacks. He cannot imaginatively change places with others because he has no place or history of his own. He, thus, cannot properly see them. He is incapable of love as Williams frames it and, in a certain sense, incapable of conversation. He is incapable of Rose's *drama of misrecognition*. This is not to say that he cannot 'misrecognise' others; but that is *all* he can do, and that is what excludes him from the drama. For Rose, the *drama of misrecognition* is a process in which mistake leads to revision, and to real gain. It is, ultimately, comedic.[111] But Myshkin, in his privation, lacks the resources to recognize mistakes, or revise them. There is no gain or progression in his drama, which ends in an idiotic silence coterminous with the ending of the histories of the novel's other central characters. Myshkin cannot undertake the work of love, which is that non-parodic *kenosis* of an entry into a drama that can only move forward, in mistake, revision and gain, through love's work. That is the most striking distance between this parody and its original. Christ is the one who is a human *an*-other in time, authoring a self, entering the drama and undertaking its attendant work of love. He is thus holy, if not 'beautiful', and it is in this way that he can be a 'last word' who vivifies the histories of others, and does not end them.

Concluding Postscript: Christ before the Inquisitor

There is one other potential Christ figure, whether beautiful or holy, yet to be engaged with. Earlier it was stated that Williams judges none of Dostoevsky's literary figurings of Jesus successful. Such a success is theologically impossible. Yet, there is an apparent exception – the Christ portrayed in *The Brothers Karamazov*, in Ivan's account of the Grand Inquisitor. As already noted, Williams returns repeatedly to this pericope for theological insight, but the question of his consistency in doing so must be asked. Williams is not unaware of this Christ's potentially parodic nature – that he might be 'transcendent but more or less powerless in the real world'.[112] Such

---

110. Williams, *Wrestling with Angels*, 215–6.

111. See Rose, *Mourning Becomes the Law: Philosophy and Representation* (Cambridge: Cambridge University Press, 1996), 71–2. The essay concerned is also the only other one by Rose cited by Williams in *Dostoevsky* (260, n. 15).

112. Williams, *Dostoevsky*, 28–9. Williams cites the work of Boyce Gibson, as well as Paul Evdokimov's reading of Dostoevsky's saints as 'a presence that does not actively engage with other protagonists but is primarily a site of manifestation and illumination' (29). See

a description is arguably not too far from the impotent eros of the beautiful soul. Nor, arguably, is this Christ completely dissimilar to Natasya's anodyne 'painting'. He 'says nothing',[113] but only bears 'a quiet smile of infinite compassion'[114] – and he is, distinctly, the Christ of *Ivan's* 'poem',[115] presented, at least at first, in a facetious manner. He is, in his inception, intended as a parody, a Christ cast into a world of absences.

But this Christ does not, despite Ivan's avowal, say 'nothing'. Two words are found, quietly, on his lips – '*Talitha cumi*' ('Little girl, get up').[116] These are Jesus's own words from Mark 5.41. They were spoken when raising a young girl from the dead, an action repeated in Ivan's poem – and here, already, is an interval of distance from Natasya's painting, an imagining where there was no help for the child/Natasya, and no salvation from *her* death. Although Williams does not draw attention to this aberration from silence, he does regard the Christ portrayed in the poem as 'the Jesus of the Gospels'. The depiction is 'naïve' he notes, but it is not that of 'an abstract and ideal figure'.[117] If all Christ figures tend towards parody, what arguably saves this intended parody is that he is, to Williams, more a repetition than a figure. He is, to Williams, even 'iconic' insofar as, despite Ivan's intentions to show him as ineffective, he effects a new possibility in Alyosha[118] – the repetition of a kiss that instantiates a divine possibility within human life. The eros of this Christ is not *utterly* ethereal. He undertakes definitional actions, such as a kiss that 'is the kind of thing that will make all the difference or none at all'.[119]

It is as if Ivan's attempted parody – almost an attempt to write his own *Idiot* – begins to cross the interval of its distance from the original.[120] In fact, if there is a truly *parodic* Christ in this account, it is the Inquisitor, a lover of mankind who takes on sin and terrible knowledge so that others may be happy.[121] The

also Rowan Williams, *A Silent Action: Engagements with Thomas Merton* (Louisville: Fons Vitae, 2011), 34–5, where Dostoevsky's saints are termed, in Evdokimov's understanding, 'useless'.

113. Fyodor Dostoevsky, *The Brothers Karamazov*, trans. R. Pevear and L. Volokhonsky (London: Vintage, 2004), 247.

114. Ibid., 249.

115. Ibid., 246.

116. Ibid., 249.

117. Williams, *Dostoevsky*, 34–5.

118. Ibid., 33. The Christ of the poem is also, unlike Myshkin in his opaque iconicity, very much recognizable. See Dostoevsky, *The Brothers Karamazov*, 249.

119. Williams, *Christ on Trial*, 119.

120. As Alyosha notes, Ivan's poem becomes an unintended act of 'praise' (Dostoevsky, *The Brothers Karamazov*, 260). See also Oenning Thompson, 'Problems of the Biblical Word', 92–3.

121. The Inquisitor 'loves mankind' (Dostoevsky, *The Brothers Karamazov*, 261), The title 'lover of mankind' is a Christological epithet in Orthodoxy. It is also given to Alyosha (18). See also Kroeker and Ward, *Remembering the End*, 115.

result, however, is the privation of their agencies as they are reduced to veritable children,[122] a diabolic authorship ultimately not unlike Myshkin's. Yet, it would still be a mistake to judge the poem's Christ as completely unambiguous. For Williams, Christ's silence and kiss constitute a refusal of the ensemble of the world's truths that, as was seen in the previous chapter, divinely disrupts the world.[123] But there is a thin line between such a refusal, and a refusal to enter a conversational *drama of misrecognition*. This Christ still does not say much.[124] Even though willing to kiss, he does not converse with the Inquisitor. And, in his silence, he is still socially noisy, with something like that 'inability to pass unnoticed' that Rose ascribed to Weil.[125] The hint of a beautiful soul perhaps lingers in this 'naïve' account.

Yet, this Christ, for Williams, still makes a salvific difference through deliberate action – even if it is the deliberate inaction of holding silence and refusing temptation – and in Ivan's poem, this is not without a terrible cost. By surrendering to the temptations of the 'dread spirit', Jesus *could* have saved humanity a millennium of suffering,[126] or at least such is the Inquisitor's charge. In the name of love, it is alleged, Christ has acted as if he did not love humanity at all.[127] In other words, to the Inquisitor, the innocence of his prisoner is really still up for question. If part of his interval of distance from Myshkin is that the poem's Christ is capable of definitional action, of making a difference in time, the goodness of that difference remains potentially opaque. And insofar as this poetic Christ is, for Williams, a repetition of the Jesus of the Gospels, this points to an interval of difference between *that* Christ and Myshkin as well. As will be seen in the chapter to come, if Myshkin is 'unfallen' in his 'beauty', Jesus's unfallenness, and therefore his claim to be holy, is complex and disputable. He may even be vulnerable to something like the Inquisitor's charge.

---

122. Dostoevsky, *The Brothers Karamazov*, 258–9.

123. Williams, *Dostoevsky*, 29–32.

124. Williams himself acknowledges this. Ibid., 35.

125. 'He appeared quietly, inconspicuously, but, strange to say, everyone recognized him.' See *The Brothers Karamazov*, 249.

126. Ibid., 252–3.

127. Ibid., 254–5.

Chapter 4

A CHRIST COMPLEXLY UNFALLEN

Introduction

Our explorations of Williams's negative Christology through parody have pushed to the fore the need for the *non*-parodic Christ to be 'holy', but not 'beautiful'. Unlike the privative Myshkin, Jesus fully inhabits his agency in time and a human context, making choices and committing to the human and historical drama in which love's work is accomplished; this is the content of his being a human *an*-other. But this becoming a human *an*-other is also something that potentially stretches and distorts the divine grammar manifest in that life. If, as was argued in our first chapter, the difference of God – understood in one idiom as *non aliud* – makes Christology possible, it is also a divine difference that complicates that Christology. In this chapter, that complexity comes to the fore. By becoming a human *an*-other in the drama of time and its misrecognitions, there is an inescapable sense in which Jesus's performance of God's life, his translation of that generative and creative *not*-other into a human life, is put at risk. His performance acquires a complex opacity, and there are elements in Williams's presentation that even imply that Jesus's innocence is up for question, that the charges laid by Ivan's Inquisitor may hold some water. Thus, Jesus might be *neither* beautiful *nor* holy. This chapter will turn on discussing that darker possibility, beginning with a discussion of Jesus's human nature.

Agency in The History We Have

To return to Williams's presentation of Myshkin: the prince is 'unfallen' in that he is naively innocent of a certain sort of history. He lacks the acumen for living in a temporal manifold inflamed by rivalry and desire. He is, thus, in an odd way, naively innocent of original sin as Williams conceives it. An important claim forwarded by Williams is that Myshkin is, thereby, something of a theological tell; he instantiates an aspect of Dostoevsky's 'implicit Christology'. In Myshkin, the ideal of an unfallen humanity, belonging to 'a timeless order and harmony', is dismissed by his creator with 'profound nostalgia'.[1] What is, thereby, also dismissed

---

1. Rowan Williams, *Dostoevsky: Language, Faith and Fiction* (London: Continuum, 2008), 55–6.

is at least one tactic for construing Christ's unfallenness: a Christ not immersed within the reality of a fallen history is parodic.

If Dostoevsky's Christology remains 'implicit' – *The Idiot* is a novel, not a dogmatics – what is interesting is Williams's all-too-brief attempt to make something explicit out of it. He frames the possibilities along the following lines: if being fallen entails being 'incapable of not sinning', and the Word assumes a humanity fallen in *this* way, then the restoration of such a humanity approaches impossibility. Although Williams does not make this logic explicit, such a 'fallenness' could only be overcome by the Word vitiating such a humanity's irredeemable will. Considering the importance in Williams's Christology of Christ's volitional human performance, this would be an unacceptable option. Yet, if the humanity assumed in Christ is *un*fallen, Williams must ask: 'In what sense does he undergo precisely the experience of fallen beings faced with potentially tragic choices?' To follow Nazianzen's classic soteriological logic, if this human tragedy has not been assumed in the incarnation, it cannot be healed. Williams tries to articulate a way through this dilemma of either irredeemable fallenness or tragedy unassumed. He pictures a schema in which 'the Word takes on the *consequences* of the Fall so far as they affect the circumstances in which human beings exercise their freedom, but does not take on the impaired judgement which distorts created freedom'.[2] Williams's explication of the concrete content of the above '*consequences*' will become increasingly significant in our discussions:

> But for Jesus to be human at all ... is for him to be faced with choices not simply between good and evil but between options that might arguably be good but also bring with them incalculable costs. The options that confront actual historical agents are not like self-contained items on a shelf or rack awaiting buyers; they are part of a continuum of human policies that may be flawed and damaging, and they will already be constrained by what has happened. This is the concrete meaning of embracing the consequences of fallenness. Even a subject whose desires are creative and altruistic has to enact those desires in a context where their objects will often appear obscure and ambiguous, so that good outcomes cannot be tightly and causally linked to good intentions.[3]

What, for Williams, must be assumed is a humanity hemmed by the constraints of a certain sort of history, and thus subject to a certain form of tragedy. It cannot be one (*pace* Myshkin) inserted into time innocent of that history. This humanity must then engage in a world of unpredictable opacity. If not 'fallen' in the sense of having an incapacity to act well, or an internal impairment in so acting, it still persists in a world where acting well has become no simple matter. In the last chapter, the definitional nature of choice was articulated as a substructure in Williams's anthropology. Here it is a substructure impacted upon by the 'Fall'. No

---

2. Ibid., 56.
3. Ibid., 57.

choice is without difficulty, and no outcome unequivocal, when every choice is enmeshed in the numerous prior choosings of a rivalrous history. It is this tragedy from which Myshkin seeks a premature exemption. It is with this post-lapsarian difficulty that Christ must engage as a human *an*-other in history's drama.

Having said that the exercise of human agency is impacted upon by the 'Fall', it must be added that Williams is not given to counter-factual accounts of what an *unfallen* exercise of human agency might entail. He largely confines himself to describing the history that we have, often blurring lines that might demarcate whether it is as it is because of the nature of created contingency *per se,* or because of some non-necessary historical trajectory of sin. This blurring is visible in his description of 'embracing the consequences of fallenness' as entailed in Jesus being 'human at all'. What is important is that the language of complexity, involvement and constraint adheres at every point to Williams's discussions of human agency in history, whether it be down to the consequences of fallenness, or just the way creaturely existence intrinsically works. In fact, part of Williams's admiration for Dostoevsky's fiction is its facility for engaging with this constraining complexity. It, to him, portrays well the 'crowded background' of human agency, where we find ourselves located as an 'immense complexity', physically and socially enmeshed at the convergence of 'countless lines of force'.[4]

For Williams, we are creatures born into multiple *milieux* we did not choose, and much of our agency is 'a confused, partly conscious, partly … instinctive response to the givenness of a world we do not dominate, a world of histories and ideas, languages and societies, structures we have not built'.[5] Our actions in this givenness have unforeseeable consequences in the lives of others, such that those actions and their interpretations cease to belong solely to our own agency, Thus, 'we have a life in other people's imaginations, quite beyond our control'.[6] This is part of the force of the point made earlier, that our life and death are with our neighbours. What was earlier portrayed as an ecclesial attribute is, in fact, a human given: the self we have depends on encounters with neighbours; it is 'dependent for its definition and realization on dialogue extended in time'.[7] Williams thus frames the social manifold as one of mutual impingement and almost aporetic enmeshment in dialogical relations that constitute selves, and part of the practical wisdom for living in this manifold is the practice of what he intriguingly calls 'remorse'. This is defined as 'thinking and imagining my identity through the ways in which I have become part

---

4. Ibid., 221.

5. Rowan Williams, *Open to Judgement: Sermons and Addresses* (London: Darton, Longman and Todd, 1994), 90. See also his 'Making Moral Decisions' in *The Cambridge Companion to Christian Ethics*, ed. Robin Gill (Cambridge: Cambridge University Press, 2001), 5–6.

6. Rowan Williams, *Writing in the Dust: After September 11* (Grand Rapids, MI: Eerdmans, 2002), 55. The context is globalization's heightening of mutual implication.

7. Williams, *Dostoevsky*, 132–3.

of the self-representation of others.[8] Remorse is, thus, an imaginative and analogical skill – a seeing of the self in the other, and the other in the self – which is necessary for dealing with our social enmeshment in a world of unpredictable opacity. Notably, by this definition, remorse is also something Myshkin cannot undertake. In his own poverty as an agent, he lacks the analogical skills to imagine others' agencies adequately, and he cannot properly see his appearances within them.

It is more than notable that Williams uses the language of 'remorse'–language loaded with moral implication and regret – to describe this imaginative practice necessary for living well in history. If the perception of our involvement in the lives of others is so coded, a judgement is already made upon the enmeshed history that we have. It is a history of, in some ways, culpable damage, marred by the 'already' of original sin, that endemic process of diminishment we come to before we can choose. Remorse is for history after the 'Fall', the history for which Myshkin lacks the necessary acumen. Yet, there is ambiguity here as well, for in aspects of Williams's presentation – which, again, lacks counter-factual accounts of potential unfallen histories – an endemic violence in relating appears to be more of a given infinitude than an artefact of fallenness. For instance, in *Lost Icons*, the book in which the discussion of remorse occurs, Williams notes Gillian Rose's insight that violence and love co-inhere. Love is 'never far from violence'; in staking a position within the social manifold it risks 'the displacement or damaging of another'. In turn, violence is 'obliquely connected with love's search for life in the other', such that one may speak of a certain 'love in violence'. Violence, in this understanding, is potentially attendant upon all social action, any instantiation of one's agency as *an*-other.[9] This is a world where acting well *is* no simple matter, and if 'violence' attends even loving action, so must remorse. What is lacking in Williams's brief discussion is any pointer to this being an abnormal or pathological condition. It is just our history.[10]

---

8. Rowan Williams, *Lost Icons: Reflections on Cultural Bereavement* (Edinburgh: T&T Clark, 2000), 104, 109–11. See also *The Truce of God: Peacemaking in Troubled Times* (Norwich: Canterbury Press, 2005), 19–21, where repentance is 'to retrieve the vision of one's own responsibility, and to learn to look in critical openness at one's own life and the shared life of the society around' (21).

9. Williams, *Lost Icons*, 178–9. Williams cites Gillian Rose's *The Broken Middle* (Oxford: Blackwell, 1992), 147–52. 'Violence' is a complex presence in Rose's work. Without it 'language, labour, love – life – would not live'. It is the 'risk' involved in creative action, 'inseparable from staking oneself, from experience as such' (151). For another reading of 'violence' as a complex and, in some way necessary, presence by Williams himself, see his *The Truce of God*, 51–2. There he dismisses the idea of violence as an 'unnatural aberration', noting that some acumen for defending the self's boundaries is necessary for maturation.

10. This militates against seeing violence *per se* as an artefact of sin or the fall. It is interesting in this context that Medi Ann Volpe critiques *Lost Icons* for failing to provide a sustained theological account of sin (see her *Rethinking Christian Identity: Doctrine and Discipleship* [Chichester: Wiley-Blackwell, 2013], 63–4). Such a critique seems to miss the apologetic intent of *Lost Icons*.

Whether Christ, in his difference from Myshkin, can be termed 'fallen' will be debated shortly. However, if in his humanity he assumes our human tragedy, then he is subject to the constraints of this history we have. In *Dostoevsky*, these constraints are deemed, at least in part, the consequences of the Fall. Like the rest of humanity, it is no simple matter for Christ to act well. This is the 'tragic shadow' he assumes, and under it – whatever is to be made of the question of 'fallenness' – the question of Jesus's *innocence* erupts. If 'remorse' is necessary for navigating an enmeshed and opaque social manifold, is it due from Jesus? Does this mean he shares in our culpabilities? Have his actions persisted in the lives of others in ways that damage or diminish? Is violence attendant upon his love? That is certainly something like the Inquisitor's charge.

Is Christ's Humanity 'Fallen'?

The intuition in *Dostoevsky* that Christ's humanity is, in some sense, impinged upon by the consequences of fallenness, and, thereby, subject to some element of tragic constraint, seems to have been one long held by Williams. It is arguably reflected in one of his earliest essays, 'The Spirit of the Age to Come' (1974). There, the humanity assumed is one 'whose mode of being is *God-less-ness*'.[11] Yet, the exact relation of this 'God-less' humanity to the status of being 'fallen' is left vague. Perhaps the best place to look for precision is in a much later essay, ' "Tempted as we are": Christology and the Analysis of the Passions' (2010).[12] It is a piece of work that reflects on some patristic understandings of the temptations of Christ. It is also a piece that had its inception at about the same time as Williams was working on *Dostoevsky*. Its close relation to that book's concerns is borne out by discussions within the essay of elements of Bakhtin's work, specifically a concept of his that will become increasingly important in these discussions – *syncrisis*.[13]

The question framing Williams's essay concerns the meaning of the claim in Hebrews 4.15 that Jesus was tempted as we are, but was without sin. Williams parses the options in regard to Jesus's vulnerability to temptation as follows: (1) Was Jesus subject merely to the external pressures of existence in a fallen finitude, or (2) was he also prey to an 'internal mobility or uncertainty of desire', or even (3) to an internal mobility exacerbated, like ours, by a prior history of sin? In considering these questions, Williams traces a trajectory of thought from Irenaeus, through Origen and Evagrius, which finds an 'ingenious and fruitful' culmination in John Cassian. What this would ultimately develop into was an understanding

---

11. Rowan Williams, 'The Spirit of the Age to Come', *Sobornost: The Journal of the Fellowship of St Alban and St Sergius* 6, no. 9 (1974): 618–9. Italics mine.

12. Rowan Williams, ' "Tempted as We Are": Christology and the Analysis of the Passions', in *Studia Patristica*, Vol. XLIV, ed. J. Brown, et al. (Peeters, 2010), 391–404. First given as a paper in 2007.

13. Ibid., 391–2, 404.

that Jesus was not subject to *every* species of testing we know. Some trials are provoked by a prior history of error, and Jesus has no such destabilizing personal history behind him.[14]

This trajectory, and Williams's framing of the possibilities of Christ's vulnerability, anticipates the possibility outlined in *Dostoevsky* of a Christ who enters into the *consequences* of a post-lapsarian history (corresponding to option 1), but who is not marked by an 'impaired judgement which distorts created freedom'. Such an impairment would certainly entail some element of internal mobility and uncertainty, and this might arise from, or be aggravated by, a history of moral failure. Thus, a Christ with an impaired judgement and compromised moral freedom is a scenario corresponding (if imperfectly) to the possibilities laid out in options 2 and 3 above – and yet, some of our previous arguments complicate this picture. If the deep mutual implication of human agents that Williams portrays is taken seriously, any rigid demarcation between external pressures and internal destabilizations starts to look tenuous. The logic of an anthropology where lives and deaths are enmeshed confuses such divisions; the actions of others in the external world come to persist, for Williams, *in* my identity. Also complex is how Williams reads, and appropriates for his own thought, the culmination of the trajectory he traces in Cassian.

To Williams, Cassian understands 'that to live in the material world is to be vulnerable to the impact of unstable circumstances', and that even Christ is subject to the destabilizing effects of life in the body and society. To recall what was said in terms of the insights Williams saw in Dostoevsky's fiction, life – Christ's and ours – is lived physically and socially enmeshed, at the convergence of 'countless lines of force'. Williams, through Cassian, understands that the external pressures brought to bear by these forces have penetrative power. Even without a history of prior error, a needy physicality and the presence of other potentially competitive agents mean that there is always the possibility of acting out of our innate vulnerability in such a way as to exceed our needs and attempt a sinful, self-protective control. These external but penetrative testings were a reality for Christ,[15] for he 'begins where we begin, in the body'.[16]

And beginning in the body is, itself, no simple matter, as is made clear by what Williams writes elsewhere concerning embodiment. The body is already a site of meaning making. Dualisms between it (coded as external) and the soul (coded as internal) are undone, as the body '*is* the soul', in that it is a '*meaning* portion of matter'. It is from our embodied orientation in the world that intelligence and the self spring; it is here, for Williams, that we begin to navigate the manifold in which our identity comes to fruition, and the needs and desires of the body, such as those for sustenance and reproduction, are always already being symbolized and organized between bodies in their sense making, such that 'we are already

---

14. Ibid., 393–4. Williams mistakenly cites the passage as Hebrews 3.15.
15. Williams, 'Tempted as We Are', 400–1.
16. Ibid., 403.

embroiled in speech and relation, and so in culture – in the life of the soul we might say'.[17] Thus, embodiment, and its attendant vulnerabilities and needs, penetrate beyond any externality and into the depths of the self, and already implicate us in the social – in our life and death with our neighbour. If Christ 'begins in the body', the walls between options 1 and 2, between an external and internal vulnerability, are flimsy, even if – in Christ's case – the wall separating off option 3, a history of error, is still allowed to stand.

So, in the modulated, and perhaps rather attenuated, sense of having no history of error, Cassian's Christ remains unfallen. Insofar as this understanding is 'ingenious and fruitful', it seems to be one Williams agrees with. He notes that it is in line with a general emphasis in Eastern Christology, not insignificantly exemplified by Maximus, on an unfallen humanity in the incarnation – and yet, Williams remains cautious about what this unfallenness might actually entail. If it appears to qualify the humanity of Christ, and exempt him from history's constraints, it proves 'on closer examination to invite a more complex and … "polyphonic" reading'.[18] Critically, it also takes on a quality of what might be called suspension. Jesus 'lives in that – for us – unimaginable place where instability is always real yet always contained, on the threshold between freedom and self-enslavement'.[19] He is, like us, subject to the convergence of numerous lines of force, and yet, he is a currently unimaginable exemplar of utter consistency in this vicissitude, suspended 'between absolute stability and the trials to which bodily, social and historical life are vulnerable'.[20]

Arguably, this quality of suspension is even subtly implicit in Williams's deployment of the musical analogy discussed earlier. Jesus performs God's love

---

17. Rowan Williams, 'On Being a Human Body', *Sewanee Theological Review* 42, no. 4 (1999): 405–7. Williams draws heavily on Merleau-Ponty in making these points. A fascinating parallel is Williams's discussion of Nyssa's anthropology in his essay 'Macrina's Deathbed Revisited: Gregory of Nyssa on Mind and Passion' in *Christian Faith and Greek Philosophy in Late Antiquity: Essays in Tribute to George Christopher Stead*, eds L. R. Wickham and C. P. Bammel (Leiden: Brill, 1993), 227–45. Part of the same Eastern ascetical tradition in which Origen, Evagrius and (liminally) Cassian are found, in Nyssa is discerned a tendency to refuse to divorce physicality from the soul or reason (see 233–7). In language similar to his 1999 essay, Williams finds that for Nyssa, the body 'is charged with making sense of itself, coming to "mean" something, to bear the task of intelligible communication in the world of what God's life is like' (240).

18. Williams, 'Tempted as We Are', 402. Note the resonances with Bakhtin's language of the 'polyphonic' novel. Here Williams seems to use the term to indicate that any rendering of Christ's unfallenness will be the product of a number of views in dialogue, but not necessarily reconciliation. For Bakhtin, polyphony encompasses 'battling and internally divided voices'. See Mikhail Bakhtin, *Problems of Dostoevsky's Poetics*, trans. C. Emerson (Minneapolis: University of Minnesota Press, 1984), 249–50.

19. Williams, 'Tempted as We Are', 402.

20. Ibid., 404.

without break or stumble, a flow of perfection in which sin was unimaginable because 'there is nothing in this performance that blocks out the composer'.[21] One can picture an audience enrapt, breath bated, willing this performance on, and yet, in such an imagining, despite Williams's contestation that such a thing might be *un*imaginable, is there not an underlying fear that the performance will *not* go on, and that the performer will stumble? After all, the place where 'instability is always real yet always contained' is not currently imaginable. This performance, insofar as it is a human engagement in body and society, is suspended over potential failure and darker possibilities.

To return to 'Tempted as we are': Williams bookends his contemplations in that essay with an already noted consideration of Bakhtin's concept, taken by him from the ancient genre of Menippean satire, of *syncrisis*. *Syncrisis* is the practice of juxtaposing within such a satirical drama sharply opposed personalities or points of view. This is a dialectical juxtaposition that is undertaken in order to test for the truth of the represented points of view within the context of a robust dialogical encounter. Importantly, for Bakhtin, the genre of Menippean satire was a literary feeder for early Christian writings, including the Gospels. For Williams, this is a contestable claim, but he does assert that a *syncrisis*-like element is palpable in such texts.[22] There is even, and importantly, an element of *syncrisis* attendant upon the dramatic person of Jesus himself. He is, for Williams, a 'liminal' figure, 'on the frontier between worlds, holding them in both union and otherness'. He is 'in the place of *syncrisis* not just between persons, states of life or systems of thought but between the world itself and its source'.[23]

In other words, Jesus is imaginable for Williams as a point of robust dialogical or dialectical encounter, the site for a collision and probing of disparate possibilities – the possibilities of the world and its source.[24] The language used in 'Tempted as We Are', of holding two worlds, or the world and its source, 'in both union and otherness' recalls Chalcedon's affirmation of the unconfused and yet inseparable presence in one person of both creature and Creator. But, as a way to speak of the hypostatic union, the semantic field around the concept of *syncrisis* introduces an element that is unnervingly conflictual. It is an element of dramatic dialectic in some tension with Williams's earlier-explored emphasis on the non-dramatic nature of that union. It also connotes, in tandem with the element of suspension and bated breath spoken of above, an open-ended, and even uncertain, aspect

---

21. Rowan Williams, *Tokens of Trust: An Introduction to Christian Belief* (Norwich: Canterbury Press, 2007), 74.

22. Williams, 'Tempted as We Are', 391–2. See also Bakhtin, *Problems of Dostoevsky's Poetics*, 135.

23. Williams, 'Tempted as We Are', 404.

24. See also Williams's *The Truce of God*, where he describes a 'crisis' running through Jesus's being (69–70), and notes – in a discussion of the transfiguration – that: 'Where he stands is not middle ground, but a space where worlds overlap. In his life and person, he defines that it is for glory and misery to come together and interpret one another' (77).

to that union. It is a dialectical juxtaposition of the world and its source that is perhaps tensely unresolved. This element of *syncrisis* is also in some tension with the musical analogy, insofar as the latter seems to imagine the hypostatic union in a more harmonious mode. Yet, *syncrisis* brings out more fully the element of suspension and bated breath that is subtly implied in that musical analogy. If Jesus is, and inhabits, that unimaginable place where instability is both courted and contained in a virtuoso performance, the metaphor of *syncrisis* draws attention to the precariousness of that recital. The 'unfallenness' of Jesus, whatever it means, is something suspended over more dissonant possibilities. It is a truth that can be discovered only in the dialectical outworking of this dramatic performance, its truth revealed only in the *syncrisis* that Jesus instantiates in his person and story.

This sense of possible failure emerges starkly in a passage from one of Williams's most intriguing essays, 'Trinity and Ontology' (1989).[25] In dialogue with the thought of Donald MacKinnon – as already noted, an important influence – Williams notes how Jesus's 'innocence or sinlessness becomes a dauntingly complex manner if it is not to be taken as a complete alienation from the realities of temporal experience'. If it is to be affirmed, it must be, in MacKinnon's words, 'historically achieved', a judgement passed on the entirety of a life.[26] But there is an inherent complexity and difficulty attached to discerning Jesus's historical innocence, one which the essay roots in factors already noted in Williams's thinking – the opaque outcomes of even well-intentioned acts, the enmeshed depths of human mutual implication, the way that 'violence' adheres to even loving action. Following MacKinnon's lead, Williams asserts: 'For Jesus to have been a temporal individual at all is for him to have changed and learned and made decisions whose full consequences he did not control; for him to have been *responsible*, as all adult persons are, for the injuring and diminution … of others.' The 'innocence' of such a life, he asserts, can only be found in the enfolding of the inevitable damage done 'by the possibility of compassionate and creative relationship'. And Williams obliquely implies that the damage done by Jesus's life includes its far-reaching historical after-effects. It includes even Christian anti-Semitism, and its dark culmination in the Shoah. The reader is left with the rhetorical question: 'Does this give a hint of what the content of "sinlessness" might be?'[27]

Whatever its content, the not-quite-drawn-out implication is that its *veracity* is suspended until time's end. If the logic Williams apparently accepts in MacKinnon is followed through, then Christ's innocence remains in abeyance. Its historical

---

25. Williams, *On Christian Theology* (Oxford: Blackwell, 2000), 148–66.

26. Ibid., 157. The phrase 'historically achieved innocence' is from MacKinnon's, 'The Relation of the Doctrines of the Incarnation and Trinity', in ed. R. McKinney, *Creation, Christ and Culture: Studies in Honour of T.F. Torrance* (Edinburgh, 1976), 97.

27. Ibid., 157. This implicating of Jesus in the history of anti-Semitism is a move borrowed directly from MacKinnon. See Donald MacKinnon, *Borderlands of Theology and Other Essays* (London: Lutterworth Press, 1968), 103, and *The Problems of Metaphysics* (Cambridge: Cambridge University Press, 1974), 128–31.

achievement can only occur when the generative possibilities it opens up enfold the damage done. If that damage includes the impact Jesus's life has had throughout the manifold of history, including perhaps its darkest moment, then that enfolding can only be an eschatological possibility. In the enmeshed tangle of interwoven lives in history's middle, Jesus's innocence remains dubitable. This is the shadow side of the already explored contention that Jesus's story includes its history of response. Bracketing more overtly perverse reactions to Christ, the life on which judgement is to be passed continues as *not*-other to a community of placeholders whose own actions entail continuing unintended consequences. If this is the case, Jesus's life continues to be caught up in a necessary remorse over its implication in others' lives, and continues even in its vulnerability to the Inquisitor's questioning.

But does this draw Jesus into the ambit of what it might mean to be 'fallen'? Insofar as his performance continues note perfect – no. In Williams's presentation, he remains unimaginably stable in vicissitude, unaffected by a prior personal history of sin. But caveats intrude: the external pressures he faces are penetrative, and his life in the body already implicates him in the lives and deaths of many others – and then, there is the continuance of his agency in perhaps far less perfect ecclesial performances. Any casting of 'unfallenness' under these strictures will be complex, even 'polyphonic' – and the 'unfallen' Myshkin remains as a parodic counterpoint. His lack of acumen for, and refusal of, the agon of a fallen world implies that Jesus must persist with acumen in that agon. He enacts within it love's work, involving 'intelligent choices made in uncertain circumstances',[28] choices that risk damaging others. He, thereby, binds himself into the potential compromise of his innocence in a performance that, by virtue of being human, is suspended over failure. To put it another way, if original sin persists in the already of mimetic violence within the social manifold, Christ both inhabits that manifold and continues, note perfectly, to refuse its terms.

Insofar as this is the work of love in the history that we have, violence's possibilities inhere within it. But, as Williams picks up from Rose, violence is brought into a different register when its oblique connection with 'love's search for the other' is preserved.[29] That search, which *is* the work of love, is an entry into what the last chapter called a *drama of misrecognition*. It is a dialectical drama, full of the risk of conflict, perhaps even of *syncrisis*.[30] But it is the only possibility for love to become visible. This insight is encoded, for Williams, in Dostoevsky's fiction. Goodness, therein, is invisible and tractionless outside of dialectic, unless it is 'engaged historically and specifically with its opposite'. This is why Myshkin's 'undialectical' attempt at goodness is a privative morass.[31] It is why Christ's

---

28. Williams, 'Tempted as We Are', 403.

29. Williams, *Lost Icons*, 178–9.

30. Rose's primary use of the phrase is to describe the movement of spirit in Hegel's Phenomenology, see *Mourning Becomes the Law: Philosophy and Representation* (Cambridge: Cambridge University Press, 1996), 72–4.

31. Williams, *Dostoevsky*, 145.

holiness is discernible only in compromising action. In the last chapter, this was spoken of as a non-parodic kenosis. In this one, it is the assumption of an agency in a constrained, and even fallen, history. Insofar as Christ's unfallen existence resists a 'Myshkinite' construal, and embraces what looks like fallenness itself, it is a dialectically suspended unfallenness that is posited.[32]

It is visible in the *syncrisis* of and around Jesus, where the world is engaged by its source. This source, as argued in Chapter 1, is fundamentally generative. But it becomes *an*-other in a manifold of remorse and violence. Jesus performs the creative presence of God, and is thus the 'last word' with which all may come into a vivifying relation. But 'last words' are known only when all other words have been spoken. It is only eschatologically that it can be known if the generative outcome of Jesus's agency has enfolded the damage done. It is a question Williams holds open, complicating both Jesus's innocence and thereby the very possibility of Christological mediation.

Christ's Suspended Unfallenness in Context

Historically, conceiving of Christ's humanity as fallen, or at least complexly unfallen, has been very much a minority report, although in modernity this possibility has gained increasing traction.[33] One problem with locating Williams within these efforts is his use of theological language. Terms such as 'fallenness' – and

---

32. These discussions have carried a number of Hegelian markers, and it is worth digressing to consider a reading of Hegel by Andrew Shanks who, along with Rose, has influenced Williams (see Rupert Shortt, *God's Advocates: Christian Thinkers in Conversation* [London: Darton, Longman and Todd, 2005], 16–7). For Shanks, the genesis of 'true religion' in the *Phenomenology* involves the coming together – *pace* the beautiful soul – of a willingness to act, with the readiness to forgive the impurity of action, and the readiness of the actors to offer themselves up for judgement (see his *God and Modernity: A New and Better Way to Do Theology* [London: Routledge, 2000], 78–9 & *Hegel's Political Theology* [Cambridge: Cambridge University Press, 1991], 36–41). In parallel to Rose's construal of the inherence of 'violence' in even loving action, Shanks discerns in Hegel the intuition that all acts carry an evil aspect, 'if only because of the impossibility of controlling the consequences, and the inevitable conflict between different duties' (*God and Modernity*, 170, n. 20; Shanks cites §642–3 of the *Phenomenology*). To transpose this into Williams's considerations – insofar as Christ acts with acumen within contingency, he binds himself to remorse's necessity. Remorse is an openness to judgement, to accountability for the sometimes violent appearances one's life makes in others. The question as to whether the generative possibilities Christ engenders can enfold the damage done is akin to the question of the forgiveability of Christ's necessarily impure actions.

33. For surveys of this subject, see Kelly Kapic, 'The Son's Assumption of a Human Nature: A Call for Clarity', *International Journal of Systematic Theology* 3, no. 2 (2001): 154–66; Thomas Weinandy, *In the Likeness of Sinful Flesh: An Essay on the Humanity of*

especially 'sinlessness' and 'innocence' in the essay 'Trinity and Ontology' – travel in ill-defined formations, and Williams shows little interest in parsing their exact differences. His language is often more provoking and suggestive than analytical. Yet, there is some mileage in locating Williams against a tensioned logic implied in the biblical and patristic literature, a logic of Christ's similarity and dissimilarity to us. Thomas Weinandy has argued that in patristic thought, the emphasis on similarity ('like us') or dissimilarity ('yet without sin') shifted on an ad hoc basis, according to need or context. It was 'recognized, consciously and sometimes not, that both must be maintained'.[34] Ian McFarland sees this tensioned intuition, which undergirds the whole enterprise of soteriology, as earthed in the text of Hebrews 4.15 itself, communicating the necessary solidarity of Christ with vulnerable humanity, as well as the necessary exceptionality of his sinlessness.[35] In Williams's brief discussion of these issues in *Dostoevsky*, cited near the beginning of this chapter, it is this logic of similarity and dissimilarity that is at work. The humanity assumed, by the logic of dissimilarity, cannot be incapable of not sinning. Yet, by the logic of similarity, it must be immersed in our tragedy and the history we have.

The under-defined and suspended mode of Williams's discussions arguably preserves as *tensioned* this logic of similarity and dissimilarity. In that Jesus's life is the, by definition different, human life of the Logos, it is unimaginably note perfect. It is a life that perfectly performs the generative *not*-other of God. In that it is *human* and indwelling the history we have, it is suspended over failure. It is the coming together of these two affirmations in the *syncrisis* of his life that creates the dialectic of this tension. If he does not draw perilously close to being incapable of not sinning, our tragedy is unassumed. If that difference is collapsed, it is unhealed. If the logic present in 'Trinity and Ontology' and *Dostoevsky* – with the parody of Myshkin in the background – pushes towards a Christ seemingly fallen, then the logic in 'Tempted As We Are' presses, at times, in the other direction. It probes, carefully, the unlikeness of Christ, a polyphonous and suspended unfallenness.

A more determinate solution might parse differences, such as that between 'innocence' and 'sinlessness', more carefully. Innocence may be impossible in an enmeshed reality, where none is 'innocent' of damaging others. Yet, insofar as Jesus might act note perfectly, with acumen and love, he could perhaps remain 'sinless', guiltless of intentional harm. However, tendencies in Williams's theology

---

Christ (Edinburgh: T&T Clark, 1993), and Ian McFarland, *In Adam's Fall: A Meditation on the Christian Doctrine of Original Sin* (Oxford: Wiley-Blackwell, 2010). Kapic, from the Reformed tradition, notes figures such as Edward Irving and Thomas Erskine as outliers in attributing to Christ a fallen human nature, with Barth bringing the idea into the theological mainstream (155–6). The Catholic Weinandy includes Balthasar in this list (65–9).

34. Weinandy, *In the Likeness of Sinful Flesh*, 37–8. See too McFarland, *In Adam's Fall*, 119–20. Weinandy argues that the grammar of this logic pushes towards an inchoate affirmation of the fallenness of Christ's human nature.

35. McFarland, *In Adam's Fall*, 118–9.

pick away at such parsings. There is a startling call to responsibility in his writings, emerging precisely out of our mutual implication, which unsettles distinctions. It is illustrated in a meditation on Zosima's dictum in *The Brothers Karamazov* – that we are each 'guilty' or 'responsible' before each and every other.[36] 'Responsibility' entails recognition of our 'complicity in the world's evil',[37] but also a hyperbolic duty to foster the flourishing of others. It involves 'imaginative penetration' into others' agencies, and 'sets no limits in advance to those for whom I am obliged to speak'.[38] The admixture of 'guilt' and 'responsibility' here (Williams prefers the latter as a translation) already blurs careful gradations of culpability – and such an unlimited positive duty creates a field of endless potential failure in our responsibilities. It necessitates what might, again, be called remorse – an imaginative penetration into how our failures continue in other lives. In the light of Zosima's dictum, any easy facility in parsing the differences between the wilfully and the unwittingly done, between sinlessness and innocence, begins to sound like an exculpatory tactic for evading responsibility and remorse. If, for Williams, these are the 'fallen' conditions in which human agents operate, they are the conditions Jesus assumes in his complex unfallenness. He is, in his similarity, responsible like us. Thus, he comes perilously close to being 'guilty'. Any assertion of innocence or sinlessness, or any attempt to parse their difference, can only be an eschatologically suspended claim. On one level, Williams asserts that this performance is perfect. On another level, this is problematized to the point of being taken back.

A Lengthy Digression Towards (and away from) Maximus

In Chapter 2, Williams's closeness to the concerns of Maximus the Confessor was marked. I opined that the deployment of the musical analogy was underwritten by something like a Maximian account of the cooperation of the wills. However, in my previous chapter, almost in passing, a potentially dissenting note was sounded. Myshkin, in his parodic unfallenness, was described as having been stripped by illness of his proper deliberative capacity, and this was perceived as a diabolical privation. Yet, *prima facie,* the lack of such a deliberative capacity (or of a 'gnomic will') is something that Maximus ascribes to Christ himself, and for precisely the reason that his is an (presumably *non*-parodic) unfallen humanity. There is a case to be made that Williams departs from Maximus on the point of the presence of a deliberative will in Christ, and making it will further illumine the status of the humanity assumed. It is more decisively *similar* to ours than Maximus, for one, allows.

For Maximus, Christ lacks a deliberative volitional procedure akin to ours for two reasons: his humanity is (1) unfallen, and (2) without a *hypostasis* of its

---

36. Williams, *Dostoevsky,* 164–9.

37. Ibid., 167.

38. Ibid., 171.

own. The will for Maximus is a faculty of the nature, but it is individuated by its particular modal deployment in a given *hypostasis*. Thus Christ, as having two distinct and yet inseparable natures, has two distinct and yet inseparable wills. They find a unique mode of harmonious deployment in Jesus, in a human life whose *hypostasis* is the Word.[39] Importantly, natures, for Maximus, as the generative sources of the will, are not fallen in terms of their fundamental rational structures (*logoi*). Rather, what is distorted by the Fall is their mode of deployment within a fallen *hypostasis*. It becomes possible for a given *hypostasis* to will self-destructively against its created nature. Human volitional deliberation, at least in terms of any species of deliberation we know, implies this capacity to act against the unfallen created structure of human nature – by sinning. It is, thus, a post-lapsarian reality residing in human *hypostases* within a fallen manifold.[40] Its presence implies internal mutability, and ignorance concerning correct courses of action. Maximus defines these traits, which we might ascribe simply to the nature of creaturely finitude, as in themselves *accidental* to the human nature. They are characteristic of a temporary (pre-eschatological and post-lapsarian) mode of that nature's hypostatic deployment. In its assumption by the *hypostasis* of the Word, however, Jesus's human nature finds its expression in a uniquely unfallen and deified mode of hypostatic existence – without instability or ignorance. This, in itself, is not an alienation from human nature, but it is, for us, only an eschatological possibility.[41]

Importantly, as gestured to above, deliberation is absent in Jesus not only because his humanity is unfallen, and thus uniquely stable and epistemically privileged within our post-lapsarian history, but also because it is what might be called *anhypostatic*. It is a human nature without a *hypostasis* of its own, but which finds its unique mode of deployment in and by the divine *hypostasis* of the second person of the Trinity. The result is a composite *hypostasis* in which the divine Logos assumes a human nature that is *enhypostatos* (given real hypostatic existence) in that assumption.[42] Deliberative or gnomic willing is definitionally excluded by Maximus from this composite *hypostasis* because it is still the *hypostasis* of the divine Word for whom there *can* be no 'wavering

39. See Nicholas Madden, 'Composite Hypostasis in Maximus Confessor', in *Studia Patristica Vol. XXVII*, ed. E. A. Livingstone (Leuven: Peeters, 1993), 191–7. Bathrellos makes the point that while hypostasis and the mode in which a nature is deployed are closely connected, for Maximus they cannot be conceptually collapsed (*The Byzantine Christ: Person, Nature, and Will in the Christology of Saint Maximus the Confessor* [Oxford: Oxford University Press, 2004], 103–4).

40. Louth, *Maximus the Confessor* (London: Routledge, 1996), 57–8, 60–1. See also *Opusc.* 7.80A-B as translated by Louth (ibid., 185).

41. Bathrellos, *The Byzantine Christ*, 127, 149, 161, and Louth, *Maximus*, 60–1. McFarland draws especial attention to the deified and eschatological mode of Christ's willing in Maximus (see *In Adam's Fall*, 95–7).

42. Madden, 'Composite Hypostasis', 181–2.

and hesitation'.[43] Rather, what the Logos accomplishes is, in Balthasar's words, 'a perfect hypostatic realization of human nature'.[44] One can perhaps hear echoes of Williams's note-perfect performance in this idea, just as one can hear echoes in Williams of Maximus's essentially *anhypostatic* Christology. But there is arguably a different quality to Maximus's perfection. Internal instability is not held off, as it is for Williams, in a pressured embodiedness; it is simply absent in the humanity given hypostatic existence by the Word. There is no suspension or bated breath in Maximus's account. Neither is there any recognizable internal history, an absence that in ' "Person and Personality" in Christology', as explored in my first chapter, Williams thought incredible. To return to 'Tempted As We Are', what Maximus as an expositor of the unfallen humanity of Christ is forwarding is an unfallenness that consists not only in a lack of instability derived from a history of sin, but also in a lack of any 'internal mobility or uncertainty of desire' at all. If there is a tensioned logic of similarity and dissimilarity at work, it is one where, compared to Williams's presentation, the accent is decisively on the latter. The question then becomes marked as to whether Maximus's Christ assumes our tragedy to heal it or, a little like Myshkin, prematurely absents himself.

It is worth returning to Maximus's exegesis of Gethsemane. He was the first theologian to unequivocally assert that both Jesus's resistance towards death, and his submission to it, were acts of his human will.[45] This apparently contradictory dual-willing *looks* like deliberation.[46] However, something different is going on. As mentioned in Chapter 2, Jesus's resistance towards death is the blameless epiphenomenon of a humanity that, by its human nature, does not will death. Yet, this humanity is the perfect hypostatic realization of that nature. Its will is 'wholly deified, in its agreement with the divine will', and 'eternally moved and shaped by it'.[47] Importantly, this divinization is not, insofar as the human nature is 'eternally moved', a temporal process; it is an artefact of the hypostatic union itself. Thus, what is on display is not a process of deliberation or of *becoming* divinized. The 'process', as such, is outside history. The human life that results is a harmonious manifestation of eternity. In a sense, Jesus's human desire to keep living in that garden has been reduced to so much white noise by the pre-determined triumph of an already divinely stabilized will.[48] It is voluble, but without any real effect on the drama. In a sense, there *is* no drama as the outcome is determined outside

43. Hans Urs von Balthasar, *Cosmic Liturgy: The Universe According to Maximus the Confessor*, trans. Brian Daley (San Francisco: Ignatius Press, 2003), 266. See also Bathrellos, *The Byzantine Christ*, 161, 168.

44. von Balthasar, *Cosmic Liturgy*, 269.

45. Bathrellos, *The Byzantine Christ*, 171; Madden, 'Composite Hypostasis', 196–7.

46. A point made by McFarland, see *In Adam's Fall*, 98–9.

47. *Opusc.* 7.80D, from Louth, *Maximus*, 186.

48. Williams, in a brief exegesis of Maximus, describes the incarnation as a double kenosis in which 'the eternal Word first empties himself of his divinity to become man, then empties himself of instinctive human passions in accepting suffering and death'. Thus,

of time. We are, arguably, not far from that unfallen humanity belonging to a 'timeless order and harmony' that Williams reads Dostoevsky as rejecting in Myshkin. Recalling Williams's historicist bent, discussed in our second chapter, we are very far from seeing the 'heart of "meaning"' as 'a human story, a story of growth, conflict and death'.[49] What we have is the de facto vitiation of a human will that is understood as irredeemable insofar as it is, like ours, mutable.

Williams is wary of any Christology 'nervous' about process and maturation. To him, it is a tendency that threatens to render a Christ 'so devoid of human psychological depth as to sound like an automaton'.[50] Maximus's Christology seems to be in danger of falling under this rubric, a divinely stable Christ for whom the pressures of life in the body have no actual penetrative power. There is no need for love's deliberative work, and the import of 'intelligent choices made in uncertain circumstances' falls away, as does that obscurity of vision that, at least in *Dostoevsky*, is associated with those consequences of fallenness that Jesus must assume. An element of Myshkin-like parody thus seems to adhere to Maximus's Christ. But Williams admires Maximus, and does not make a habit of open disagreement with him. In 'Tempted As We Are', he only goes so far as to describe his theology of the unfallenness of Christ – indicative as it is of the Eastern post-Chalcedonian tradition – as 'controversial'.[51] To find him speaking more directly, you would have to go back to the early '"Person" and "Personality"', and read footnote 17. There Williams admits to parting company 'with the post-Chalcedonian tradition in so far as it affirms the unfallen-ness of Jesus's humanity and the absence in him of a "gnomic" or dispositional free will'. Williams 'cannot make either historical, psychological or theological sense of this'.[52] He later modulates his stance to a 'polyphonic' acceptance of Christ's unfallenness, but here – in one footnote – in a move of the like one would be hard pressed to find elsewhere in his writings, he repudiates an entire swathe of the theological tradition.[53] If his later stance is more

---

the divinization of the humanity is seen in the overcoming of the natural desire not to suffer (Rowan Williams, *The Wound of Knowledge: Christian Spirituality from the New Testament to St John of the Cross*, 2nd Rev. edn. [London: Darton, Longman and Todd, 1990], 122).

49. Ibid., 2.

50. Rowan Williams, 'The Seal of Orthodoxy: Mary and the Heart of Christian Doctrine', in *Say Yes to God: Mary and the Revealing of the Word Made Flesh*, ed. Martin Warner (London: Tufton, 1999), 19.

51. Williams, 'Tempted as We Are', 402.

52. Rowan Williams, '"Person" and "Personality" in Christology', *The Downside Review* 94 (1976), 258, n. 17.

53. It is also a significant departure from the theology of his earliest Orthodox interlocutors. In an early article on Christos Yannaras, Williams reads that theologian as also looking back to Maximus's understanding of Christ's unfallen will ('The Theology of Personhood: A Study in the Thought of Christos Yannaras', *Sobornost: The Journal of the Fellowship of St Alban and St Sergius* 6, no. 6 [1972]: 427–8) – and, in a thesis interlaced with numerous explorations of Lossky's debt to Maximus, Williams acknowledges Lossky's

careful, what Williams finds wanting in Myshkin remains as an implicit question to the tradition Maximus represents.

Intriguingly, ' "Person" and "Personality" ' is a defence of precisely that *anhypostatic* Christology which, for Maximus, was a reason for repudiating the presence of a deliberative will in Christ. But Williams takes the doctrine in quite the opposite direction. For him it allows us 'to say unequivocally that his experiences were precisely the same as ours'.[54] He argues that, while much classical Christology may be 'implicitly Apollinarian' and 'appallingly confused' about Christ's ignorance and maturation, the *anhypostatic* model is patient of a Christ with an 'internal history' akin to ours.[55] To quote a much later essay, it encodes the 'theological mystery' wherein 'Jesus really does grow and learn as a human being; yet that maturation is a constant bringing to light, bringing to particular life, something that is *already* real at the centre of his being, that is more than just a human psyche – the given, abiding presence of God the Word'.[56] To understand why this is so, we need to return to the final section of our first chapter. There it was argued that Williams's grammar of divine difference grounds his *anhypostatic* Christology. God's difference is generative of a created reality that is profoundly different from God, but to which God is profoundly present. Transposed into Christology, this means that the Word is the *hypostasis* of a real human subjectivity, *not*-other to a human *an*-other in all its variegated fullness. It was also argued that there was 'no "drama," no dialogue of resistance and engagement and submission, between Jesus and the Word'.[57] Now this claim must be qualified.

Williams, *with* the post-Chalcedonian tradition, rejects any Nestorian drama of two centres of consciousness in Christ, but he has room for drama of a different kind – one of bated breath. The humanity to which the Word is *not*-other is our mutable humanity, enmeshed in a complex and often agonized social manifold that penetrates into, and disrupts, any boundaried interiority of the self. It is a humanity that begins, precariously, in the body. God's very dissimilarity to us, for Williams, allows for the presence of God in maximal similarity to us, in one whose 'experiences were precisely the same as ours'. This is the vector for a twofold drama. First, the question already raised persists – Can a humanity that is in this way similar to ours maintain a note-perfect performance, or is it 'incapable of not

---

agreement with Maximus on the gnomic will ('The Theology of Vladimir Nikolaievich Lossky: An Exposition and Critique' [Doctoral Thesis, University of Oxford, 1975], 96–7), as well as his tying it to an *anhypostatic* Christology. See also Lossky's *The Mystical Theology of the Eastern Church*, trans. Fellowship of St Alban and St Sergius (London: James Clarke, 1957), 125–6, 145–9.

54. Williams, ' "Person" and "Personality" ', 257–8.

55. Ibid., 256.

56. Williams, 'The Seal of Orthodoxy', 21.

57. Rowan Williams, 'Augustine's Christology: Its Spirituality and Rhetoric', in *In the Shadow of the Incarnation: Essays on Jesus Christ in the Early Church in Honor of Brian E. Daley, S.J.*, ed. P. W. Martens (Notre Dame: University of Notre Dame Press, 2007), 185–6.

sinning'? This question remains, arguably, eschatologically suspended, and it passes into a second aspect – our breath is bated over the very integrity of God. A God invested in this humanity within the history we have is stretching his grammar to the breaking point. This is gestured towards in 'Trinity and Ontology' – the God who is *not*-other to this fraught temporal life cannot have an integrity secured outside of it; there is 'no concrete language for the unity of God but this story of risk and consummation.'[58] The questions of a human performance and of divine integrity are then dramatically intertwined in a *syncrisis* – itself a term drawn from drama – where the world and its source meet within a singular life.

'Trinity and Ontology' draws on MacKinnon, who himself draws on Balthasar, in many ways the consummate theologian of drama. In a 1982 essay, Williams 'fairly freely' paraphrases the programme of von Balthasar's *Theodramatik*. Drama, in a remark that recalls the concept of *syncrisis*, is characterized as 'truth manifest in dialogue'. It is also a form of manifestation that, importantly, resists facile closure. On one level, the drama of God's activity in history, where God's truth is manifest in dialogue with what God is not, is sourced in an eternal form – the divine life. On another level, resisting any facile closure, there is a level of indeterminacy as this form is dramatically 're-presented' in contingency.[59] This re-presentation, whose apogee is Jesus's human performance, is thus not a univocal repetition of eternity. Such a 'repetition' would look more like Maximus's harmonious (and rather drama-less) Christ. There is, instead, in Williams's reading of Balthasar, some element of risk implied, of the performance potentially going astray. This drama is bound to have a certain feel of *syncrisis* to it.

Perhaps the greatest locus of dramatic risk for Balthasar is in God's re-presentation of God-self in the crucified one who proclaims his abandonment by God and descends into hell.[60] This is an emphasis that shows up early in Williams's own thought, in the proclamation of Christ's '*God-less-ness*' in 'The Spirit of the Age

---

58. Williams, *On Christian Theology*, 158–60. This is an echo of MacKinnon, for whom 'God's consistency with himself, his very unity, is at risk in the ministry and especially the Passion of Jesus' (Donald MacKinnon, *Themes in Theology: The Three-Fold Cord* [Edinburgh: T&T Clark, 1987], 158).

59. Rowan Williams, *Wrestling with Angels: Conversations in Modern Theology* (Cambridge: Eerdmans, 2007), 96. Ben Quash has questioned the degree to which von Balthasar leaves room for indeterminacy, noting his tendency to surrender to the 'epic'. This is brought up in a number of places in his *Theology and the Drama of History* (Cambridge: Cambridge University Press, 2005), including in the context of discussing the Williams article cited (see 133–8). Williams takes this critique seriously, but sees in Balthasar 'a willingness to cleave to the saving discomfort of historical/temporal difference as a necessary element in thinking through the analogy between history and the divine life'. See Rowan Williams, 'Balthasar and the Trinity', in *The Cambridge Companion to Hans Urs von Balthasar*, eds E. T. Oakes and D. Moss (Cambridge: Cambridge University Press, 2004), 43.

60. See Williams, 'Balthasar and the Trinity', 37–8.

to Come' [61]– and this divine acumen for being *not*-other to a reality that is, *prima facie*, self-alienating can only make sense, for Williams, in the light of Balthasar's construal of God as 'intrinsically that life which exists only and necessarily in the act of "bestowal", in a self-alienation that makes possible the freedom and love of an other that is at the same time itself *in* otherness'. The concrete possibility of this statement's coherence is God's presence in a victim of execution.[62] But that divine presence in that death is also the dramatic re-presentation within contingency of an eternal form – the Father's pouring of his divinity, without remainder, into the Son. Here, Williams notes, Balthasar draws on Sergii Bulgakov. This is an act of '(divine) godlessness' that constitutes God. The Son, in the sameness of his divinity, is yet an infinite difference from the Father, and this is the formal possibility of the utterly different God's presence in maximal similarity to our godlessness.[63]

What began as a detour through Maximus has evolved into a digression towards Williams's reading of Hans Urs von Balthasar. The point of these meanderings is to make the argument that if Williams's conception of the difference of God allows for the Word to be *not*-other to a humanity whose unfallenness is 'polyphonic' to the point of '*God-less-ness*', then this is because it is, as was argued in Chapter 1, the difference of a Trinitarian God. Insofar as Williams makes common cause with what he finds in Balthasar, this Trinitarian difference is the possibility for a divine entry into a dialectical relationship with what God is not.[64] To recall what was said earlier about goodness only appearing in relation to what it is not, this is the space where God's goodness can obtain visibility for us. The truth of God appears, and is tested, in a dramatic *syncrisis* that is God's re-presentation in a human life lived, however perfectly, under the constraints of fallen human history.

That what Williams reads in Balthasar is in the territory of what he himself affirms is evident in the essay 'Deflections of Desire', already cited in discussions of the Trinitarian inflection he gives to the concept of *non aliud*. It was noted then that the re-presentation of God's Trinitarian difference in the contemplative takes the

---

61. Williams, 'The Spirit of the Age to Come', 618–9. The article is heavily dependent on MacKinnon, and through him, Balthasar.

62. Williams, *Wrestling with Angels*, 81.

63. See Williams, 'Balthasar and the Trinity', 38–40. The phrase '(divine) godlessness' is taken by Williams from von Balthasar's *Theo-Drama: Theological Dramatic Theory*, vol. IV: *The Action*, trans. G Harrison (San Francisco: Ignatius Press, 1994), 323–4. Williams notes that Balthasar draws upon Bulgakov's concept of the 'self-devastation' of the Father in the Son, and translated a relevant excerpt from Bulgakov's *The Lamb of God* (1933) on the subject. See *Sergii Bulgakov: Towards a Russian Political Theology* (Edinburgh: T&T Clark, 1999), 194–5. He also comments on Bulgakov's influence on both Balthasar and MacKinnon (172, fn 32).

64. Williams notes that this theological move is implied in Augustine's Christological exegesis of Psalm 22, which he reads as foreshadowing Balthasar. See his 'Augustine and the Psalms', *Interpretation* 58, no.1 (2004): 19.

form of a 'dark night', and that the prototype for this was Jesus's dereliction.[65] What Williams is driving at is that, in the transposition of the eternal form into a drama of encounter, the result, at least at first, is devastation.[66] This is no harmonious repetition of the eternal in time, not even in the psyche of Jesus:

> To be included in the love of the Son for the Father is to participate in a love without satisfaction or closure – an endless love; and for us as creatures, that *can only* be felt as pain and privation before it is recognized as freedom (and continues as pain even within recognition). Even for the human subjectivity of Jesus, the *non aliud* of the Father's unreality, the excess and exclusiveness of the Father's love, appears concretely as the black void of Gethsemane and Calvary, the 'annihilation' of the dereliction on the cross.[67]

To return to Maximus, it must be asked to what extent Gethsemane is, for him, a 'black void'. In his vision, the agony is contained in a far-less dramatic frame. For von Balthasar, in his reading of Maximus, 'the inevitable question is how this struggle, already decided beforehand, can still be called serious. If [Christ's] human nature has no process of its own, no *gnōmē*, no indecision, does it not fail to merit its crown?'.[68] There is no *syncrisis* here, no drama in the dialogue, no question asked of Christ's human holiness or God's integrity. No one's breath is bated. If Maximus's Jesus is the 'last word', he is an undialectical one. He is eschatological before he begins, and decides all possibilities beforehand. Such a word does not invite others into vivifying dialogue; the conversation is already closed. The questions Williams suspends, Maximus resolves before beginning. To speak in a Rosean register, there is no 'anxiety' in this beginning.

What, for Williams, is at stake in those suspended questions emerges in his discussion of the icon of the transfiguration, already cited in Chapter 2's exploration of the musical analogy. Observing the presence in both episodes of Peter, James and John, he juxtaposes the transfiguration with the story of Gethsemane and notes:

> The extreme mental and spiritual agony that appears [in Gethsemane] is the test of what has been seen in the transfiguration. We are shown that God can be God even in the very heart of human terror: the life of Jesus is still carried along by

---

65. 'The Deflections of Desire: Negative Theology in Trinitarian Disclosure', in *Silence and the Word: Negative Theology and Incarnation*, eds O. Davies and D. Turner (Cambridge: Cambridge University Press, 2002), 120–22.

66. Williams is not as bold as, at least, Bulgakov in reading this devastation back into the divine life. See his *A Margin of Silence: The Holy Spirit in Russian Orthodox Theology/ Une Marge De Silence: L'esprit Saint Dans La Théologie Orthodoxe Russe* (Québec: Éditions du Lys Vert, 2008), 23–4.

67. Williams, 'Deflections of Desire', 121.

68. von Balthasar, *Cosmic Liturgy*, 269. Greek transliterated from the original.

the tidal wave of that which the dark background of glowing blues and reds in the icon depicts, the life of God.[69]

For Williams, the Word is *not*-other, the *hypostasis* and hinterland, of *an*-other human life in 'the very heart of human terror', or – as in 'The Spirit of the Age to Come' – in a humanity that is godless. This is one whose holiness is contestable, whose life can be pictured as a dialectical argument that has yet to be clearly won. His performance is unimaginably perfect. But, if it should falter, if Gethsemane is a 'test' and not a foregone conclusion, then what is at stake is the hinterland from which Jesus emerges. When it was stated earlier that the incarnation involves a stretching of the divine grammar, a grammar that both makes possible *and* complicates Christological mediation, this is something of the content of what was meant.

69. Rowan Williams, *The Dwelling of the Light: Praying with the Icons of Christ* (Norwich: Canterbury Press, 2003), 11.

Chapter 5

The Complexities of Mediation

Introduction

If the innocence of Christ must be historically achieved, but can only be a suspended and dubitable reality within time, this presents a question for Christological mediation. If this human life is a divine performance, then it must open up generative possibilities that enfold and heal the damage done. Only then can the *an*-other who is Jesus mediate the generative *not*-other of God, and present a 'last word' with whom all may find a life-giving relation. The complex and suspended nature of Christ's innocence, therefore, implies a complexity within Christological mediation itself, and the question of Christ's innocence is not the only place where this complexity persists. This chapter will explore, from a number of angles, the nature of mediation within Williams's Christological presentation by looking at the places where it appears strained. I will argue that these strains are the unsettlements caused by the friction between two tendencies within Williams's thought: (1) his understanding of the divine agency (understood in one idiom as *non aliud*) as fundamentally peaceable and generative to the whole of what is, and (2) his understanding of that creational whole as, to some extent, tragically agonized. These two tendencies will be shown to be correlated with two tensioned and intertwined logics of mediation that persist within and throughout Williams's work.

Two Logics

To find a place where Christological mediation looks complex and strained, one need only begin where the previous chapter ended, with Williams's juxtaposition of the transfiguration and Gethsemane. Gethsemane reveals the extent of the transfiguration's implicit claim: 'God can be God' in precisely *this* contorted humanity – even at the heart of its terror and awful decision. Yet, by the logics already traced, it cannot be taken as a *given* that 'God will be God' in this pressured humanity. The success of this performance, if it is truly human in the history we have, is yet to be decided. What Gethsemane arguably constitutes is a moment of heightened *syncrisis*, in a life that is itself a place of *syncrisis,* a sharp point in the narrative of a testing drama where the dialectic of God appearing in what God is not is excruciatingly tensioned, and, thereby, allusive of the depths of what is being claimed in the incarnation.

It is not unimportant that Williams's discussion of the icon of the transfiguration is one of those places where he deploys the analogy of a musical performance. It is also a discussion that envisions Jesus's life as 'sustained from the depths of God without interruption and without obstacle'. It is a life that translates 'into human terms what and who God the Son eternally is'. What seems to be connoted here is a pacific harmony, an utterly successful flow of mediation; this performance is perfect. And yet, there is also a language of extremity present in this discussion, which belies any connoted harmony. The icon described is one 'of quite violent force'. It has an 'explosive quality'. The experience depicted by it is 'extreme'. The claim it makes about Jesus's humanity and its divine implications, a claim expanded by the allusive terror of Gethsemane, is 'shocking, devastating'.[1] What is given in the transfiguration is a 'rare moment of direct vision',[2] of something close to demonstrably successful Christological mediation, but it is a moment attended by adjectives of disruption, and one framed against Gethsemane's darker narrative. This is evocative of a discernible tendency in Williams to restrict such moments of near clarity to occasions of extremity. Despite rhetoric around Jesus's life being – as a whole – saturated with the divine, the moments in Williams's writings when this becomes most visible are not quotidian ones. Rather, they are moments of sharp juxtaposition, even of *syncrisis*. If God can be God in the extremes, it seems that this is visible only *in* the extremes. The point alluded to in the previous chapter stands: goodness becomes visible only against a contrastive dialectical background, in engagement with what it is not.

Two tensioned but intertwined mediatorial logics are implicit in the discussion of the transfiguration and Gethsemane, logics that reappear throughout, and beyond, Williams's Christological presentation. The first is a logic of harmony and the whole, perhaps most visible in the musical analogy. It is conceptually tied to Williams's construal of the divine life as *non aliud*. God so coded is able to be generatively and non-competitively *not*-other to a *whole* human life in its complex difference. The difficult aspect of this first logic is that in no isolatable *part* of that whole is God then demonstrably locatable. To repeat a refrain: 'God is never going to be an element, a square centimetre, in any picture.' Rather, God is present to the entirety of the picture as its possibility to be. It is to Jesus's human performance as a *whole*, including the multitude of responses it evokes, that God is *not*-other.

But there is a second logic. It finds some of its voice in the unnervingly conflictual language of *syncrisis*, as well as the semantic field of extremity. It is a logic of revelation in dialectical encounter, most profoundly when the world meets its source in Jesus. It is conceptually related to what can tentatively be called a tragic construal of contingency. The world is, in some sense for Williams, in a conflictual relation with its source as well as being, in itself, riven by conflict.

---

1. Rowan Williams, *The Dwelling of the Light: Praying with the Icons of Christ* (Norwich: Canterbury Press, 2003), 11–12.

2. Ibid., 18.

Thus, as I will show, the encounter between Creator and creature is often coded as fraught. Christologically, this works out in complex ways. Internally to the person of Jesus, as we have seen, his humanity – that of the Logos – is 'God-less', only complexly unfallen, and a hair's breadth from being 'incapable of not sinning'. Thus, he himself is a place of *syncrisis*. Externally, insofar as his life is a performance of the peaceable God, it is pictured as paradoxically in dramatic friction with the violent *milieu* in which it persists. This harks back to the discussions in Chapter 2 of the ways this life judges our violence. Thus, internally and externally, Jesus's life is a sustained *syncrisis*, a sustained series of dialectical encounters where the truth is tested in a life where, as a whole, the world meets its source. But there are moments when this reaches a crescendo, extreme moments where allusive (if also elusive) possibilities occur and Christological mediation attains to a degree of visibility, as what is true of the *whole* is hinted at in particularly tensioned *parts*. Gethsemane is one such moment. It is an internal *syncrisis* (*pace* Maximus) over Christ's willingness to forego any evasive manoeuvre, especially a resort to external violence (see Mt. 26:51ff). The transfiguration is also such a moment. If it is a 'mountain-top' experience, it is for Williams an explosively disruptive one.[3]

So, according to the logic of the whole, God is generatively *not*-other to the whole of Jesus's performance. But this only attains to visibility in the momentary sparks from a friction that occurs when that performance is lived through a humanity, and in a contingency, beset by tragic division. These allusive moments belong to a logic of *syncrisis*. The former logic is conceptually tied to God's *non aliud* nature, the latter to the world's tragic agon towards God and itself. The former is the basis of the latter – if God is not *not*-other to Jesus, there is nothing to reveal. The latter is the possibility of glimpsing the former – for the 'good is neither knowable or effective if it is not engaged historically and specifically with its opposite'.[4] To return to the Christological foil of Myshkin, there is no mediation of God in that parodic Christ because, *pace* the logic of the whole, there is no divine hinterland behind him. And, *pace* the logic of *syncrisis*, his goodness is undialectical, a 'premature embrace of harmony' that has no purchase which might ignite sparks of illumination. It is only in dialectical friction that love's work is accomplished; the moments of *syncrisis* are when love's work is most strained, and, paradoxically, most visible.

---

3. It is framed in the Synoptic Gospels by Jesus's predictions of his death, and what is spoken of with Moses and Elijah is his 'exodus'. Williams elsewhere juxtaposes the transfiguration with the pericope of the epileptic youth that follows in Mark, noting that Jesus stands 'in a space where worlds overlap', defining 'what it is for glory and misery to come together and interpret one another' (See Rowan Williams, *The Truce of God: Peacemaking in Troubled Times* [Norwich: Canterbury Press, 2005], 77). This sounds like *syncrisis*.

4. Rowan Williams, *Dostoevsky: Language, Faith and Fiction* (London: Continuum, 2008), 145.

Much of the remainder of this chapter will be taken up in tracing these two intertwined logics. They are often intriguingly visible on the borderlands between Williams's theological and literary interests. Thus, he reflects on the ambiguous nature of Christological mediation in the concluding remarks of his early lectures on Eliot's *Quartets*. There, as time is devoid of 'obvious and unambiguous theistic reference', Christ's temporal life shares this opacity. The Gospels cannot compel belief, and Jesus 'remains a point of *krisis*, the object of *doubt* as much as faith'. This opacity arises because the realm of time is itself in dialectical disjuncture from its source; it is a world of 'practical "Godlessness"'.[5] This language of worldly 'Godlessness' recalls the language of Jesus's 'God-less' humanity in the slightly later 'Spirit of the Age to Come'. The language of '*krisis*' perhaps hints at the much later language of Christ as *syncrisis*. The logic of *syncrisis* would seem to dominate these discussions. But, if one were to look to a later discussion of the *Quartets*, one would also find the logic of the whole. The elusiveness of the divine presence there is a consequence not so much of the godless nature of time, as of the nature of 'a God who will not be restricted but whose presence is so elusive, so dark and so mysterious precisely because it is everywhere, and not obvious because it is not to be restricted to a religious area'.[6] This, implicitly, is the logic of a God who is not discernible in any isolatable part, but is animatingly present as the whole's possibility.

Incoherent Cries and the Cradle

We will return later, with a discussion of poetical mediation, to the borderlands of literature and theology. First, we will look at another place where the skilful deployment of language and theological thought come together – in preaching. In Williams's infamously misunderstood sermon 'Being Alone', he employs a rather daring metaphor. He compares the presence of God in Jesus's passion to God being present as a 'spastic child who can communicate nothing but his presence and his inarticulate wanting'.[7] The context in the sermon is a reflection on the increasing solitude of Jesus as he moves towards his death. It is a solitude born out of a failure of language and communication. Disciple and interrogator alike increasingly fail to comprehend Jesus. In turn, the latter, especially, faces his silence or evasiveness. Finally, in the dereliction, language fails even towards the Father. It is replaced

---

5. Rowan Williams, 'The Four Quartets' (1975), lecture 3, 7–8. Greek transliterated from original.

6. Rowan Williams, *Christian Imagination in Poetry and Polity: Some Anglican Voices from Temple to Herbert* (Oxford: SLG Press, 2004), 37.

7. Rowan Williams, *Open to Judgement: Sermons and Addresses* (London: Darton, Longman and Todd, 1994), 145. The language is more shocking now in its datedness. In a remarkably partisan piece, this analogy was held up as an exemplar of all that is wrong with Williams's theology of revelation. See Garry Williams, *The Theology of Rowan Williams: An Outline, Critique and Consideration of Its Consequences* (London: The Latimer Trust, 2002), 4–5.

by a wordless cry, an exclamation of the type a profoundly disabled child might give. This failure of language stems from Jesus being the manifestation 'of a reality which so resists definition and limitation that it can only appear utterly strange in our world. It doesn't belong, and so, as Bonhoeffer said, it is "edged out of the world and onto the cross"'.[8] Arguably both logics are at work in this sermon. The inability of the Word to appear in that part of the world known as language is sourced in its resistance to 'definition and limitation', to being confined to any particular part. This life is 'utterly strange' because it is *non aliud, not-*other to the whole. Yet, it does appear dialectically in the friction, backlit by the aggressive incomprehension that edges it out of the world. It is alluded to, as will become increasingly clear, in a silence and inarticulacy that is itself a form of *syncrisis*.

The trope of an inarticulate child reoccurs in Williams's writing and preaching. If it is not that of a disabled child, it is of one who has not yet found language. This travels with a belief that the incarnation encompasses the presence of God in the most pre-articulate of human beginnings. For Williams, the mediatorial logic of the whole entails a belief that the Word is *not*-other to the *whole* narrative of a human organism, even an inchoate foetus 'not yet active and distinct'.[9] It is also *not*-other to the disruptive cries of a neonate. In the sermon 'Not to Condemn the World', Williams draws attention to a baby's 'insistent presence without shame or restraint, crying and clutching'. It is in the mode of this disruptive inarticulacy that the Christmas child confronts us. His note-perfect performance is, here, through the communication of urgent infantile need, a vector for 'the shattering strangeness of God'. It is also a communication oddly transposable with the wordless cry of the cross.[10] In the words of Williams's poem 'Advent Calendar', which obliquely recalls Bonhoeffer's language of 'being edged out of the world', the one who comes 'like a child', comes 'like blood, like breaking/as the earth writhes to toss him free'.[11]

For Williams, 'the free God of stable and cross' comes to us as the 'wordless stranger', not amenable in that wordlessness to partial interests, and, thereby, 'there for all'.[12] It is in Christ as disruptively inchoate before language, as well as disruptively inarticulate beyond language, that a logic of the whole is alluded to. What is gestured towards is that *non aliud* difference that takes no part and, thereby, paradoxically, is present to the whole.[13] But that reality only attains to

---

8. Williams, *Open to Judgement*, 144–5. The Bonhoeffer quote is from *Letters and Papers from Prison*. No pagination or edition is specified by Williams.

9. Rowan Williams, *Ponder These Things: Praying with Icons of the Virgin* (Norwich: Canterbury Press, 2002), 45–6.

10. Williams, *Open to Judgement*, 34–6.

11. Rowan Williams, *The Poems of Rowan Williams* (Oxford: Perpetua Press, 2002), 15.

12. Williams, *Open to Judgement*, 37.

13. In a later Christmas sermon, it is the child's status as 'displaced', occupying no recognizable place in the given social manifold, that alludes to 'another reality, another order'. See Rowan Williams, *Choose Life: Christmas and Easter Sermons in Canterbury Cathedral* (London: Bloomsbury, 2013), 61, 66.

visibility as a consternation for the world. Its *loci* are two points of extremity, cradle and cross, where communication fails. The logic of the whole, predicated on the *non aliud* God, is inextricably interwoven in these reflections with the language and logic of crisis, and *syncrisis*, of a world obdurately related to its peaceable source. This source comes into phenomenal reach in its disconcerting impact. But this focus on extremities and wordlessness, on an early childhood rendered cruciform, and a crucifixion rendered through the metaphor of an inarticulate child, begs a question. Whither all the days in between, and the many words and gestures, quotidian and extraordinary, they contained? The Gospels are full of interactions, teachings and parables. It will be an open question throughout these discussions as to whether these intertwined logics work together, or whether they constitute a tension wherein one wins out. At points, it seems that the logic of *syncrisis* overcomes the logic of the whole, as the extraordinary and pressured eclipses the prosaic.

Silences and the Cross

To shift the primary focus from cradle to cross, it is worth turning to the silences and failures of language around Jesus's end. In Williams's account of the Markan narrative in *Christ on Trial*, he notes the silence of Christ when questioned about his messianic identity. He argues that for Jesus to have spoken openly could only have resulted in misapprehension. In the tragically conflictual 'midnight world' in which Jesus is placed, such talk could only be construed in the native idioms of competition and power. In that context its generative nature is lost. It is only in the moment of extremity that is Jesus's midnight trial, when any claims to worldly authority become manifestly absurd, that he can speak the simple and theologically evocative words – 'I am'. It is only in this pressured moment of dramatic *syncrisis* that the truth can be alluded to, and something like successful mediation occur. Even then, judging from the interrogators' reaction, it is not unambiguously successful. After this point, in Mark's narrative at least, Jesus essentially holds silence. To Pilate he is evasive. His one articulate cry on the cross (given first in a foreign language) is a plaintive accusation of desertion, and then there is that wordless cry, elsewhere reminiscent of a disabled child's.[14]

The logics already noted are again replicated here. The *non aliud* difference of God has no place in the world beyond a point of allusive extremity; it emerges – obliquely – in the *syncrisis* of a testing encounter. Yet, the silences leading to and

---

14. Rowan Williams, *Christ on Trial: How the Gospel Unsettles Our Judgment* (Grand Rapids: Zondervan, 2000), 5–9. For a similar point made in relation to Luke's account, see Williams, *The Truce of God*, 70. It is notable that, in the Markan discussion, Williams elides Jesus's words concerning the vision of the 'Son of Man' from Dan. 7:13 that follows (Mk. 14:62).

following that trial and its briefest of admissions also have an aspect of *syncrisis*, insofar as we are speaking of a testing of the truth through dialectical juxtapositions and, even, a particular form of dialogue. Jesus's willed silence is, paradoxically, a form of dialogue with a reality that misapprehends or distorts speech. It is, as alluded to in Chapter 2, a judgement that is also a potentially transformative telling of the truth about an inability to speak in peaceable idioms. It is a silence in an intentioned and communicative sense, still an engagement in the drama, and in its own way the work of love. That this is a possibility inherent within silence is alluded to in one of Williams's most recent writings, *The Edge of Words* (2014). There, when speech becomes 'corrupted and facile', silence can become 'significant as protest', its signifying power being in its juxtaposition with what it, by silence, denies.[15]

The communicative silence of Christ moving towards death is a silence like that of Christ before the Inquisitor. It is indicative of agency. It takes its meaning in dialogue, and in a dialectic of juxtaposition, with the mendacious speech that surrounds it. This is what differentiates it from the parodic silence of Myshkin's idiocy. If Myshkin is an 'undialectical' non-entity, Jesus's silence is precisely dialectical. It is a response to, and a sharp break with, the untruthful speech of a 'world' that has come to (mis)construe itself as in a competitive relationship with its source.[16] In *that* world, it is 'as if the silence of [Jesus's] dying is the only rhetoric for his gospel'.[17]

But a *syncrisis* of silence is not just deployed externally by Jesus, it is arguably deployed internally against him. If his narrative proposes a testing encounter between him and the world, one in which his silence becomes a communicative crisis for that world, silence and a communicative crisis finally also occur within him as the meeting of that world and its source. For Williams, in 'Deflections of Desire', silence reflexively comes back upon Jesus to thrust itself between his human subjectivity and its divine ground. As was seen, in the dereliction, divine difference re-presents itself as the loss of any discernible consolation for this human subject. There is only the profoundly painful silence of divine absence.[18] This is where *syncrisis* as a dialectical silence potentially becomes unnervingly conflictual in terms of the hypostatic union. But it is also where the truth of that union perhaps becomes most visible – in the silence that erupts in a juxtaposition between an only complexly unfallen humanity and its divine ground. For Williams, 'Jesus

---

15. Rowan Williams, *The Edge of Words: God and the Habits of Language* (London: Bloomsbury, 2014), 157–8. Williams discusses this communicative possibility of silence in the context of Cordelia's silence before her father Lear. See also 57–8.

16. See Williams, *Christ on Trial*, 87. The context of this discussion is the theological freight given to the term 'world' (*kosmos*) in the Johannine literature.

17. Rowan Williams, 'Resurrection and Peace', *Theology* 92, no. 750 (1989): 486.

18. Rowan Williams, 'The Deflections of Desire: Negative Theology in Trinitarian Disclosure', in *Silence and the Word: Negative Theology and Incarnation*, eds O. Davies and D. Turner (Cambridge: Cambridge University Press, 2002), 121–2.

faced with the absence of the Father is also Jesus endowed with the resource to give himself so wholly to the Father that he is free to act for the Father in the world.[19]

It is for Williams as if *here*, when the skies become a dialectical silence even to Jesus, is the most truly successful point of Christological mediation, because 'what is "left" is the purpose and act of God'.[20] This is a point reiterated in *The Edge of Words*, in reference (as is the case in 'Deflections') to the work of John of the Cross. The narrative of Jesus's dereliction 'represents the unrepresentable God by tracing a movement towards silence and motionlessness'. It reveals the dispossesive nature of God's power in a temporal re-presentation of the eternal pattern of divine self-giving. In entering into that moment is found 'a new freedom ... to represent the God whom Jesus decisively represents in his own displacement and dispossession'.[21] The implication not quite drawn out here is that, until this point in Jesus's narrative, it cannot be made clear that the objects of even Jesus's desires are not worldly, that he isn't working in the world's divisive idioms. Up till this point, his innocence and the mediation of the divine life are opaque. But at this pressured point, when a *syncrisis* of silence engulfs the human person of the Word, the reality that is the generative possibility of the whole of his life becomes emergent in its dialectical friction with that humanity's godlessness. Here is where the logics of the whole and of *syncrisis* lie most closely together, and where they are also in the most excruciating tension.

Something of this is alluded to in a 1978 tribute to Thomas Merton. There Williams affirms that 'Christian belief finds the ground of truth in the silence of Christ'. The one who at his end utters nothing, 'but suffers only', is the one who is 'transparent without qualification to the shape of reality'.[22] Here silence and suffering are the apogee of Christological clarity, even if the later predication of an alienating silence *within* Jesus's psyche is absent. This is approached from another angle in the 1991 Pitt Lectures at Yale. Williams again reflects on John of the Cross, and argues that 'in the emptiness and stripping of Jesus' death, we understand and are touched by the love which keeps nothing back, which does not claim and defend a place over against us in the world but is unequivocally *for* us'.[23] Here the locus of silence is death, the biological endpoint of the dereliction's abandonment. This is where the *syncrisis* of Jesus's existence is at its most pointed, where the very life of God is *not*-other to a cessation of existence. This is a supremely dialectical point, but it is also where the *non aliud* God who claims no place, but is every place's possibility, can cease to be *negatively* dialectically related to the world. In this equivocal place, the generative possibility of God that Jesus performs reaches the status of unequivocal.

---

19. Ibid., 128.

20. Ibid., 121.

21. Williams, *The Edge of Words*, 176–7.

22. Rowan Williams, *A Silent Action: Engagements with Thomas Merton* (Louisville: Fons Vitae, 2011), 18.

23. Williams, *Open to Judgement*, 275.

For Williams, it seems that mediation's intensity and opacity co-inhere. The generative reality of God comes to us most decisively through the *syncrisis* of silence and inarticulacy that is a tortured and incoherent body dissolving towards death. The silence and demanding inarticulacy of an infant is a proleptic gesture towards this event, sharing in its *syncrisis*. This is a genuine *theologia crucis* in which, to cite words already quoted in Chapter 2, 'God himself is the great "negative theologian", who shatters all our images by addressing us in the cross of Jesus'.[24] In that chapter, the argument was made that the cross, as Christianity's generative negative moment, is an 'anti-representation' that is, yet, supremely significant of God's utter difference from the world; it, thereby, persists as a judgement against the world. Now this intuition is found to rest within the very mediatorial logics of Williams's Christological presentation. The utter difference of God, which cannot be located in any conceptual or linguistic place, in any *part* of this world, is, yet, disconcertingly emergent in allusive moments of dialectical friction, when the peaceable God is performed in *an*-other human life within a divisive and agonized manifold. The cross is the epicentre of this *syncrisis* – the point of greatest internal and external tension for Christ, and, thus, the locus within opacity of the most strangely clarified Christological mediation.

Christ, Truth and History

As I have already suggested, the 'world' is a home for mendacious speech. For Williams, this world – insofar as it conceives of itself as its own source of value over and against its true source – 'is always bound to various sorts of untruthfulness'.[25] This is arguably the context for his sympathy with the following statement by Dostoevsky: 'If someone were to prove to me that Christ was outside the truth, and it was really the case that the truth lay outside Christ, then I should choose to stay with Christ rather than with the truth.'[26] What keeps this from being an irrational leap is that Williams reads the 'truth', which Dostoevsky prefers Christ against, as that of a world caught up in the false consciousness of its opposition to God, the 'truth' of a world bound in untruth. On one level, Williams reads Dostoevsky's statement as a protest against technical modernity's reduction of 'truth' to the rational-mechanical ensemble of empirically discernible propositions, as well as the use of violence to enforce such rationality.[27] But it is built on an understanding that a Christ 'outside truth' is one free in regard to the world's valuations and

---

24. Williams, *The Wound of Knowledge: Christian Spirituality from the New Testament to St John of the Cross*, 2nd Rev. edn. (London: Darton, Longman and Todd, 1990), 149.

25. Williams, *Christ on Trial*, 87.

26. Williams, *Dostoevsky*, 15. The statement is found in an 1854 letter, written shortly after the author's release from incarceration. The original text is in *Pol'noe sobranie sochinenii*, 30 vols. (Leningrad: Nauka, 1972–90), 28:2, 176.

27. Ibid., 15–21.

violences, in some sense excessive of a history of tragic alienation – the kiss of Christ in the Inquisitor poem is held as emblematic of such a freedom.[28]

What is being claimed is that the one whose human life is a transcription of God is not mediating that which can easily be plotted as *an*-other among the ensemble of the world's truths; the truth of the *whole* takes no mere *part*. It is evasive of worldly purchase and idioms; its rhetoric is finally a *syncrisis* of silence. But this immediately introduces a tension with other aspects of Williams's presentation – for it is in becoming *an*-other in our drama, and in our *world*, that Christ heals it. Any evasion (even through excess) of a tragic history begins to smack of Myshkin, a potential flight to a false timelessness. To return to the Inquisitor narrative, as discussed at the end of Chapter 3, this tension is visible there in the still open question as to the degree to which *its* Christ truly escapes the parodic. His freedom to keep silence, and to enigmatically kiss, comes close to an ethereal beauty without purchase. The equation of Jesus's freedom from 'truth' with this poetic figure does not come without some complications.

In a 2001 conference paper, Williams makes a point, using Kierkegaard's *Philosophical Fragments*, which resonates with that made in *Dostoevsky* about Christ and the world's truth. It also recalls what was said earlier in his lectures on *The Four Quartets* – that Jesus as a temporal figure is an object of '*doubt* as much as faith'. In the 2001 paper, he argues that the truth of the incarnation, while mediated *in* history, is not in itself a historical datum. Historical data cannot deliver 'a resolution that will make faith easier', and there is no straight line from the Jesus of history to the Christ of faith.[29] The Christ of faith is not part, in any simple manner, of the ensemble of this world's truths. There is, again here, an evasiveness to purchase and an elusiveness to empirical reduction in Christological mediation. But there is also, again, a tension with previously made points. As argued in my discussion of Williams's incarnational historicism in Chapter 2, it is only by becoming *an*-other in the historical manifold that history is transformed. The Jesus of history, there, cannot be disposed of without substantial theological damage being incurred.

The tension of a Christ who is *an*-other, embracing the tragic muddiness of history, but who is also oddly evasive of history and historical truth, is the tension enshrined in the two mediatorial logics under discussion in this chapter. According

28. Ibid., 30–1.

29. Rowan Williams, 'Looking for Jesus and Finding Christ', in *Biblical Concepts and Our World*, eds D. Z. Phillips and M. von der Ruhr (Basingstoke: Palgrave MacMillan, 2004), 149–50. *Philosophical Fragments* is also referenced in a 2004 lecture on Michael Ramsey. There, Williams suggests that 'the unbreakable association of the infinite God with the material Jesus' paradoxically reinforces 'that God is never part of the system of the universe'. It demonstrates a divine liberty 'to be ... in the place of death and hell'. See Rowan Williams, 'Theology in the Face of Christ', http://rowanwilliams.archbishopofcanterbury.org/articles. php/2100/addresses-given-to-celebrate-the-centenary-of-the-birth-of-archbishop-michael-ramsey.

to the logic of the whole, this is the one who can appear unequivocally in no *part* of a divisive and delusional manifold. His life may be a virtuoso performance, but this only attains to visibility in a strange sort of dissonance as, according to the logic of *syncrisis*, it comes into friction with history's tragic divisions. Even then, the illumination is allusive and resistant to assimilation. History and empirical truth provide no royal road to Christological knowledge. But this raises a question similar to one raised earlier. Just as the focus on extremity and *syncrisis* threatens to devalue the quotidian and less obliquely communicative aspects of Jesus's narrative, so the focus on Christ's evasiveness to history and intra-worldly 'truth' threatens the already noted import of history in William's Christological presentation. In both of these situations, the logic of *syncrisis* potentially threatens to derail the intuition that the Word is truly *not*-other to the whole of a historical career.

An Illustrative Side Step – Poetical Mediation

Earlier I noted that Williams's mediatorial logics are often visible where theological and literary concerns come together. Eliot and Dostoevsky have already come into our considerations, but there is another figure, previously discussed in this book, who can also be brought to bear – the Welsh poet and priest R. S. Thomas – and with Thomas also comes, at least in Williams's work, the figure of Kierkegaard. In the concluding section of the essay 'Suspending the Ethical: R. S. Thomas and Kierkegaard' (2003), Williams characterizes Thomas's poetic enterprise as 'the pursuit of presence – but a presence that can only be obscure when it is actually present'. It is a pursuit carried out by 'pushing the inner tensions of language to the point of new discoveries in form and metaphor'. Its success is in 'speaking in such a way as to open up what is not said', an 'unsaid' with a distinctly theological flavour. It 'is reality as the manifestation of God, God as the ground of what is perceived'.[30]

The grammar emergent for Williams in Christological mediation is essentially replicated here in this discussion of poetry. The 'presence' sought in poetical mediation is that of the 'unsaid'. This recalls Williams's use of de Certeau, explored in Chapter 1, to speak of an un-encompassable 'un-said' behind all discourse, another register in which to speak of divine difference. Here the unsaid is allusive of the divine 'ground' of all perception, which is only ever obscure in its presence. This unsaid seems to carry the same weight as it did in the discussions of de Certeau, as adjectival of the *non aliud* God who is the unspeakable possibility of the whole created and linguistic manifold. The logic of the whole is here, but so too is the logic of *syncrisis*. The very possibility of bringing this presence to an allusive light – 'pushing the inner tensions of language' – recalls *syncrisis'* semantic field of

---

30. Rowan Williams, 'Suspending the Ethical: R. S. Thomas and Kierkegaard', in *Echoes of the Amen: Essays after R.S. Thomas*, ed. D.W. Davies (Cardiff: University of Wales Press, 2009), 217–8.

extremity and tension.[31] It is this linguistic extremity in Thomas that, as Williams elsewhere notes, makes him useful for a theologian seeking 'an appropriately difficult, distancing register' in which to speak appropriately of God.[32]

If I spoke first of the conclusion of Williams's 2003 essay on Thomas, it should also be noted that the essay's considerations begin with Thomas interacting with the thought of Kierkegaard. If Kierkegaard understands faith as the 'unspeakable reality' of a relation beyond language,[33] Thomas is one for whom 'God enters discourse … in a very particular kind of interruption of speech'.[34] What comes arrives as speech's disruption, a wordlessness indicative of the divine presence that might recall the *syncrisis* of silence – and, ultimately, the tie between poetical and Christological mediation is emphasized in this essay on poetry by a discussion, within it, of Christology. Williams reads Thomas as working 'toward a Kierkegaardian conclusion: The Incarnation … is the brick wall which confronts thought, imagination and management.' It is 'the presence of God's dream as a kind of wound in the fabric of history'.[35] Just as poetical mediation comes as a tensioning of speech, and ultimately its interruption, Christological mediation appears as a 'wound' in temporality. Christ is, again, outside history's truth, and the truth he mediates is not part of the ensemble of worldly factual data. Where this truth finds elusive visibility are the edges of the wound, in those dialectical moments of extremity and friction where the poetic disruption Christ mediates encounters a violently prosaic world.

These discussions of poetical mediation, conducted in relation to R. S. Thomas, have something of a coda in Williams's more recent work *The Edge of Words*. It is a book where, admittedly, Thomas is not mentioned and Christological mediation *per se* is often only discussed obliquely. In it, what poetry and speech about God have in common (the latter more profoundly than the former) is a certain tendency to linguistic eccentricity and disruption. If God is the ground Thomas's poetry alluded to in its pushing of language to a *syncrisis*-like crisis, it is a ground that, for Williams, frames finite being itself. Speech about God attempts to speak about that which concerns 'all possible subjects of discourse', the whole, but is itself not such a subject of discourse. It frames the whole, but is not a part of it. Its resultant linguistic eccentricity thus entails an accompanying importance for silence[36] – and

31. The emphasis on tension is also found in Rowan Williams, '"Adult Geometry": Dangerous Thoughts in R.S. Thomas', in *The Page's Drift: R.S. Thomas at Eighty*, ed. M. Wynn Thomas (Bridgend: Seren, 1993). For Thomas, 'there might be a legitimate word or thought, an utterance beyond suspicion, if it is held to a point of pure tension' (93).

32. Rowan Williams, '"Is It the Same God?" Reflections on Continuity and Identity in Religious Language', in *The Possibilities of Sense*, ed. J.H. Whittaker (Basingstoke: Palgrave, 2002), 211–12.

33. Williams, 'Suspending the Ethical', 206–8.

34. Ibid., 210–1.

35. Ibid., 213–4.

36. Williams, *The Edge of Words*, 30–1.

it is an eccentricity that must include, as Thomas's poetry does, some elements of linguistic extremism, even language framed as 'carefully calculated shocks' and 'metaphorical violence', to upset our habitual perception of the world and its truths.[37] Williams's is, then, a theology of language, and thus of poetry, which looks for mediation in the extremes of words, and in the silences between them.

Tracing the Issues of Christological Mediation – Scriptural Mediation

If poetical mediation formally replicates the grammar of Christological mediation, this does open up a further question. Insofar as poetry's possibilities are language's possibilities at their most ambitious, what does this mean for mediation in the language of scripture? What emerges in Williams's thought is that scriptural mediation evidences the same dynamics found in poetical and Christological mediation – and, in examining scriptural mediation in Williams, we are ultimately returned to distinctly Christological considerations.

For Williams, in the essay 'Historical Criticism and Sacred Text' (2003), it is of the nature of a text, sacred or not, to have an excessive quality. Every text emerges from a particular context, embodying its assumptions and contradictions, and yet many texts seek to surpass their context. A perceptive reader is one who then discerns a text's excessive quality, how it 'establishes its difference from the context', and how it, thereby, initiates 'a new chain of textual reflection and response, as well as seeing how it repeats what is received'.[38] To put this differently, some texts mediate something to attentive readers, a freedom from the ensemble of what has been previously assumed. They do this, precisely, in disjunctions, in straining at the givenness of their contexts to open up new possibilities. One example of this is Williams's own reading of the Inquisitor narrative, and of the excessive freedom mediated within it by the kiss of Christ. It opens up new possibilities of response, new ways to read situations and a new repertoire of action – including Alyosha's mimesis of that kiss.

The additional qualitative difference brought into play by a *sacred* text, for Williams, has to do with an aspect of its context being, itself, excessive. The context of such a text is 'always something more than the social-ideological matrix', something more than the phenomenal ensemble of the world's truths. It initiates a 'conversation with a presence that is not a rival speaker, a participant in the exchange and negotiation of empirical speakers'. Insofar as it has a hinterland in this expansive context, such a text instantiates a liberating interruption in normal speech. In other words, the context of a *sacred* text is that *non aliud* presence that

37. Ibid., 148–9.

38. Rowan Williams, 'Historical Criticism and Sacred Text', in *Reading Texts, Seeking Wisdom*, eds David F. Ford and Graham Stanton (London: SCM Press, 2003), 224. See also 221, where Williams references Derrida's concept of *différance*.

cannot be mapped at any point in a rivalrous manifold and thus, if it appears, does so as an interruption and *syncrisis* for that manifold. It initiates two unsettlements, the first being that possibility already implicit in non-sacred texts of an excessive difference from the given social-ideological context, and the second being the unsettling excessiveness of what is utterly different from *any* context. One is 'driven into contradiction, by the address of God, as well as by the tensions of the social-ideological context'.[39]

What Williams offers is a hermeneutics of scripture that looks for mediation in the breaks, in the unsaid and that which strains saying. This reflects what has already been said of poetic mediation, and is a hermeneutical analogue to the tendency to look for places of contradiction, pressure and extremity in Christological mediation. The *non aliud* God does not appear as a given datum or object in scripture, any more than God so appears in Christ's career. The idea that God might be so rendered is correlated with 'unsustainable doctrines of biblical inerrancy'. It improperly places God within the ensemble of the word's empirical truths. Thus, 'a theological exegesis is not one that assumes such transparency in the text, but one that looks for those contradictions between intention and performance, those marks of excess and intra-textual strain that might have to do not only with immediate ideological context but with God'.[40] Scripture, insofar as its context is the *non aliud* God, refers allusively to that context through *syncrisis* and contradiction. As in Thomas's poetry, God is a reality that appears as a 'wound' in the given.

But, if Williams's thinking on scriptural mediation is analogous to his understanding of Christological mediation, then an analogous question to one already raised persists. Just as the emphasis on pressured moments of *syncrisis* in Jesus's career seems to belie that the Word is *not*-other to the whole of his existence, so it must be asked if this emphasis on the marks of excess and strain constitutes a similar problem for the scriptures. If one asks of Jesus: 'Whither the quotidian aspects of his existence?', one might also ask of scripture: 'Whither its plain sense, the (revelatory?) import of its historical context, and the critical methods used to study it?'. Quotidian words and quotidian history seem not to be the stuff of mediation, and ordinary language, just as ordinary time, needs to be stretched to the breaking point to serve. If, as already argued, there is no

---

39. Ibid., 224–5.

40. Ibid. See also Rowan Williams, 'Scriptures in Monotheistic Faith', http://rowanwilliams.archbishopofcanterbury.org/articles.php/2114/paper-for-seminar-scriptures-in-monotheistic-faith-at-st-egidio-conference-naples-italy, where Williams warns against the failure to read scripture 'without ever noticing the persistent ironies and critical moments within the text'. Ben Quash, who draws heavily upon 'Historical Criticism and Sacred Text', argues for a very similar approach, which looks for the 'gaps and tensions', or even (following Halivni) 'maculations', in the text 'which may be regarded as divine provision for some generative purpose'. See his *Found Theology: History, Imagination and the Holy Spirit* (London: Bloomsbury, 2013), 56–7, and Chapter 3 *passim*.

simple line between the Christ of faith and the Jesus of history, so there is no easy correlation between the deliverances of historical-critical study and scripture's revelatory possibilities. 'Otherwise theology itself ... puts itself in thrall to a theory of religion, phenomenological and historical in character.'[41]

Fundamental questions are provoked here. I have argued already for Williams's incarnational historicism. I have also argued that the Word, in his Christological presentation, is *not*-other to *an*-other humanity mired in the tragic mechanisms of a fallen history. God, and God Incarnate, are not 'beautiful souls' reticent about sullying their hands in time; the incarnation is God's demonstrable acumen for doing so. Yet, in these discussions of mediation, a contrapuntal reticence has emerged. It is revealed in the grinding together of two theological tectonics: (1) a *non aliud* God, *not*-other to his entire creation but unequivocally locatable in no part of it, and (2) a creation coded as tragic, divided from its source and within itself. Such a reading of creation perhaps makes it acidic to mediation's possibilities, unless they come as a fracturing of creation's tortured and deceived manifold – and such an understanding of God as *non aliud*, as had been argued, both makes possible and *complicates* mediation. This dynamic complexifies the investment of God in history, words *and* Christ. But, for now, these questions will be bracketed, as we return to scriptural mediation and note how it pulls us back towards Christological considerations.

In Williams's sermon 'Reading the Bible', similar themes to those explored in the essay 'Historical Criticism and Sacred Text' emerge. Citing as programmatic for the biblical text Jacob's belligerent encounter with the angel in Gen. 32, Williams characterizes the scriptures as 'the record of an encounter and contest': 'Here in scripture is God's urgency to communicate, here in scripture is our mishearing, our misappropriating, our deafness and our resistance. Woven together in scripture are those two things, the giving of God and our inability to receive what God wants to give.'[42] If a physical altercation between a theophanic being and a man at the desperate turning point of his life, set on a night of sublime extremity, is programmatic for scripture, then what Williams is implicitly claiming is that scripture, like Jesus, is a site of *syncrisis*. It is the locus for a forceful dialectical encounter, as Word and words written share the character of being a space where the world and its source grapple. This correlation makes it unsurprising that Williams moves quickly from speaking of Jacob's striving to the repeated misapprehensions of those who wrestle with Jesus's words in the Gospels, especially the parables.[43]

---

41. Rowan Williams, 'Historical Criticism and Sacred Text', 227. Elsewhere, Williams notes how a proper theological reading of scripture probes the places in the text where the pressure of divine difference is felt. See his 'Afterword: Knowing the Unknowable' in *Knowing the Unknowable: Science and Religions on God and the Universe*, ed. John Bowker (London: I.B. Tauris, 2009), 260–1.

42. Williams, *Open to Judgement*, 158.

43. Williams particularly notes the parable of the Unjust Steward (Lk. 16:1-13), which even the Gospel writer seemed not to comprehend (ibid.). Quash notes how, for

In the previous chapter, I noted that an element of *syncrisis* is palpable, for Williams, in early Christian texts, especially the Gospels. The focus, then, was on the temptation narratives. But, insofar as in reading the Gospels *per se* there is a grappling with that which resists, with what is heard but not understood, there is also what might be termed a *syncrisis*, a dialectical struggle for truth. Like the figure they depict, the Gospels share with the rest of scripture in the quality of *syncrisis* – and that is, ultimately, because they point to the one who meditates the *non aliud* in time, a reality that attains to visibility only in dialectical friction.[44] To return to a point made earlier in relation to Williams's lectures on Eliot, these are not documents that compel faith, but communicate the one who 'remains a point of *krisis*'.

Williams has commented more than once on the fourfold and differing nature of the Gospels. In their non-systemized plurality, they point to the idea that 'there is in Jesus a dimension not contained', an elusiveness to capture that is like 'a face coming to light at the mouth of a cave, the light falling this way and that, but never turning full glare into unreachable darkness'.[45] This imagery perhaps recalls Williams's discussion of the averted faces of Rublev's icon, with *their* elusiveness to capture – communicative both of the measure of divine difference, and of the invitation within that difference. The elusiveness of Jesus to capture in the Gospels serves a similar purpose; it draws the reader into a grapple for the truth with the one who mediates God's difference. In the essay 'Does it Make Sense to Speak of Pre-Nicene Orthodoxy?' (1989), Williams speculates that the refusal to systematize the Gospels into a unified whole preserves, even, a memory of the '*way*' in which Jesus's story was told. Early Christian preaching was less about 'the communication of principles', and more about inducting 'the hearer into a "dramatic" relation with the subject of the story', drawing them into the tensions of the narrative.[46] Thus, that in Jesus which is 'not contained', but escapes into a polyphonic fourfold telling, is that which meets us as an involving challenge, even an entry into a dramatic *syncrisis*.

But the language of *syncrisis* is, ultimately, not widely deployed in Williams's work; it is confined to the essay ' "Tempted as We Are" '. And yet, as the discussions of this chapter have shown, the concept it represents – of a dramatic and dialectical

---

Williams, Christ's teachings are '*generatively*, perhaps even *deliberately*, underdetermined'. Consequently, the tensioned and difficult aspects of Scripture are a 'faithful registration of generative uncertainty'. Quash, *Found Theology*, 75.

44. In his essay 'Trinity and Revelation' (1986), Williams makes it clear that the 'revelation' of God in Jesus – communicated through the Gospels – is in his ' "initiation of debate" at an unprecedentedly comprehensive level' (Rowan Williams, *On Christian Theology* [Oxford: Blackwell, 2000], 138).

45. Williams, 'Looking for Jesus and Finding Christ', 148.

46. Rowan Williams, 'Does It Make Sense to Speak of Pre-Nicene Orthodoxy?', in *The Making of Orthodoxy: Essays in Honour of Henry Chadwick*, ed. Rowan Williams (Cambridge: Cambridge University Press, 1989), 15-6.

testing of the truth, even to the point of extremity – inheres throughout Williams's discussions of mediation. In 'Does it Make Sense to Speak of Pre-Nicene Orthodoxy?' another language, that of parables, is in fact used by Williams to a curiously similar effect. They are cast as realistic narratives that invite hearers to 'find an identity' within them. Furthermore, Jesus's narrative is read as having a parabolic quality. It 'is remembered in diverse and less than wholly coherent narrative forms', which portray a figure not exhaustible in 'word or system', but enunciated 'as a questioning and converting presence in ever more diverse cultures and periods'.[47] 'Beginning with the Incarnation', written in the same year, echoes this idea. The proclamation of Jesus's lordship is likened to the proclamation of 'a kind of parabolic drama: this is what has happened, and you must discover where you stand as you discover your response to this'.[48]

Thus, if Christ and the scriptures both have a quality of *syncrisis* to them, they both have a parabolic quality; they involve us in a wrestling where truth and identity are at stake. Jesus's narrative is the parabolic drama wherein we 'find an identity', where, as was argued in Chapter 2, we are judged and re-created. Jacob's wrestling, as paradigmatic for scripture, leaves him with a new name and identity – Israel. For Williams, a Christian reading of scripture is unavoidably dramatic and involving, and a particularly significant instance of this is Jesus's parables. They 'invite the hearer's or reader's identification'.[49] They are 'a cardinal example' of texts 'intended to effect change … the result of being forced to identity yourself within the world of the narrative, to recognise who you are or might be'.[50] And these parables within scripture only make sense themselves within the greater parable that is Jesus's story.[51]

But the parables are also a cardinal example of the *elusive* quality of Jesus's teaching and life[52] – a reminder that mediation, through incarnation and

47. Ibid., 16–7.

48. Williams, *On Christian Theology*, 81. For a more recent discussion of parables by Williams that reiterates many of the themes discussed here, see his *The Edge of Words*, 89–90, 149–50. Parables there are a 'dramatic metaphor' that invite the hearers' identification and involvement. Also discussed is the way some of the more challenging parables (such as the Unjust Steward and the Unjust Judge) are a transposition into narrative form of the sort of linguistic extremity that encodes the 'carefully calculated shocks' (149) already spoken of in the discussions of poetic mediation.

49. Williams, *On Christian Theology*, 50.

50. Rowan Williams, 'The Bible Today: Reading and Hearing', a lecture given in Toronto on 16 April 2007, http://rowanwilliams.archbishopofcanterbury.org/articles.php/2112/the-bible-today-reading-hearing-the-larkin-stuart-lecture.

51. See Williams, *On Christian Theology*, 40–1.

52. MacKinnon, whose interest in parables may be one of the wellsprings of Williams's own approach, has commented on their elusive quality (see, especially, Donald MacKinnon, *The Problems of Metaphysics* [Cambridge: Cambridge University Press, 1974], Chapter 6 *passim*).

scripture, is only ever *allusive*. It is in the context of the Parable of the Sower that the possibility of seeing and yet not seeing, hearing but not understanding, is raised by Jesus himself (see Mt. 13:13-14). These are words alluded to by Williams in *Dostoevsky*: he discusses Christ's iconic possibilities as being 'in the form of an image that is, inevitably, caught up in the process of seeing and not seeing, understanding and not understanding'. Christ is, like any phenomenon in history, 'vulnerable to being made sense of in diverse ways', 'not naturally or visibly the last word in history as it proceeds'.[53] To go to another of Williams's sermons, 'What is Truth?', Christ's kingship is that 'of a riddler', promulgated in 'enigmatic words which oblige us to imagine ourselves anew: as a child, as homecomer, as discoverer of hidden treasure; as afraid of compassion and jealous of gifts given to another; as Pharisee and tax-collector'. These examples are allusions to well-known parables, but, ultimately, this enigmatic kingship is mediated most powerfully through silence, and in death.[54] The enigmatic silences around the cross, where the *syncrisis* is at its sharpest, are the culmination of the parabolic narrative that is Jesus's story.

The Problems of Mediation – Conclusion

I have explored the complex nature of Christological mediation in Williams's thought at a number of points, including through the related grammars of poetic and scriptural mediation. The divine reality that Christ mediates is, like his innocence, an occluded reality in time. He is an enigmatic parable, which may be seen and not seen, heard and not understood. Thus, his status as the 'last word' is not a given within history's procession. It is an eschatological datum, and so – as will become increasingly clear in the next two chapters – is the success of Christological mediation. At several points in these discussions, questions have surfaced concerning whether the tensioned logics that underlie mediation might, in the end, come apart. The tendency for Williams to restrict points of allusive success to moments of extremity and *syncrisis* seems to work against his understanding that the Word is *not*-other to the whole of who Jesus is. This tension is earthed in two already mentioned tectonic intuitions – God's *non aliud* generativity, and the tragic nature of a riven contingency that misconstrues its relation to God. It seems, at times, that Williams's construal of creation's tragedy makes history an impossible space for God; divine generativity can only come as an interruption to such a history, a wound within its woundedness. If this is the case, then much of what has been said positively about Williams's commitment to history – to the 'drama of misrecognition' that Jesus enters in time – potentially comes undone. Whether it *is* the case must await a more detailed exploration of Williams's understanding of creation's tragedy in the coming chapter.

---

53. Williams, *Dostoevsky*, 207.
54. Williams, *Open to Judgement*, 131.

Chapter 6

TRAGEDY

Introduction

The problem carried over from the previous chapter is one of Christological mediation – whether, in Williams's tensioned logics, his construal of history's tragic nature compromises mediation's possibilities. But this sense of the tragic impacts upon more than just Christology; it arguably translates into a pervading ethos of difficulty within Williams's work. Even Williams's theological sympathizers have concerns about the 'unremittingly agonised' nature of his thought.[1] One vector for this sense of difficulty seems to have been the recurring figure of Donald MacKinnon, who consistently argued for the place of tragedy in Christian theology. He was also a thinker whose semi-legendary ability to agonize is perhaps unparalleled.[2] Williams's early allegiance to MacKinnon is evidenced in his almost breathless praise of the latter's essay 'Theology and Tragedy' in 'The Spirit of the Age to Come' (1974). Williams there dubs it 'the most profound and moving defence of the presence of tragedy in its most classical form in the basic documents of the Christian faith that I know of'.[3] Later, MacKinnon is cited as, 'above all', one of those teachers who have 'shared their wisdom with me'.[4] And then there is that pivotal essay of Williams's already discussed, one written in dialogue with MacKinnon, 'Trinity and Ontology'.[5]

---

1. Mike Higton, *Difficult Gospel: The Theology of Rowan Williams* (London: SCM, 2004), 36. See also Benjamin Myers, *Christ the Stranger: The Theology of Rowan Williams* (London: T&T Clark, 2012), 116–17.

2. See Rowan Williams, 'Living the Questions: An Interview with Rowan Williams', http://www.christiancentury.org/article/%252Fliving-questions. Another illuminating perspective is offered by George Steiner in his *Errata: An Examined Life* (New Haven: Yale University Press, 1997), 149–53.

3. Rowan Williams, 'The Spirit of the Age to Come', *Sobornost: The Journal of the Fellowship of St Alban and St Sergius* 6, no. 9 (1974): 618–9. The essay 'Theology and Tragedy' is to be found in Donald MacKinnon, *The Stripping of the Altars: The Gore Memorial Lecture and Other Pieces* (London: Fontana, 1969), 41–51.

4. Rowan Williams, *The Truce of God* (London: Fount, 1983), 10.

5. For another assessment of MacKinnon, see Williams's essay 'Theology in the Twentieth Century', in *A Century of Theological and Religious Studies in Britain*, ed. E. Nicholson (Oxford: Oxford University Press, 2003), 244.

But MacKinnon has had his critics, and some of them are vociferous. David Bentley Hart has offered an aggressively pitched critique of twentieth-century theology's taste for the tragic. To him, it is a penchant that offers only a 'narcotic metaphysical solace', inspiring an ethos of 'resignation and masochism'.[6] MacKinnon, specifically in his use of classical tragic drama as a theological datum, is seen by Hart as culpable in this development. To Hart, he has imported into Christianity an alien element from the religio-political world of the Greek *polis*.[7] Such ancient tragedy proposes a 'metaphysical horizon of cosmic violence'. Its wisdom is 'one of accommodation, resignation before the unsynthesizable abyss of being, a willingness on the part of the spectator to turn back to the polis as a refuge from the turmoils of a hostile universe, reconciled to the regime and its prudent violences, its martial logic'.[8]

To Hart, tragedy as a theological datum is fundamentally problematic because it radically ontologizes violence and evil – although the implied conflation of violence and evil will itself be queried in our coming discussions. Tragedy represents a world wherein they are a primal existent, lurking at the roots of everything. Christianity, on the other hand, historicizes them. Violence and evil are, in Hart's theological understanding, the artefacts of a non-necessary history of wrongdoing. Their presence is likened to 'the superscribed text of a palimpsest, obscuring the aboriginal goodness of creation'.[9] John Milbank, a thinker to whom Hart is indebted, mounts a similar argument. In the same *festschrift* in which 'Trinity and Ontology' originally appeared, he terms MacKinnon's recourse to tragedy an 'extremely subtle version of the aesthetics of the sublime'. In its insistence on the tragic as the 'surd' element in creation, it imports the notion of an abyssal radical evil, and undermines a proper Augustinian vision of evil as contingent and privative.[10]

These criticisms raise questions for Williams insofar as he is indebted to MacKinnon. If a theology informed by tragedy proposes a created manifold wherein

6. David Bentley Hart, *The Beauty of the Infinite: The Aesthetics of Christian Truth* (Grand Rapids, MI: Eerdmans, 2003), 374–5.

7. Ibid., 380–4. Larry Bouchard makes a similar point about classical tragedy's extrinsic relation to Christianity, but views the relation between them as potentially generative. See *Tragic Method and Tragic Theory: Evil in Contemporary Drama and Religious Thought* (University Park, PA: Pennsylvania State University Press, 1989), 51.

8. Hart, *The Beauty of the Infinite*, 383.

9. Ibid., 384.

10. John Milbank, 'Between Purgation and Illumination: A Critique of the Theology of Right', in *Christ, Ethics and Tragedy: Essays in Honour of Donald Mackinnon*, ed. Kenneth Surin (Cambridge: Cambridge University Press, 1989), 178–81. Ben Quash notes Hart's dependence on Milbank, but also questions their critiques of MacKinnon. See his essay 'Four Biblical Characters: In Search of a Tragedy', in *Christian Theology and Tragedy: Theologians, Tragic Literature and Tragic Theory*, eds Kevin Taylor and Giles Waller (Farnham: Ashgate, 2011), 20–3.

evil is a radical reality, it would be a manifold in which mediation is problematic. This 'world' would not be self-deceived in construing itself in a negative relation to God. The conceptual field of *syncrisis*, with its semantics of conflict and extremity, might become the only dialect for speaking of the relation between such a world and its source. If there is at least a *part* of creation to which God is indelibly in enmity, the logic of God's generative presence to creation's *whole* becomes untenable. What is potentially at work is a severe irony. In Chapter 2, MacKinnon was cited as one of the sources of Williams's incarnational historicism. But it now seems that aspects of MacKinnon's thought push in a contrary direction, towards a view of history as tragically allergic to divine possibilities. However, in this chapter I will argue that there are resources in Williams's theology for escaping this irony. While he is indebted to MacKinnon, there are movements in Williams's thought, and even departures from MacKinnon, that ameliorate, without dissolving, history's tragic nature. Williams, in dialogue with both Augustinian and Hegelian thought, adopts a more eschatological bent than MacKinnon might be comfortable with. Ultimately, the adoption of this bent is tied up with Christological considerations.

The Tragic – An initial foray

For MacKinnon tragic drama, especially classical tragedy in its Attic origination, is 'a form of representation that by the very ruthlessness of its interrogation enables us to project, as does no other available alternative, our ultimate questioning'.[11] It confers an acumen for pressing uncomfortable questions, and thus constitutes an essential part of theology's 'system of projection', its conceptual apparatus for approaching the realities it seeks to deal with.[12] But what did tragic drama enquire into with such ruthless facility? MacKinnon probes this question by looking, paradoxically, at what Plato found objectionable about tragedy. Among the reasons why, in *The Republic*, he would have removed the tragic poets from the *polis* are (1) tragedy's transgressive theology, which refuses theodicy's exculpation of the divine from responsibility for evil, (2) its intuition that a virtuous life is no protection against disintegrating catastrophe and (3) the attention it draws to diverse, and often discordant, stories as opposed to any harmonious whole. It is in foregrounding these realities that tragedy is, in fact, instructive.[13] For MacKinnon,

---

11. Donald MacKinnon, *The Problems of Metaphysics* (Cambridge: Cambridge University Press, 1974), 136.

12. MacKinnon, 'Theology and Tragedy', 51. For more on 'systems of projection', see Giles Waller, 'Freedom, Fate and Sin in Donald Mackinnon's Use of Tragedy', in *Christian Theology and Tragedy: Theologians, Tragic Literature and Tragic Theory*, eds Kevin Taylor and Giles Waller (Farnham: Ashgate, 2011), 102.

13. MacKinnon, 'Theology and Tragedy', 43–6. To Dennis Schmidt, Plato sought to exclude the tragic for reasons both political and spiritual. Politically, tragedy worked

it is a literary and dramatic form that presents 'a sense of the sheerly intractable in human life'.[14]

However, for Williams, in 'The Spirit of the Age to Come' – in the very essay where MacKinnon's work on tragedy comes so warmly recommended – it is to Hegel's insights about tragedy, and not Plato's objections to it, that he goes in thinking through the genre and its significance. For Williams, following Hegel, the historical intuition behind tragic drama emerges from 'an awareness of present reality as divided, fragmented, liable to internal struggle and frustration'. This is not so much an intuition of the surdish presence of radical evil, as it is an apprehension of the inescapable conflicts that arise between conflicting *goods*. Good, in the history that we have, is not experienced as unitary; it comes in partial forms and lays countervailing claims upon us – and it is to Hegel's interpretation of *Antigone* that Williams goes to explicate this. Hers is a situation, in the clash between civic and familial duty, obedience to the king or the imperative to secure a seemly burial for her brother, 'where good is divided against itself'.[15]

For Hegel, fundamentally, the motive forces behind the conflicts in tragic drama are partial, but real, goods. These fragmented goods bear the 'stamp of the Ideal', and are 'universal', 'eternal' and justified in and of themselves.[16] In contrast, evil is a negativity that cannot provide the motive force for dramatic action. In the light of Hart's and Milbank's critique of tragedy, there is something to note here. Insofar as Williams follows *Hegel*, the charge that he might be engaging in a project that ontologizes evil loses some of its potential traction. If there is a surd present, it is not found in the presence of a radical evil, but in the tragic incompossibility of some goods. Hegel's description of evil even looks a little like Milbank's desired privative account; it is an absence that fails to inspire agency. Hegel's Devil (perhaps a little like Williams's Myshkin) is 'an extremely prosaic person'.[17] What is important is that, even in an early essay such as 'The Spirit of the Age to Come' where Williams praises MacKinnon, he also begins to depart from him with an appreciation of Hegel that hints at things to come. That this is, in fact, a *departure* is intimated by MacKinnon's own scepticism towards Hegel's reading of *Antigone*, and his assignment of tragedy to conflicting goods. MacKinnon is concerned that Hegel's interpretation elides the curse of Antigone's incestuous lineage, as well as the murkiness of the motivations in play within the drama.[18]

---

against the unity of the polis, presenting 'images of death that remind us of our apartness'. Spiritually, it damagingly appealed 'to the speechless desires and fears of the soul'. Thus, tragedy presents that within human life which is destabilizing to both community and soul. See his *On Germans and Other Greeks: Tragedy and Ethical Life* (Bloomington: Indiana University Press, 2001), Chapter 1 *passim*, especially 43–4.

14. Donald MacKinnon, *Explorations in Theology 5* (London: SCM Press, 1979), 186–7.

15. Williams, 'The Spirit of the Age to Come', 616.

16. G. W. F. Hegel, *Aesthetics: Lectures on Fine Art, Volume I*, trans. T. M. Knox (Oxford: Clarendon Press, 1975), 220.

17. Ibid., 222.

18. See MacKinnon, *Explorations in Theology 5*, 187–9 and *The Problems of Metaphysics*, 123–4.

Where Williams also departs from MacKinnon is in a relative lack of interest in classical tragedy, at least within his writings to date.[19] While MacKinnon gave the Attic tradition fulsome attention,[20] citing Hegel on *Antigone* is about as far down that road as Williams has gone.[21] Yet, what both thinkers *do* share is a more general interest in literature and its theological import, including its ability to foreground that which is difficult within human existence. If MacKinnon finds tragic drama efficacious in interrogating the world's intractable aspects, Williams finds something similar in certain modern poets. Eliot, he notes, does not offer a 'pessimistic' vision, but rather a 'tragic' vision. His world, in the previous chapter painted as empirically godless, is such that 'waste and failure' are ubiquitous.[22] His 'sensibility' is that 'of a man for whom the consciousness of being human was so constantly and nakedly the consciousness of pain and failure, loss of simplicity and single-heartedness'.[23] R.S. Thomas offers a similar 'tragic' vision to Williams.[24] But, more so than Eliot, he is a poet whom Williams is willing to criticize. In Thomas's understanding of humanity as 'condemned to the tantalising knowledge of a non-negotiable horizon ... variously represented by death, time, failures of control, pain',[25] the intractable is brought into view. Where Williams becomes critical is when Thomas obliquely locates this intractability 'in the fractures of God's own will or desire'. At this point, a theologically unacceptable option is broached: 'the assumption that conflict and rivalry ... are somehow native to our being, because, explicitly or implicitly, the relation of beings to their final origin is itself a kind of flaw, "wound", violence'.[26] In Williams's reading, Thomas draws close to rendering evil or violence ontologically radical, something that emerges from a primal fracture either within God, or between God and the world. Williams rejects this, and in this rejection there is something like an implicit rejection of any totalizing

19. At the time of writing, Williams is finishing a book on tragedy. It remains to be seen if this will include a fuller investigation of the classical tradition.

20. Besides 'Theology and Tragedy', see *The Problems of Metaphysics*, 122–4, 143–5; and *Explorations in Theology 5*, 187–91. MacKinnon also employed Shakespearean tragedy. See ibid., 182–7; *The Problems of Metaphysics*, 137–8, 145.

21. Shakespearian tragedy does appear in Williams's writings (see his 'The Spirit of the Age to Come', 617 and Rowan Williams, *The Truce of God: Peacemaking in Troubled Times* [Norwich: Canterbury Press, 2005], 195–6), and Lear holds a special fascination; see Williams, 'Living the Questions'.

22. Williams, 'The Four Quartets', (1975), lecture 3, 9.

23. Rowan Williams, *Open to Judgement: Sermons and Addresses* (London: Darton, Longman and Todd, 1994), 215. Myers implies that Eliot is as much an informer of Williams's tragic vision as MacKinnon. See Myers, *Christ the Stranger*, 24–7.

24. Williams, 'Living the Questions'.

25. Rowan Williams, ' "Adult Geometry": Dangerous Thoughts in R. S. Thomas', in *The Page's Drift: R.S. Thomas at Eighty*, ed. M. Wynn Thomas (Bridgend: Seren, 1993), 87.

26. Ibid., 96. Williams equates this unacceptable theological option with Milbank's idea of 'foundational violence'.

of the logic of *syncrisis*. In such a one-sided and totalized logic, to recall language from our previous chapter, mediation can *only* appear as a 'wound'. Here the rendering of our relation to God, finally, in terms of a wound is the rejected option.

For Williams, as much as for MacKinnon, there is an intractability to the world. To dwell in it is to live at the antipode of all that the beautiful soul longs for. It entails a horizon of failure and conflict, the loss of innocent singularity of heart. Poets inform this vision, as do authors like Dostoevsky, through creations such as the parodic Myshkin. So too does Hegel, at least in 'The Spirit of the Age to Come' – and we have also argued that the Hegelian rejection of the beautiful soul is an intuition that Williams takes to heart. Williams's is a vision where, to quote 'The Spirit of the Age to Come', 'all genuinely moral dilemmas are essentially tragic', entailing conflictual imperatives, and even the very process of maturation is 'bound' to involve tragic collisions with others in the same process.[27] This is why, in a later book, he says that 'a degree of self-assertion, even aggression, is necessary for the individual's growing process', and violence cannot be dismissed as an 'unnatural aberration'.[28] It is, potentially, more than the superscription on a palimpsest.

This is a world, as noted in Chapter 4, where acting well is – tragically – no simple matter and violence's possibilities inhere in even loving action. Also noted in that chapter was the opacity within some of Williams's writings as to whether this is an artefact of the 'Fall', or the given nature of contingency. But, if conflict is innate in contingency, then Williams seems to draw close to what he backs away from in R. S. Thomas. He seems, in his openness to the tragic, to radicalize the violently conflictual in the very way Hart and Milbank feared tragedy might. This is why it is important that, in a 1989 essay entitled 'Resurrection and Peace', Williams makes the claim that an affirmation of conflict's inevitability does *not* translate into conflict's ontological radicalization; it is not a 'metaphysical statement about the inevitability of mutual exclusion and strife'. 'Conflict', in that essay, is the ineluctable product of the resistances the world offers us. It is inherent to what Chapter 4 termed the pressures of life in the body and society. 'Strife' and 'exclusion' have a different aetiology; they derive from a self-defensive and accidental mode of living in one's body and society, 'from the conviction that we possess a territory to be safeguarded'.[29]

To tie this in with previous Christological discussions, to be human – even for Christ in his complex *unfallenness* – is to live in a *conflictual* world of multiple pressures. What is not automatically entailed in this is a *fall* into a particular history of strife and exclusion, an exacerbation of conflict into something darker. That possibility, in 'Tempted as We Are', was labelled as living our innate vulnerability in such a way as to exceed need and exert a self-protective control. Its accidental nature is demonstrable – if in the most suspended of manners – in Christ's human

---

27. Williams, 'The Spirit of the Age to Come', 616–7.

28. Williams, *The Truce of God*, 51–2.

29. Rowan Williams, *On Christian Theology* (Oxford: Blackwell, 2000), 273.

refusal of it. I will argue in this chapter that the eschatological aspect of Williams's thought, ultimately inseparable from the Christological, enables a trajectory in which, gradually and never cleanly, the inherent difficulties of living in creation are uneasily separated from a particular historical condition of fallenness. In a sense, and *pace* tendencies in Hart and Milbank, *violence* (inherent, in some form, to creation's manifold) is separable from *evil* (a tragic enflaming of that manifold in a given history). Evil is, thereby, rendered non-radical, even if some aspect of the conflictual is not. In making this argument, Williams begins to separate himself from MacKinnon, but at the same time from the theological approach typified by Milbank and Hart.

The Nature of Contingency – Continuities and Departures from MacKinnon

It is worth returning to Williams's understanding of the nature of created existence, and noting its complex relationship to MacKinnon's construal of the same subject matter. There are some fairly straight lines to be drawn between MacKinnon and Williams when it comes to the inherently conflictual nature of contingency. Despite MacKinnon's reticence about Hegel's reading of *Antigone*, he does understand the incompossibility of some goods to be part of the world's intractability. Likewise, there is a sense in MacKinnon that maturation is an agonized process. But, as I will show, this is also the site of a departure between him and Williams, one made along an eschatological horizon. A further departure is found in their different approaches to theodicy, a discussion that will also foreground Williams's differences from Hart and Milbank.

For MacKinnon, the most seemingly innocent of human limitations – finitude – is part of the tragedy of our contingent frame; it is an intractable limit that fragments our efforts – even, he notes, for Jesus: 'To leave one place for another is to leave work undone; to give attention to one suppliant is to ignore another; to expend energy today is to leave less for tomorrow'.[30] In a world where we are confined to a singular flow of agency in time, every positive choice entails a negative foregoing of other goods. MacKinnon intriguingly illustrates this with a striking counterfactual reading of the Good Samaritan; he notes a defence for those who passed by the injured man – they made a calculation between real goods. To aid someone potentially beyond aid would have entailed a loss of liturgical purity, which cannot be consigned to the purely fictive or obscurely pharisaical.[31]

Echoing themes later found in Williams, MacKinnon argues that if choices have moral significance, they are tragic in that what is not chosen is gone. What further inflames this is the fallible nature of human insight when making such choices.

---

30. Donald MacKinnon, *Themes in Theology: The Three-Fold Cord* (Edinburgh: T&T Clark, 1987), 162–3.

31. MacKinnon, *The Problems of Metaphysics*, 88–9.

Bracketing the issues of culpable self-deception, which MacKinnon did not,[32] he was burdened by the intuition that limitations in knowledge and foresight bind us into frustration. In words that recall Williams's insights about the damage done by any agent in the complexity of an enmeshed social manifold: 'No one who goes to the aid of another ... fails to run the risk of greater human damage both to himself and to the object of supposedly spontaneous concern, and indeed to others bound up with both of them in the bundle of life.'[33] Like Williams's, MacKinnnon's is a world of mutual implication, where acting well is no simple matter, where even (recalling words from Williams's *Dostoevsky*) 'creative and altruistic' desires are hobbled by the opacity of insight.[34] This, for both MacKinnon and Williams, is part of the world's tragedy.

Also part, for both, is the agony of maturation in time. In an occasionally opaque essay, 'Some Notes on the Irreversibility of Time' (1975), MacKinnon explores the structures of temporality in which the human self comes to be. As an ongoing construction, the self (including Jesus's) is a painful achievement, hard-won 'in the ragged piecemeal succession of human actions, performed in circumstances not entirely foreseeable, and even when foreseen, still in the cruel impact of angry exchange, always less manageable than even the clearest foresight can make the wise man realise'. Thus, time arrives to us as a jarring set of discordances in which the self is (just about) held together. It is a medium of distension and estrangement.[35] The language of 'angry exchange' echoes Williams's insight that part of this distension arises from the presence of others in the same process of becoming, others with whom there will be conflict. But, to the theologically literate reader, this discussion might also suggest Augustine's considerations, in *Confessions* XI, of time and the distension of the soul.[36]

Augustine is not mentioned in MacKinnon's essay, but making this connection opens up a potentially fruitful avenue of comparison with Williams. In terms of his theological anthropology, Williams is an Augustinian. The self, as he understands it, is characterized as fundamentally desirous, motivated by its foundational lack of God as its ultimate good. This is an insight Williams worked out in a series of closely connected essays in dialogue with Augustine's writings, produced

---

32. See his readings of *Oedipus Rex* in ibid., 143–5 and *Explorations in Theology 5*, 190–1.

33. MacKinnon, *The Problems of Metaphysics*, 89. MacKinnon illustrates this, in a different counterfactual reading of the Samaritan parable, by speculating about the unwitting negative outcome if the Samaritan's hands had been infected, or his oil rancid (140).

34. Rowan Williams, *Dostoevsky: Language, Faith and Fiction* (London: Continuum, 2008), 57.

35. MacKinnon, *Explorations in Theology 5*, 96–7.

36. See, especially, Paul Ricoeur's meditation on this text, which notes the pathos implied in Augustine's discussion, in his *Time and Narrative: Vol. I*, trans. K. McLaughlin and D. Pellauer (Chicago: Chicago University Press, 1984), Part I, Chapter 1 *passim*.

over several years in the late 1980s and early 1990s.[37] However, in the later *Lost Icons* (2000), this Augustinianism is refracted through a curiously Hegelian prism. Williams there draws upon Hegel's idea of the 'unhappy consciousness' in considering the role that frustration and conflict play in the production of the self. The self is haunted by a desire for self-presence, but this desire springs from an already experienced dispersal and instability of the self. Thus, the self is always already in distension before the incumbent nature of its desire, persisting in a world where nothing will bestow 'a rounded and finished identity'.[38] This vision echoes MacKinnon's insofar as the existence of the self in time is rendered, to some extent, discordant, its unity an elusive possibility. Where Williams departs from MacKinnon is in his insistence that this self's agony is ultimately rendered as *non*-tragic against an eschatological horizon.

This is visible in the essay '"Know Thyself": What Kind of Injunction?' (1992). Once it comes to recognize its 'utter and irreducible difference' from its desired *summum bonum* in God, the self's distension is transposed into a different register. Seeing that there is no immanent fulfilment for its lack, it can find that implied in God's difference is 'unlimited time' to move towards God. The desire of a distended self for self-presence thus passes into a desirous search for the one whose *non*-presence is paradoxically saving because, against an unlimited horizon of deferral, 'there is always a resource for the renewal or conversion or enlargement of myself'.[39] Thus, for Williams, the self's distension obtains an almost eudaemonic register against an eschatological horizon. This is reflected, in a different way, in his talk, in *Dostoevsky*, of Christ as the 'last word'. There, what is offered in Christ is not an angry exchange within a discordant jostle, but a vivifying dialogue in which the self is expanded. This dialogue is also the gift 'of a future without fear of the other, an assurance that within other and more conflictual dialogues there is still the potential for life'.[40] In other words, not only is the distended self given life in relation to an eschatological horizon, but the social manifold is also in

37. See Rowan Williams, 'Language, Reality and Desire in Augustine's *De Doctrina*', *Journal of Literature and Theology* 3, no. 2 (1989), 138–50; 'Sapientia and the Trinity: Reflections on the *De Trinitate*', in *Collectanea Augustiniana: Mélanges*, eds T. J. van Bavel, et al. (Leuven: Leuven University Press, 1990), 317–22; 'The Paradoxes of Self-Knowledge in the *De Trinitate*', in *Collectanea Augustiniana: Augustine, Presbytr Factus Sum*, eds J. T. Lienhard, E. C. Muller and R. J. Teske (New York: Peter Lang, 1992), 121–34; '"Know Thyself": What Kind of Injunction?', in *Philosophy, Religion and the Spiritual Life*, ed. Michael McGhee (Cambridge: Cambridge University Press, 1992), 211–28. In many ways these essays are an extension of Williams's chapter dealing with Augustine in *The Wound of Knowledge: Christian Spirituality from the New Testament to St John of the Cross*, 2nd Rev. edn. (London: Darton, Longman and Todd, 1990), Chapter 4 *passim*.

38. Rowan Williams, *Lost Icons: Reflections on Cultural Bereavement* (Edinburgh: T&T Clark, 2000), 145–53. A similar argument is made in 'Know Thyself', 213–4.

39. Williams, 'Know Thyself', 220–3; quote from p. 223.

40. Williams, *Dostoevsky*, 139.

movement towards repair. Its discordances against this horizon – be it coded as 'unlimited time' or a Christological 'last word' – become potentially life giving. The tragic intractabilities of living as a self and a social being are here ameliorated through being set within an eschatological frame – and it is not incidental that both Augustine and Hegel are invoked in these discussions.

This eschatological amelioration is a deep-seated intuition in Williams's thought. It is present as early as the 1970s in 'The Spirit of the Age to Come'. In that essay, it is the Spirit that is coded as eschatological, 'the bearer of a *new* mode of being'. It provides an energy 'which has not been atrophied by tragic experience and tragic knowledge'.[41] Williams intriguingly juxtaposes the work of the tragic poets with prayer as the Spirit's work. If the poets' words can be read as a protesting 'demand for the saeculum, the order which is totally different', so can the practice of prayer. Pneumatologically empowered, prayer provides 'the "artistic" presupposition of unity', the intuition that the tragic conflicts that grow from human maturation in a world of partial goods do not propose a final fracturing.[42] Thus, there is an intuition already at work in this early bit of Williams's writings: what is conflictual, and even tragic, about existence finds some element of repair in being set in an eschatological frame. To understand the full import of this intuition, we must first look at theodicy.

Theodicy

It is not insignificant that MacKinnon inverted the Platonic love of harmony to describe the tragic. Tragedy, in his understanding, refuses to soften existence's discordances, and theodicy is, for MacKinnon, just such a softening. It places the tragic in a teleological providential order, which, ultimately, dissolves its astringency. Theodicy as an enterprise is even cast as in surreptitious service to a form of monism. It effaces multiple intractable particulars in the service of a blander whole. Tragedy, therefore, is a countervailing force to theodicy. It defends a realist pluralism, one that foregrounds the discordant and particular.[43] Another way to put this is to say that theodicy, for MacKinnon, occludes history, or at least the history that we actually live in. Tragedy, in acknowledging that there is 'nothing here which is not Zeus',[44] nothing from which the divine can be excused through theodicy, returns us to history. This is the context for what is perhaps MacKinnon's

41. Williams, 'The Spirit of the Age to Come', 619.

42. Ibid., 624.

43. Donald MacKinnon, *The Problems of Metaphysics*, 128–9, 134–5; *Borderlands of Theology and Other Essays* (London: Lutterworth Press, 1968), 104. For Williams on this aspect of MacKinnon's thought, see *On Christian Theology*, 154–6.

44. The concluding words of Sophocles' *The Women of Trachis*, taken by MacKinnon as the epitome of tragedy's rejections of theodicy. See his *The Problems of Metaphysics*, 122 and *Explorations in Theology 5*, 189–90.

boldest theological move, his rejection of the primary Western theological approach to evil – privation theory. He sees it as emerging in Plato's *Republic*, and characterizes it as a view that has 'only to be stated clearly, and worked out in terms of concrete examples, to be shown to be totally inadequate as an analysis either of moral or physical evil'.[45] *Prima facie*, there is some potential merit to MacKinnon's case. To take one example: Milbank (who critiques MacKinnon's departure from privation theory) has argued that, eschatologically at least, the tragic evils of human history will be forgotten – 'revised out of existence' – because only the good participates in being.[46] Such rhetoric seems close to the effacing monism that MacKinnon fears might lurk behind the enterprise of theodicy.

Aspects of Williams's thought concerning theodicy head down this same route of scepticism as MacKinnon's. In 'Trinity and Ontology', he notes the mendacity of resolving suffering particulars into 'comfortable teleological patterns', an attempt to explain suffering that forgets it '*as* suffering'.[47] In his essay in dialogue with McCord Adams, he critiques theodicy as an enterprise. It is, to him, 'more religiously imperative to be worried by evil than to put it into a satisfactory theoretical context'. Such worrying 'keeps obstinately open the perspective of the sufferer';[48] it holds our concentration on those intractables of particular human sufferings in history that tragedy foregrounds. However, even in 'Trinity and Ontology', where Williams's concerns lie so proximate to MacKinnon's, there are also signs of departure. In a criticism similar to Hart's fears of a 'narcotic metaphysical solace', Williams worries that an emphasis on the tragic might enervate transformative action to ameliorate suffering[49] – and, elsewhere, he does accept a form of theodicy, even one that relies on an understanding of evil as privative. In tracing this, we can locate not only another departure from MacKinnon, but also a differentiation from Milbank and, insofar as his approach echoes Milbank's, Hart.

In a review essay of Milbank's *Theology and Social Theory,* Williams notes Milbank's cautions around tragedy and the potential radicalization of evil it entails. Yet he argues, in turn, that in a history of incompossible goods 'shaped by privation', a conception of the tragic must be retained. Thus far, barring the use of the word 'privation', there is no obvious departure from MacKinnon. But then Williams makes an important distinction. He differentiates between the pressures, inherent to 'what it *is* to be created', that make for tragedy (the incompossible nature of temporal goods), and those exacerbating factors that are accidental to creation, but render it a 'life threatening as well as life nurturing' context. These are primarily the self-subverting choices sentient beings make for untruth. Thus,

45. MacKinnon, 'Theology and Tragedy', 143–5.

46. John Milbank, *Being Reconciled: Ontology and Pardon* (London: Routledge, 2003), 54.

47. Williams, *On Christian Theology*, 155.

48. Rowan Williams, *Wrestling with Angels: Conversations in Modern Theology* (Cambridge: Eerdmans, 2007), 172–3.

49. Williams, *On Christian Theology*, 162. Williams also sees a positive role for the tragic in transformative change (163–5).

for Williams, there are evils – if they are rightly called such – that are inherent to creation, and evils that are artefacts of an accidental historical series. Williams also interrogates Milbank around his rhetoric of violence, and questions what he means by a view that the tragic must succumb to a 'myth of necessary violence'. Implicitly recalling the argument in 'Resurrection and Peace', Williams implies that the acknowledgement of some level of conflict does not necessarily entail a mythic violent ontology. Williams also makes a move that joins up with the point I made earlier about the eschatological amelioration of the tragic, arguing that even the inevitability of conflict in contingency does not exclude an eschatological 'healing or mending'.[50]

In thus invoking eschatology to help refuse violence a sacral character, Williams makes a significant move. He sets creation against an eschatological horizon, as something 'whose good will take time to realise'.[51] This is in counterpoint to Milbank's trademark move in *Theology and Social Theory*, where Trinitarian theology 'is the coding of transcendental difference as peace'.[52] To Milbank, this becomes a claim that peaceable difference is ontologically primordial in creation, whereas violence and contestation are superscriptions. But, for Williams, there can be no conceptually univocal move from Trinitarian to creational difference. The absence of contestation in the divine life is not indicative of contestation's presence in creation being a fall from primordial grace. Instead, the non-repetitious difference of creation from God is the establishment of a *process* in which creation's goodness is emergent. It is a process 'pregnant with the risk of tragedy, conflicting goods, if the good of what is made is bound up with taking time'.[53]

To Williams, it seems, creation's good is not so much primordial as *eschatological*; creation is a process moving towards fruition. Thus, the primordial presence of contestation does not imply violence's *ultimate* reification, for the weight of meaning is at the end, not the beginning. And, since contestation should not be collapsed into 'evil', nor violence too easily conflated with evil, conflict's primordial presence does not necessitate evil being primordial. Thus far Williams's defence of leaving space for the tragic in relation to the charges that might come from Milbank or Hart. In terms of his difference from MacKinnon, it is Williams's description of these theological moves as caught up with the 'minimalist theodicy of Augustinianism' that raises eyebrows.[54] Not only is theodicy invoked, but so too is the great Christian advocate of privation theory.

The Augustinian underlay of Williams's approach to creation is evident in the essay '"Good for Nothing?" Augustine on Creation' (1994). There, all creaturely

---

50. Rowan Williams, 'Saving Time: Thoughts on Practice, Patience and Vision', *New Blackfriars* 73(1992): 321–2. Later in the article, Williams describes his questions to Milbank as 'MacKinnonesque' (325).

51. Ibid., 323.

52. John Milbank, *Theology and Social Theory*, 2nd edn. (Oxford: Blackwell, 2006), 6.

53. Williams, 'Saving Time', 323.

54. Ibid., 322.

good 'is the product of process', and 'Augustine's is a universe in motion whose order, beauty and purpose is only properly discernible as a whole'. It speaks of God in its (non-repetitious) difference from the divine nature, a temporal movement towards equilibrium that can be understood, analogically, as desire.[55] That Williams is moving towards an Augustinian account of *privation* is confirmed in the essay 'Insubstantial Evil' (2000). There he notes Augustine's fundamental conceptual breakthrough in departing from Manichaeism – the idea of a mode of being that is not spatially extended. God becomes conceivable as persisting in a non-extended mode in relation to the 'interlocking system of action and passion' that is creation. God is not mappable within the system, but is its generative ground – essentially the *non aliud* grammar explored in Chapter 1. Evil, importantly, can be understood in a strangely analogous manner. It too lacks extension, and is not locatable as an item in the system. Rather, it 'is a failure of the appropriate balance' between items, 'paradigmatically' a human agent giving priority to 'selfish and materially defined goals' in such a way as to impact upon other creatures – that earlier-mentioned self-defensive and sinful mode of living in body and society. Thus, evil is privative because it is not a *thing*, but a parasitic distortion *between* things, the systemic disruption caused by sentient vanity.[56] If creation is a process in movement to its good, evil is not innate to its workings; it is their frustration.

'Insubstantial Evil' as an essay also further underlines the idea of creation as a process. Creation is home to a divergence of complexity and capacity, a variety necessary when things 'become' through interaction, dependence and complexification. The good of this movement that is creation is not discernible at any one point, but is found in the unfolding as a whole. Likewise, the good of any one creature within creation cannot be discerned apart from its place in this process.[57] Importantly, creation's movement cannot, in and of itself, issue in a discernible state of final goodness. In a parallel grammar to that of the human self's desirous distension towards a God never had as an immanent good, creation's final good is not available in time. It is 'the work of grace and, thus, ultimately a victory never produced by history itself'.[58] In other words, it is an *eschatological* realization.

55. Rowan Williams, '"Good for Nothing?" Augustine on Creation', in *Doctrinal Diversity: Varieties of Early Christianity*, ed. Everett Ferguson, *Recent Studies in Early Christianity* (New York: Garland, 1999), 36–7. See also his article 'Creation', in *Augustine through the Ages: An Encyclopaedia*, ed. Allan D. Ftizgerald (Grand Rapids: Eerdmans, 1999), 252. There, Augustine's creation is 'the setting into being of a living system destined to grow into beauty and order, even if this beauty and order is not at any given moment apparent'.

56. Rowan Williams, 'Insubstantial Evil', in *Augustine and His Critics: Essays in Honour of Gerald Bonner*, eds R. Dodaro and G. Lawless (London: Routledge, 2000), 107–10.

57. Ibid., 114–16.

58. Ibid., 118–9.

The parallels with Williams's understanding of Christological mediation are striking. Taking the questions of Christ's innocence and the world's goodness in tandem, neither is clearly discernible *within* history, but both are eschatological determinations. Strikingly, by definition in this Augustinian schema, Christ as *an*-other agent *within* creation has a goodness only discernible in relation to creation's totality in process. That is the nature of creaturely goodness. Chapter 4's discussions, in fact, probed what this might mean: the data set for determining Christ's innocence encompasses the afterlife of his agency in the enmeshed manifold of history, including all the lives patterned upon or affected by his, and those they in turn affect, and onwards *ad infinitum*. If Christ is the 'last word' with whom all may find a vivifying relation, this can only be an eschatological word, spoken not from history's middle but from a temporally impossible vision of the whole. The same is true of the final word concerning creation's goodness.

In fact, as the essay 'Good for Nothing?' suggests, the grammars of Christ and creation are not just paralleled, they are interlocked. In Williams's reading of Augustine, a creation construed as process entails a commitment to a salvation worked out in process and time. The 'definitive clue' to these processes 'is the event in which the everlasting Word and Wisdom shapes and speaks in and acts out a human and material history, telling us that there is no way to God but through time'.[59] Christ is elsewhere described, in another essay on Augustine's thought, as 'the supreme *signum*, the point of greatest transparency within the world to its divine origin'.[60] In an Augustinian idiom, this is that 'incarnational historicism' spoken of in Chapter 2, wherein the meaning of history (i.e. the goodness of creation itself) is only had through one consummately significant life. But the meaningfulness of that life, *its* goodness, is a suspended reality – for the process in which it has its meaning is still ongoing – and the opacity of its mediatoral power is intensified by a reading of that process as, in some sense, tragic. This is where Williams's adoption of a 'minimalist' Augustinian theodicy begins to rescue the situation.

In the essay 'Insubstantial Evil', there is a change in Williams's linguistic usage. 'Tragedy' comes to be associated not, as in the much earlier 'The Spirit of the Age to Come', with the conflictual aspects of creation resulting from the partial nature of temporal goods, but, rather, with those exacerbating factors that have to do with a non-necessary distortion in the process. To the Augustinian, in this understanding, tragedy resides not in the system, but in the contingent vanity that unbalances it. Williams even implies that a departure from this assumption is a substantial departure from a Christian doctrine of creation. It would return one to a dualist ontology of cosmic struggle.[61] Williams now sounds more like Hart or Milbank, and less like his younger self. To some extent, this development must be treated with caution. Williams is prone to deploying terms and concepts

---

59. Williams, 'Good for Nothing?', 40.
60. Rowan Williams, 'Augustine and the Psalms', *Interpretation* 58, no. 1 (2004): 23–4.
61. Williams, 'Insubstantial Evil', 120.

divergently in different contexts. In an interview published in 2005 he stated the following, associating it with Augustine: 'The world is different from God and yet activated by God. Because it's different from God, it's subject to possibilities of tension, collision. The way in which laws and regularities unfold will, from a human point of view, lead to tragedy from time to time.'[62] Here the tragic is still associated with the functioning of creation's processes, but it is also given the additional nuance of being tragic 'from a human point of view'. The implication is that these tensions and collisions may, perhaps, be understood as, ultimately, *non*-tragic. Arguably, Williams has come to inhabit a more Augustinian world where there is a 'variety and oscillation of circumstances as agents act upon each other, never at any point obtaining a balance within the world's history'. It is a world of variegated freedoms, dependencies and constraints. But these are not ultimately *tragic* constraints, because they are constraints intrinsic to the good of finite things.[63] We are leaving behind the MacKinnonesque register of temporal experience and finitude, of contingency itself, as tragic – and we have already left behind the danger of ontologizing evil. As the *truly* tragic exacerbation of contingency's processes by self-deceived agents, evil has been properly historicized. It belongs not to the medium of creation, but to that medium's malfunction.

A question, however, remains: To what extent does Williams's proposal of an eschatological horizon, entwined with a 'minimalist' Augustinian theodicy, threaten to replicate that teleological providential order which, under MacKinnon's aegis, he was so concerned about? Has Williams stopped worrying about evil and learnt to love theodicy? It is worth going to a recent commentator on Augustine and evil, Charles Mathewes, to find some resources for thinking through this question. To Mathewes, an Augustinian reading of evil is not, as MacKinnon might fear, about dissolving the tragic. It is 'about bringing into focus the real problem, the absurdity and inexplicability of evil's reality, in order to better face it, to have courage when one confronts evil'.[64] Thus, an Augustinian approach is, to Mathewes, a 'therapy', not a 'theory'. Far from tidying away the intractable through a metaphysical sleight of hand, it arises from practical insights about the intrinsic malignancy of evil, and yet the almost unavoidable attestation of the world's fundamental, if occluded, goodness. Human resistance to evil, funded by the insight of its privative absurdity, is a 'provisional witness' to that goodness, entailing moral practices and grounded in the stubbornness of human loves.[65]

In other words, a therapeutic Augustinian understanding of evil does something similar to what Williams reads both the practices of prayer and tragic poetry as accomplishing in 'The Spirit of the Age to Come'. It protests and prays

62. Rupert Shortt, *God's Advocates: Christian Thinkers in Conversation* (London: Darton, Longman and Todd, 2005), 8–9.

63. Williams, 'Insubstantial Evil', 115–6.

64. Charles Mathewes, *Evil and the Augustinian Tradition* (Cambridge: Cambridge University Press, 2001), 76–7.

65. Ibid., 70–2.

out of a hope – however occluded – for something better. It also enables what Williams, in 'Trinity and Ontology', feared at least some modes of discourse about tragedy might disable; it acts as a force for transformation – and among the moral practices such an Augustinianism might entail could be the practice enjoined by Williams in his essay on McCord Adams, of worrying at suffering and attending in stubborn love to its particular damages in human lives.[66] These points go some way towards answering the charge of the malignancy of an Augustinian approach. That Williams is, himself, looking for a therapy that confronts evil in history, and not a theory that evacuates it, is reflected in words written in the wake of 9/11: 'He [God] has made the world so that evil choices can't just be frustrated or aborted … but have to be confronted, suffered, taken forwards, healed in the complex process of human history, always in collaboration with what we do and say and pray.'[67]

Finally, if we return to the interlocking grammars of creation and Christ's goodness, Mathewes's insights open up another confluence. It has already been established that creation's good is in its process as a *whole*, finding its fruition eschatologically. In a sense its goodness is known by what, in our previous chapter, was labelled a logic of the whole. It is not a datum in any one *part* of the process. Thus, like its Christological parallel, creation's goodness is suspended in time; it can be tragic 'from a human point of view' – and yet, if Mathewes is correct, moments of 'provisional witness' do arise when, acting on the allusive intuition of creation's goodness, humans resist evil. This looks like the logic of *syncrisis* – the allusive mediation of creation's goodness in moments of dialectical tension. Goodness, in this case the world's, appears in time when backlit against what it is not.

A Trajectory of Change

What has been proposed is a trajectory of departure by Williams from aspects of MacKinnon, and towards an amelioration of the tragic. In part, this is important for stabilizing the possibilities of Christological mediation: an intractably tragic world is one where God can only appear as a wound, and not as a last vivifying word. It is a world wherein the logic of *syncrisis* becomes the only one available. If there is something to this trajectory, then its effects should appear elsewhere in Williams's thought. Thus, if one were to trace the distances between essays nearly two decades apart – 'Trinity and Ontology' (1989) and 'Tempted as We Are' (given first in 2007) – it is arguable, as I argued in Chapter 4, that the latter is more clearly a statement of Jesus's unfallen status. However, even then, Jesus's status is 'polyphonic'. Christological mediation is more thinkable, but not less complex.

---

66. Mathewes expresses concern that Williams's propensity to worry may go too far towards the 'renunciation of our theoretical reflexes'. Ibid., 39–40.

67. Rowans Williams, *Writing in the Dust: After September 11* (Grand Rapids, MI: Eerdmans, 2002), 8.

But a close consideration of 'Tempted as We Are' also supports the distinction made in 'Insubstantial Evil' between the pressures of contingency and the, truly tragic, evils of sin. The pressures that Jesus comes under are those that arise from the inherent nature of contingency, from the vulnerability of a material creature in the process of maturation with others.[68] The essay implies that, in contingency per se, such testing is inevitable. As gestured towards in 'Resurrection and Peace', conflict is native to a world of partial temporal goods. But, in Jesus's refusal of temptation, any *necessary* connection between those inherent pressures and a history of sin is undone. In a sense, the ontological non-necessity of evil is established in Jesus's narrative, in that the potentially traumatic nature of creation in process does not, in him, pass over into the tragedy of sin. If conflict's primordial presence is not a claim to strife's metaphysical ultimacy, this cannot be unrelated to the idea in Williams that one consummately significant life is the key to history, and that life is one wherein conflictual pressures do not cede to tragic sin.

The claim that Christ is sinless or innocent is thus more than a claim about Christological mediation; it passes into a claim about creation itself. If Christ's human agency is not of a different species from ours, and is yet without sin, then sin and evil are not necessary, not ontologically radical, in at least one creature. If this creature is the 'definitive clue' to creation's process, then the implications for creation and history are profound. If it is an 'Augustinian' intuition that the grammar of Christ and creation travel together, then the grammar of the respective goodness of Christ and creation must be similarly paired. Williams's thought implies, even if it does not clearly pronounce, that the goodness of creation is more a Christological datum than one derived from the proposing of a primordial peace – and, if it is a Christological datum, it is also an eschatological one. Christ's ultimate meaning, and the establishment of his goodness, only comes when all the damage done has been enfolded and healed, and when every agent finds in him a 'last word' that gives life. In relation to that 'last word', as argued earlier, the social manifold finds repair, and creation moves towards healing.

But there are places besides the immediately Christological to look for modulations in Williams's thought. To take his 2005 re-write of his 1983 Lent book *The Truce of God* (a book wherein MacKinnon was noted as an inspiration), most of it was done to bring a work written in the Cold War into the age of terror. But there are also intriguing changes of theological content, one of which bears directly on these discussions. While the original speaks of the (sometimes necessary) use of force, 'violence' is still 'a tragedy nothing can soften'.[69] But the later text drops this language. Instead, there is a meditation on the nature of political virtue, and the lawfulness of force.[70] It seems that the language of violence as intractable tragedy

---

68. See Rowan Williams, '"Tempted as We Are": Christology and the Analysis of the Passions', in *Studia Patristica*, ed. J. Brown, et al., Vol. XLIV (Peeters, 2010), 398–401.

69. Rowan Williams, *The Truce of God* (London: Fount, 1983), 35.

70. Williams, *The Truce of God* (2005), 33.

does not completely suit a more mature Williams, the same one who cautioned Milbank about his own use of such language.

One could also look to Williams's 2006 essay in honour of Richard Harries, 'The Health of the Spirit'. In it, tragic art is affirmed as a resource with the potential to show us that God lives in the spaces where there is 'a simultaneous awareness of inevitable failure and finitude and a perpetual "reopening" of our possibilities'. There is a certain ambiguity here. Finitude is brought under the rubric of the tragic, a recoupling of what was decoupled in 'Insubstantial Evil'. But Williams's terminological imprecision has already been remarked upon, and more in line with a trajectory towards amelioration is the notion of a perpetual reopening of possibilities. Tragedy does not persist as an intractable fate because an (eschatological?) future is always being opened up.[71] This is also an essay wherein Williams expresses wariness at the ethical role of tragedy. While he does not go back on the intuition that genuine moral dilemmas involve the tragic incompossibility of goods, what concerns Williams is that this can be deployed 'as a vehicle for absolution'. The acknowledgement of the incompatibility of goods in time – again, back to finitude as falling under the rubric of tragedy – should not pass over into a claim that all goods are equal, presenting a flattened set of ethical options. Some goods have a more 'absolute' claim. Some wrongs, by nature, 'diminish the spirit's wholeness'. Thus, Williams is 'more anxious than Richard [Harries] has sometimes been about the stoical acceptance of lesser evils as a tragic feature of a fallible and fallen world'.[72] These concerns go back at least as far as 'Trinity and Ontology' and its caution that the tragic might enervate moral action. They also echo Hart's concern that the tragic promotes an ethos of prudential resignation. But it is worth noting that in an essay where the tragic is ameliorated by being perpetually re-opened to the future, it is also being relativized as an ethical datum.

A Hegelian Turn

Thus far, a trajectory towards the amelioration of the tragic has been traced primarily in terms of a dialogue with Augustine. But there is an important parallel dialogue that can also be traced, one undertaken with Hegelian thought. The interlocking relation of these two dialogues should not be underestimated, and has perhaps been inchoately intimated already. There is his previously mentioned use of Hegelian forms in *Lost Icons* to make an essentially Augustinian anthropological point. There is also an intuition, in Williams's discussions of Augustine on creation, that there are continuities to be found between Augustine and Hegel in those matters.[73] Hegel, of course, has never been absent from our discussions. He

71. Rowan Williams, 'The Health of the Spirit', in *Public Life and the Place of the Church: Reflections to Honour the Bishop of Oxford*, ed. Michael Brierley (Aldershot: Ashgate, 2006), 218.

72. Ibid., 219–21.

73. See Williams, 'Good for Nothing?' 37, 45 (note 24).

has informed our reading of Myshkin as a beautiful soul, and his understanding of tragedy is integral to 'The Spirit of the Age to Come'. But, in Williams's earlier work, Hegel is still an ambiguous figure. He is even cast as a potential monist, one who collapses the proper distinctions between God and the world.[74] Yet, from the early 1990s onwards, a more affirmative reading of Hegel begins to emerge. It arises, as noted earlier, partially from the influence of Gillian Rose. Importantly, it is a reading with a distinctly anti-tragic component to it.

In the essay 'Between Politics and Metaphysics: Reflections in the wake of Gillian Rose' (1994), Williams notes that Rose's reading of Hegel proposes not an idealism tending to monism, but 'a continually self-adjusting, self-criticising corporate practice', a politics of venture, error and reconsideration in which history is projected as a process of communal pedagogy through frequent misadventure.[75] This is that construal by Rose of history as a *'drama of misrecognition'* that I have already referred to. There is, importantly, no immanent resolution to this drama. In time it is never mended. Thus, the already discussed persistence in Rose's thought of 'violence' as 'inescapably involved in our position towards others and towards ourselves'.[76] But this violence is not a pure negative; it is simply the risk involved in any instantiation of one's agency as *an-*other in time and the social, or any formal ordering of society through law.[77] It is akin to that conflictual element that Williams elsewhere deems native to history as a process of change, where life is had in the body and society. If Williams understands conflict as attending the processes of maturation, Rose draws our focus to its persistence in maturation on the political and social level, in all our individual and communal misrecognitions – and, like Williams, Rose refuses to see the persistence of the violent or conflictual as translating into a metaphysical claim about its ultimacy. This is, at least, Williams's reading of her. Her work is to him 'a protest against the essentializing of violence', because it refuses to mystify it as a dark or surdish substrate.[78] In Rose's own words, violence is not to be 'isolated', 'hypostatized' or theorized; it is simply to be 'presupposed' in its entailment in ethical action.[79] This amounts almost to a claim that violence is not a *thing* in and of itself that *can* be ontologically radical – and while Rose's understanding of violence does not reduce to evil, Williams notes the similarity of her account to Augustine's theory of evil as privative.[80]

---

74. See Williams's 1979 essay on Barth in his *Wrestling with Angels*, especially 139–8; and in the essay 'Trinity and Ontology', Hegel is associated with a monism where God 'is the whole rational principle of the universe' (*On Christian Theology*, 156).

75. Williams, *Wrestling with Angels*, 66–7. See also ibid., 60–1 and Rowan Williams, 'Beyond Liberalism', *Political Theology: The Journal for Christian Socialism* 3, no. 1 (2001): 66.

76. Williams, *Wrestling with Angels*, 59–60.

77. Ibid., 61–2. See also Gillian Rose, *The Broken Middle* (Oxford: Blackwell, 1992), 151. For her, violence is the 'risk' that is 'inseparable from staking oneself, from experience as such'.

78. See Williams, *Wrestling with Angels*, 64.

79. Rose, *The Broken Middle*, 151–2.

80. Williams, *Wrestling with Angels*, 75, note 20.

To reduce the conflictual to a 'wholly negative definition' – which would reduce it to evil – is, again in Williams's reading of Rose, a false move. It suggests a mythic primordial equality that has been disarranged by violence, as opposed to recognizing that inequities of potency and power are 'always already' realities that entail environmental resistance and agonistic negotiation.[81] Although Rose is talking more about human society than creation per se, this 'always already' of inequity recalls Williams's reading of Augustine on creation as entailing divergences of complexity and capacity, and this being intrinsic to creation's good as a process in becoming. For Williams, Augustine's is not a creation that *begins* in equilibrium, but it moves towards an equilibrium that is not had in time – in this sense, like Rose's sociality, it is a process never temporally mended.

This is, again, where a gap opens up between Williams's reading of Augustine (and now Rose), and the theological construals of Milbank and Hart. They propose a beginning without the conflictual. Williams, insofar as he follows his readings of Rose and Augustine, does not. While Milbank, for one, allows for difference, it is coded as a peaceful repetition of divine difference, an equilibrium only disarranged by violence's superscription. How such a peace gains traction within any history that we actually know is left hanging, and Williams is left concerned, at least in his review essay on *Theology and Social Theory*, that the reparative ecclesial ethic Milbank proposes out of this understanding constructs a peace both 'totalising and ahistorical'.[82] *Sotto voce*, what Williams seems to be suggesting is that Milbank is too enthraled to an ultimately mythic primordial vision, and thus tin-eared when it comes to history's exigencies.

To bring Rose to bear, Milbank's account carries a perverse similarity to her reading of the 'gnostic' prelude in Thomas Mann's *Joseph and His Brothers*. In Rose's understanding of that work, time is abrogated to eternity's repetition and Mann's narrative is the working out of this primordial prelude. Rose understands this as an attempt to 'abolish the ethical' – to deny 'the violence to be found in love, the love to be found in violence'.[83] It is, in other words, an attempt to prefer the primordial in such a way as to avoid the difficult work of love in time. It is not, then, accidental that Milbank's resort to the primordial calls forth the critique from Rose, echoing Williams's, that his project is 'ahistorical',[84] and a denial that 'mediation is necessarily violent'.[85] We could call this the denial of the element of *syncrisis* in mediation. To Rose, the danger of such a move is that its hypertrophied investment in a primordial peace evacuates the 'broken' nature of time's middle, replacing it with a harmonious 'holy middle'.[86] But the conflictual or violent, which such an 'evasive theology' refuses to think, then returns in a darker form, and

81. Ibid., 61–2.
82. Williams, 'Saving Time', 325.
83. Rose, *The Broken Middle*, 147. See also Chapter 4 *passim*.
84. Ibid., 282.
85. Ibid., 284.
86. Ibid., 284–5.

the 'City of Death' is 'remorselessly' imported.[87] In other words, if – as argued by Williams – Rose holds the view that a negative construal of violence, conflating it with evil, suggests a mythic primordial non-conflictual equilibrium, it is likewise the case that holding to a mythic primordial equilibrium inflames the conflictual into something darker. If the conflictual cannot be 'presupposed' – and it cannot be if all difference is aboriginally peaceable – then the work of love in time cannot be undertaken with a knowing eye towards its own potential violences. Violence simply becomes an inexplicable evil other, the very surd Milbank tries to exclude. It is perversely hypostasized by the very theology that wishes to deny its ontological power.

This resort to a timeless primordial peace, and the consequent evacuation of time's middle to the violent coded as evil, is arguably the metaphysical analogue to the Christological point Williams makes in Myshkin. To Rose, in Williams's reading, beginning with the primordial is a symptom of thinking afraid to begin, that prefers not to risk its purity in an 'uncontrolled middle' where enacting one's agency means inhabiting the conflictual.[88] This replicates on another level Myshkin's beautiful soulism, a deathly purity that abnegates its agency in an enthralment to prehistory. In Myshkin, the result is a diabolical timelessness that communicates its privation to others, and is 'bound up with *death*'.[89] If one likes, it remorselessly imports the 'City of Death' into the narratives of those around him. Thus, Myshkin is a Christological 'holy middle', a primordial harmony forced upon time with disastrous consequences. But a non-parodic Christology embraces the *broken middle*, moving knowingly as *an*-other into time and time's conflicts, the pressures of life in the body and society, the pathos of choice and the agon of maturation. Likewise, thinking unafraid to begin, begins in this broken middle. It moves into the drama of misrecognition, and, thereby, opens itself to potential failure in an act of 'self-dispossession and self-gift'.[90] It is the epistemological analogue to that *non-parodic* Christological *kenosis* traced in Chapter 3, and not accidentally elucidated in *Dostoevsky* with reference to Rose and Hegel. These discussions give some hint

---

87. Ibid., 293. At this point, the discussion in *The Broken Middle* has left Milbank behind, looking, instead, to Fackenheim and Metz. However, in a 2015 essay, Williams acknowledges that the same formal critique is applicable, in Rose's eyes, to Milbank. There, Williams offers some defence of Milbank from the full force of Rose's accusations (Milbank was present at the conference where the essay was first given as a paper), while allowing that the fundamental questions that Rose raises remain 'serious and constructive' for any theology of a 'holy' community that might be tempted to elide the need to remember self-critically its complicities. See Rowan Williams, '"The Sadness of the King": Gillian Rose, Hegel, and the Pathos of Reason', in *Telos* 173 (Winter 2015), 26–8. It is the potential danger of just such an elision of memory that Williams critiques Milbank for in the earlier 'Saving Time' (see p. 323).

88. See Williams, *Wrestling with Angels*, 62–4.

89. Williams, *Dostoevsky*, 49.

90. See Williams, *Wrestling with Angels*, 64.

to the importance of the insight that if there is a 'beginning' that does not render the conflictual as evil, it is to be found in a Christological middle, and not a primordial peace. What, for Williams, keeps conflict from dark metaphysical ultimacy is the way it is lived through in one consummately significant life. It is this Christological middle, what in Chapter 2 was called time's centre, that gives history a meaning that refuses tragic evil a radical status – and, as the definitive clue to history and creation, this life gestures towards a mode of kenotic thinking from the middle that, likewise, refuses the inflation of the conflictual into the malevolent.

If Rose, along with Augustine, gives Williams some of the conceptual tools to think in this manner, there are other ways in which her thought reinforces an ultimately non-tragic vision. It is not accidental that her reading of Hegel is, in one sense, a *politics*. The Hegelianism she bequeaths Williams reinforces his intuition of the deep mutual implication of agents, that our life and death are with one another. Thus, Williams reads Hegel as insisting that our 'concrete freedom' only comes with the realization that we have no unmediated identity, and no purely private interests, separable from community.[91] This is the Hegelian analogue to the Augustinian intuition that the good of any one creature is inseparable from its place in creation's manifold. In a sense, creaturely goodness is only expressible in the 'concrete freedom' of creation's whole – which itself is good as a whole in process towards fruition – and for this Hegelianism, as much as for Augustine, that fruition is not a temporal datum.

In his essay 'Hegel and the Gods of Postmodernity' (1992),[92] Williams notes that Hegelianism proposes a '*telos*', a reconciliation towards which all acts of understanding and negotiation move. Vitally, it 'is not *representable* (not present) in the structure of any given historical consciousness or set of consciousnesses, not *a* meaning which a speaker or writer could articulate as a piece of communicable information'.[93] This grammar of an end that is not representable, not '*a* meaning' within the world, echoes Williams's grammar of God as *non aliud*, an un-said and unsayable that occupies no square centimetre and yet undergirds all.[94] It also echoes the grammar of the non-immanent equilibrium or divine good towards which Augustine's creation and Augustine's self tend; self and cosmos are summoned towards an end not had *in* time. In other words, this Hegelianism reinforces Williams's eschatological vision of creation's good, which functions to ameliorate the tragic without dissolving it.

It cannot be dissolved because there is no *temporal* mending of the drama. The world and its end cannot be brought into sameness, and the end never appears as a datum. Rather, as with Augustine, the infinite distance between creation and God

---

91. Ibid., 44. The citation is from 'Logic and Spirit in Hegel' (1998) in *Wrestling with Angels*, 35–52. It is a direct essay at Hegel's thought, but Rose lurks in the endnotes. See 51–2, notes 32 and 43.

92. In Williams, *Wrestling with Angels*, 25–54.

93. Ibid., 29.

94. Williams explicitly relates Hegel's concept of God with *non aliud*. See ibid., 39–40.

is maintained as an infinite time of reparative movement towards what is not had. This is part of the import of Williams's acceptance, through Rose, that Hegel does not propose a monist collapse of God and the world; Hegel's is not a philosophy of 'return to identity'.[95] Thus, the teleology enunciated does not pass over into the bad monist theodicy that MacKinnon, and a younger Williams, might have feared. It does not efface the particular and intractable. Rather, a Hegelian doctrine of 'grace' is one where otherness is overcome 'not by reduction to identity, but by the labour of discovering what understanding might be adequate to a conflictual and mobile reality without excising or devaluing its detail'.[96] One might term this 'labour' the work of love, and the distance between God and the world gives that work the (infinite) time it needs.

The ultimately non-tragic nature of this is perhaps best illustrated through Rose's essay 'The Comedy of Hegel and the *Trauerspiel* of Modern Philosophy'. As has been alluded to, she reads the plot of Hegel's *Phenomenology* as an ultimately comedic '*drama of misrecognition*'. It is 'a ceaseless comedy, according to which our aims and outcomes constantly mismatch each other, and provoke yet another revised action'.[97] Although sociality is never mended, there is progression. Yet, this cannot be blithely said, for the drama is also one of what Rose calls '*inaugurated* mourning' – there are always errors and violences within it that must be grieved if there is to be forgiveness and movement.[98] Thus, if engagement in this drama is the work of love, it is also a work of mourning. But this *inaugurated* mourning is juxtaposed by Rose with a darker possibility. There is also the potential for an '*aberrated* mourning', which is another species of the refusal of the drama and its attendant labour. Rose associates this more pathological grieving with the figure of Walter Benjamin. To her, he paradigmatically refuses 'any dynamic of mutual recognition and struggle'. Convinced of the irredeemable tragedy of history, Benjamin's grief has become stuck in a melancholia that allows no progression.

95. Ibid., 66. See pp. 40–1, 47 and 60 for Williams's rebuttal of the idea that Hegel proposes any easy identity between God and the world or consciousness. See also Williams, 'Good for Nothing?', 45 (note 24): 'The one thing that Hegel does not teach, despite the assumptions of some, is that there is an augmentation of Spirit through the process of creation, or that God is in any sense a subject of history.'

96. Williams, *Wrestling with Angels*, 30. Ben Quash, in his *Theology and the Drama of History* (Cambridge: Cambridge University Press, 2005), has argued that Williams's (and Rose's) reading of Hegel is too optimistic, and that he ultimately gives in to an overly determinate 'epic' approach. See pp. 99–108.

97. Rose, *Mourning Becomes the Law: Philosophy and Representation* (Cambridge: Cambridge University Press, 1996), 72.

98. Ibid., 76. See also p. 71. In his 'The Sadness of the King', Williams emphasizes the non-tragic nature of Rose's thought, while also acknowledging that the 'comedy of misrecognition' she proposes is about a 'liberty to re-form thinking' that travels, in her own words, with '*uncontrollable* tears' (31–2, Williams cites Rose, *Mourning Becomes the Law*, 144).

He can only look to a darkly messianic 'divine violence' for its interruption.[99] This can be called a world of absolutized tragedy, where a violent *syncrisis* can be the only mediatorial register. And if, in Williams's reading, the character of Myshkin is a place-holder for one who refuses, out of a hypertrophied purity, to begin the drama, Rose's Benjamin is perhaps closer to the figure of Stavrogin discussed in Chapter 3. He is not so much a beautiful soul, as someone who has given into a parodic *apatheia* and darker dreams. He has given in to that enervating resignation that Hart feared would result from a valorization of the tragic.

To take a wider perspective, if history is a comedy of *inaugurated* mourning, there is no final reduction of the tragic in time, even while creation becomes a process with a non-tragic trajectory. History involves the work of grieving, but it is also love's work and willingness to stake a place as *an*-other in the realm of error. This is the shape of a non-parodic *kenosis*, the prototype of which is Christological. History's definitive clue is found in its Christological middle, but that middling appearance as *an*-other human life is proleptic of an end, for the last Christological word is an eschatological word. It is the end – not had in time beyond the allusive frisson of *syncrisis* – that summons the whole to a reparative and life-giving movement. Even if any given coordinate within history is acidic with tragedy, still history is opened up by a future not immanent to it. By the logic of the whole, in the concrete freedom of its entire manifold from which no one creature's good can be extracted, history's ultimately non-tragic goodness is rendered as a process in eternal distension towards fruition. In saying all this, however, we are, to some extent, anticipating discussions to come in the next chapter.

To conclude this chapter, what our venture through Rosean Hegelianism shows up are the dangers in aspects of MacKinnon's approach, and where the initial critiques of Hart and Milbank strike close to home. If Rose is correct, there *is* an orientation to tragedy that induces an aberrated mourning, a frozen withdrawal from history's drama that is unnerved in terms of action, but secretly hopeful of violent interruption. This is, in its own way, a radicalization of violence as a divine possibility. Such a mourning could be called a tragic piety, and it is arguably critiqued by Rose in the form of what she calls 'Holocaust piety'. In the essay 'Beginnings of the Day – Fascism and Representation' she notes a tendency, visible in Adorno and Habermas, as well as in Christian and Jewish essays on 'Holocaust theology', to associate the Shoah with 'the ineffable': 'According to this view, "Auschwitz" or the "Holocaust" are emblems for the breakdown of divine and/or human history. The uniqueness of this break delegitimizes names and narratives as such, and hence all aesthetic or apprehensive representation.'[100]

Such a dark ineffability, destructive of representation, approaches that aesthetics of the sublime that Milbank worries about in MacKinnon. It is as if the

---

99. Gillian Rose, *Judaism and Modernity: Philosophical Essays* (Oxford: Blackwell, 1993), 209. See also her *Mourning Becomes the Law*, 64, 70–1. For Williams's comments, see his *Wrestling with Angels*, 66–7.

100. Rose, *Mourning Becomes the Law*, 43.

Holocaust is the ultimate *syncrisis*, a totalized wound that admits no words and leaves only silence. But, if representation stops, thinking and erring stop, and the tragicomedy of history freezes into a sheerly tragic and mute agony. To Rose, *this* ontologically radicalizes evil. In her words, after the death camps, 'Heideggerian and post-Heideggerian' thought came to see representation itself as the place where 'murderous complacencies' occur. Genocide granted evil a kind of positive existence, which, in such thinking, passed over into *'the evil of the positive'*, the evil of any positing. The result is a thinking that halts thinking, in which evil is located in any thinking that seeks a 'ground' and engages in a 'refusal of the abyss'. [101]

This *would* be a stuck manifold inflamed by tragedy, one wherein any positive staking of a place, any attempt at representation, is an evil. In it, the mediation of the good could only appear negatively, as an abyssal wound or messianic violence that draws nothing forward. What is offered is an engorged *syncrisis*, be it of silence or interruptive violence, as the only mediatorial logic operative. Thus, it is not accidental that in an essay wherein Williams essentially follows the lines of Rose's critique of post-Heideggerian thought, criticizing some theologies written in the light of Derrida, the concern he expresses is that these theologies can only speak of the sacred in terms of an 'absence' or 'rupture'. In such a schema, all that is temporal is relegated to the profane.[102] The world, in such an understanding, is cast into an utterly negative dialectical relation to God, and the register of One generatively *not-*other to the whole is lost. Nor is it accidental that when Williams does touch on the question of silence after the Holocaust, he is careful to argue that it is a *framed* silence, itself part of a process of representation and communication (as communicative in its own way, perhaps, as Christ's silence). It is a silence in response to an 'utterly concrete historical atrocity', a silence enacted in a specific location – in its own way an answer and comment that invites consideration and, however obliquely, continues the conversation. What is rejected by Williams, and cast as dangerous, is a construal of this silence as total rupture or representation's absolute denial.[103]

To claim that MacKinnon – whose work is deeply inflected by the memory of the Holocaust[104] – succumbs to the tragic piety that Rose lambasts is unfair. Nor

101. Ibid., 55–7.

102. Williams, *Wrestling with Angels*, 27–8.

103. Williams, *The Edge of Words*, 159–67 (quote from p. 159). Among Williams's concerns is that totalized silence entails the silencing of criticism, and thus ends the possibility of criticizing the silence caused by oppression.

104. It informs, as was seen in Chapter 4, his understanding of Jesus's difficult innocence. Referring to Jesus's trial he notes: 'There is a line traceable from the hall of judgement to the death camps of twentieth century Europe where millions of the Jewish people perished in circumstances of unspeakable indignity.' See Donald MacKinnon, 'Some Reflections on Hans Urs Von Balthasar's Christology with Special Reference to Theodramatik II/2, III and IV', in *The Analogy of Beauty: The Theology of Hans Urs Von Balthasar*, ed. John Riches (Edinburgh: T&T Clark, 1986), 166. These events 'rob any serious theologian of the remotest excuse for ignoring the tragic elements in Christianity' (MacKinnon, *The Problems of Metaphysics*, 130).

is it fair to claim that he ultimately radicalizes evil, let alone that he seeks to cast representation itself as an evil. But it is not unfair to see in his thought elements of what Rose would call an aberrant mourning. His insistence on tragedy's intractable nature, and abjuring of any theodicy or teleology that ameliorates it, heads in such a direction. Williams, on the other hand, does not ignore the tragic, but – more clearly than MacKinnon – he refuses to succumb to a tragic piety. It is, in part, the work of Gillian Rose that equips him to do this. By using conceptual tools, both Hegelian and Augustinian, he is able to picture a teleological/eschatological trajectory in which tragedy is ameliorated, but not effaced. The shape of that eschatology will be filled out in the next chapter, but here what it grants is a world where the mediation of that good towards which all things tend becomes more thinkable, even if it is not representable in time except through the allusive power of *syncrisis*.

A Christological Recapitulation

It is worth rehearsing, for emphasis, the Christological moves implicit in this, and other, chapters' discussions. Although not always clearly enunciated in Williams's work, they are implied by its logics. Something like this can be said: the incarnation is God 'staking a place' in history; within the broken middle of error and conflict, the Author of the universe undertakes what Rose calls the 'agon of authorship'.[105] Because there is no temporal mending of this middle, Christological mediation remains opaque, and the logic of *syncrisis* operative. And yet, insofar as Christ is the appearance in the '*drama of misrecognition*' of the good towards which the whole tends, this event renders history (ultimately) a comedy. Christ, in his story, decouples the conflictual pressures of contingency from the fated inevitability of sin, rendering – more than does any story of primordial harmony – evil non-radical. He also, to return to discussions in Chapter 2, teaches us to recognize ourselves and others in truth-telling judgement, to see our violences. This could be called the recognition of our misrecognitions, a process in which mourning is inaugurated. Such mourning would look like the 'remorse' enjoined in *Lost Icons*. It might also look like worrying at evil, attending to its victims in stubborn love. It is a therapy, not a theory, and it is not aberrated because, in the resurrection, new possibilities are opened. As will be explored in the coming chapter, a new community is made possible to which tragedy is not all.

---

105. See, for instance, Rose, *The Broken Middle*, 296. Cited by Williams, *Wrestling with Angels*, 65.

Chapter 7

An Endless End

Introduction

My final chapter is concerned with Williams's eschatological vision, that very vision which allows him to escape a purely tragic construal of history. This chapter is thus also concerned with the resurrection of Jesus, which in a Christian theology is where eschatology must start. But, harking back to concerns touched upon in Chapter 2, we begin with a consideration of the ecclesial community that the resurrection creates. We then move on to consider the wider shape of Williams's eschatology as an endlessly reparative, and ultimately joyful, movement of all things towards God. The efficient cause of this movement is the appearance in time's middle of creation's Christological 'last word', the transcription into time of the final cause of creation's process.

An Ecclesial Politics – the end in the middle

I proposed in the previous chapter that for Williams, following Rose, Christ is the ameliorative appearance of the world's end within its broken middle; this is how he is the world's 'last word'. This is an intuition with deep roots, visible as early as Williams's use of Florovsky's proposal (explored in Chapter 2) that Christ is the centre of history because he is the *eschaton* in its midst. For all Florovsky's scepticism about idealism, and for all Rose's Hegelianism, Williams finds similar things useful in their work. Both bring an emphasis upon history as open but shaped; it is a realm of error (Rose) and indeterminacy (Florovsky), but one graced with a *telos* that grants it form and progression. In Williams's adoption of Rosean Hegelianism, that *telos* lifts history's mourning from aberration to inauguration. For Florovsky, without the incarnation there can only be a stuck history of an eternal return of the same.

It is implied, if not clearly enunciated, that Christ is history's *non*-tragic end because his biography establishes *in* history the possibility of tragic evil's non-necessity. The conflictual pressures of life in body and society do not pass over, in him, into an exacerbated tragedy of strife and exclusion, a self-defensive and sinful mode of living. Instead, his is a precarious but note-perfect performance of God's life in a human medium. As outlined in Chapter 2, part of what marks his performance as divine is the way in which, in the resurrection, it creates (*ex nihilo*) a community attuned to the non-tragic possibility that his life reveals. To recall 'The Spirit of the Age to Come', this community 'has not been atrophied by tragic experience and tragic knowledge'. The lives within it are unfrozen, able to move beyond aberrated mourning. In a sense this community represents, in an ecclesial mode, that reparative politics of error entwined with progress that is Rose's reading of Hegel.

Further recalling Chapter 2's discussions, this community is the place-holder in time for the one who is *not*-other to it; they 'stand where he stands'.[1] But, despite the distinctiveness of this Christological standpoint, it marks out a universal possibility. To Williams, the church exists as God's 'Pilot Project' for the world,[2] the most decisive possibility for a global community.[3] It is caught up in what was termed a binding irony (an idea, not incidentally, explored through an essay on Rose), representing the 'interests' of a disinterested God. To speak 'mythologically', God surrenders 'the no-place of abstract absolute being' and, in kenotic dispossession, stakes a place in historical process. This is the grammar of the incarnation *and* of the church. Christ's community incarnates itself as an *an*-other polity within the broken middle, but it lives in the consistently self-ironizing paradox of being dispossessed 'as an "interested" or sectional presence'.[4] It takes on a life analogous to the *non aliud* nature of the end whose place in time it holds. If God's grammar of difference always displaces itself from any simple location in creaturely levels of action and causality, then, analogously, the community formed by Christ 'is not a political order on the same level as others, competing for control, but a community that signifies, that points to a possible healed human world'.[5] It eschews that self-defensive mode of living that Christ's life demonstrates to be non-necessary. It points to history's healing, in part, by showing this non-necessity. This is what Chapter 2 called the *theosis* of human possibilities in the lives constellated around Christ, mediating a divine discontinuity in history's violent sameness.

The form this communal life takes is kenotic, but it is not the parodic *kenosis* of Myshkin. That would be the establishment of an ecclesial beautiful soulism, in which the church abnegated its political agency. It could not then be ironic towards its sectional claims because it refuses to acknowledge their existence. This would constitute an ecclesial holy middle, unwittingly a potential vector for the 'City of Death' because it refuses to think through the conflictual, which will necessarily

---

1. Rowan Williams, 'Christian Identity and Religious Plurality', *The Ecumenical Review* 58, no. 1 (2006): 70–1.

2. See Rowan Williams, 'The Church: God's Pilot Project', http://rowanwilliams. archbishopofcanterbury.org/articles.php/1779/the-church-gods-pilot-project.

3. Rowan Williams, *The Truce of God: Peacemaking in Troubled Times* (Norwich: Canterbury Press, 2005), 119.

4. Rowan Williams, *Wrestling with Angels: Conversations in Modern Theology* (Cambridge: Eerdmans, 2007), 72.

5. Rowan Williams, *Faith in the Public Square* (London: Bloomsbury, 2012), 60–1.

attend its life. This is why to Williams, *pace* Milbank, 'the peace of the Church is going to be vacuous or fictive if it is not historically aware of how it is *constructed* in events of determination which involve conflict or exclusion of some kind'.[6] The church is called to love's difficult work, which includes mourning its acknowledged violences and errors in an ultimately comedic drama of misrecognition.

This difficult ecclesial work is characterized by Williams in a different register in a 2005 lecture, drawing upon Bulgakov. There he describes the church's ethical life as 'the kenotic and sophianic search for a justice which is beautiful, a justice which uncovers what the world fundamentally is; a world of interdependence and interaction, a world in which self-forgetting brings joy, common, shared joy'.[7] Thus, the ironized political practice of the church reveals the world's goodness in the concrete freedom of its whole, as 'a world of interdependence and interaction'. It does so through that kenotic move into the middle whose prototype is Christological. Through a 'self-forgetting' that is unafraid to begin, what is discovered is 'joy' – the nature of the whole drama as an ultimate comedy. Thus, insofar as the church holds the place of the Christological end that ameliorates time, its ethical and political life enacts that amelioration and alludes to the world's goodness even in time's misrecognitions.

In a sense, this is what it is to be 'catholic'. For Williams, this is not an adjective to describe a style of Christianity; catholicity is, rather, of Christianity's quintessence. It denotes a pervading logic of the whole implied by the etymology of the term. A 'catholic' community is unrestricted by conventional ethnic or political categories of belonging, encompassing 'the fullest "*variety*" of gifts and excellencies' as it 'endeavours to *tell the whole truth* about God and God's human creation'.[8] Even the Reformation displayed this catholicity in its endeavour to correct the medieval church's attempt 'to occupy and defend a portion of the world's territory'.[9] To territorialize the church as *an*-other collectivity, without irony, replicates the tragic move that Christ eschewed, a non-necessary choice for self-defensiveness. It departs from catholicity because, as merely *an*-other territory in a shifting mosaic of rivalry, the church has surrendered its logic of the whole. As I suggested in Chapter 5, that logic is underwritten by the grammar of *non aliud*, of God as occupying no one space, but generatively present as every space's possibility. Insofar as the church is catholic, it is formed in analogy to this *non aliud* end.

6. Rowan Williams, 'Saving Time: Thoughts on Practice, Patience and Vision', *New Blackfriars* 73 (1992): 322.

7. Rowan Williams, 'Creation, Creativity and Creatureliness: The Wisdom of Finite Existence', http://rowanwilliams.archbishopofcanterbury.org/articles.php/2106/creation-creativity-and-creatureliness-the-wisdom-of-finite-existence.

8. Rowan Williams, 'Teaching the Truth', in *Living Tradition: Affirming Catholicism in the Anglican Church*, ed. J. John (London: Darton, Longman and Todd, 1992), 29–30.

9. Rowan Williams, 'The Lutheran Catholic: The Ramsey Lecture, Durham', http://rowanwilliams.archbishopofcanterbury.org/articles.php/2102/ramsey-lecture-durham-the-lutheran-catholic.

As much as the church instantiates the reparative politics that Rose read in Hegel, there is also a certain 'Hegelian' quality to Williams's catholicity. This has been noted by commentators in registers ranging from the neutral[10] and mildly critical,[11] to the oddly trenchant.[12] Williams draws upon Hegelian categories primarily because he sees them as more positively informed by Christian theology than some allow.[13] In a 2001 article, mainly concerned with Rose, he notes Hegel's intuition that a 'myth' of self-reflexivity – of 'spirit' as self-staking and risking – is politically necessary if there is to be 'a full account of the good that is irreducibly social and humanly universal'. In other words, Williams is claiming through Hegel that any politics needs a kenotic movement to begin, an impetus to stake a place in the temporal and social – the broken middle – for there to be a good that might be called catholic. He notes that this 'myth' of self-reflexivity is not produced *de novo* by Hegel, but is recognized by him as already persisting with revelatory power in the Christian narrative, as 'the rationale of creation and then the content of the story of Jesus and the call of the believing assembly'.[14]

In the published lecture 'Mission and Christology' (1994), Williams notes that even the *mission* of the church can be rendered in Hegelian terms. This mission assumes a (catholic) good, 'open to any and every human subject', and imagines 'a community in which the good of each is inseparable from the good of all'.[15] It thus posits the hope of a harmony of the personal and political that, for Williams, has been present in Western thought since Augustine, and – to reprise a paring already seen – is promulgated in modernity by Hegel:

10. For Myers, Williams 'interprets Hegel's philosophy as catholic ecclesiology'. See Ben Myers, *Christ the Stranger: The Theology of Rowan Williams* (London: T&T Clark, 2012), 57.

11. Hobson sees Williams's 'catholic' vision as a distinctively Anglican 'globalization of Hegel', uniting humanity 'in a fully socialized form of Christianity' in Theo Hobson, 'Rowan Williams as Anglican Hegelian', *Reviews in Religion and Theology* 12, no. 2 (2005): 296–7.

12. Carys Moseley sees in Williams a Hegelian vision that amounts to a sinister 'management' of religious and political difference. See her article 'Rowan Williams as Hegelian Political Theologian: Resacralising Secular Politics', *Heythrop Journal* 53, no. 3 (2012): 362–81. It is difficult to know what to do with an article that accuses Williams of a flirtation with astrology on the strength of being a member of the 'Gemini Poets' (365).

13. Williams notes both Hegel's indebtedness to Lutheran categories (see his *Wrestling with Angels*, 32), and to Trinitarian thought forms (ibid., Chapter 3 *passim*). Moseley, on the other hand, regards Hegel's 'philosophical theology' as 'Hermetic and Rosicrucian at heart' ('Rowan Williams as Hegelian Political Theologian', 367). Perhaps Milbank puts it well when he notes that Williams reads Hegel, in part through Rose, with an interest shorn of the more 'Gnostic' elements of Hegelian thought. See John Milbank, 'Scholasticism, Modernism and Modernity', *Modern Theology* 22, no. 4 (2006): 658.

14. Rowan Williams, 'Beyond Liberalism', *Political Theology* 3, no. 1 (2001): 70–1; see also Williams, *Wrestling with Angels*, 71.

15. Rowan Williams, 'Mission and Christology: J.C. Jones Memorial Lecture (1994)', (Brynmawr: Welsh Members Council, Church Mission Society, 1994), 7–8.

His conviction was that the supreme political goal was a condition where the individual, in full freedom and integrity, recognized that her or his welfare and purposes could only be understood and realized in and through the welfare and purposes of the entire community; a condition in which personal and common good were really seen to be identical.[16]

This condition is what the previous chapter termed 'concrete freedom'. Elsewhere, in Williams's thought and in this book, it is framed as the acknowledgement that our life and death are with our neighbour. It is predicated upon an account of the self that is shaped by the aforementioned narrative of self-reflexivity.[17] It is shaped, ultimately, by the narrative of one who, beginning within the pressures of social and bodily life, refused to live self-defensively.

Mission thus implies a political vision patient of Hegelian description, but mission is not an invitation to an earthly *polis,* or to any final political settlement. Insofar as Hegel is read through Rose, there is no temporal mending of the social. To Williams, while the church may be described – following biblical usage – in the language of national or ethnic solidarities, it is a collectivity present with a difference that subverts given forms of belonging.[18] Its ' "belonging" … sits at an angle to all particular loyalties and identities'. It is 'given in relation to something never possessed, never wholly within our grasp, a horizon to which we look'. Thus, mission must be pursued under a self-ironizing 'imperative of dispossession'.[19] If it proposes a politics of repair, and is the ecclesial work of love, it does not itself own the possibility of its fruition. Its possibility is, instead, that of the infinite time for reparative movement spoken of in the previous chapter.

Thus, concrete freedom, be it a political vision prefigured in the church or the wider freedom of a creation that is good as a catholic whole, is only an eschatological possibility. It is the horizon towards which the church's mission/ethical life/work of love strains. The church stands in the place of the one who, in time's middle, mediated its end in such a way that mediation became thinkable, and history became unstuck from the frozen return of its tragically exacerbated conflicts. If Williams's catholicity and politics is 'Hegelian', it is so in a particular way. It has an eschatological inflection wherein the end that gives time its shape is not present in any determinate temporal arrangement. 'God' in Williams's understanding of

16. Ibid., 6. For Williams's reading of Augustine on this matter, and Augustine's critique in the *City of God* of the Roman state's failure to formulate a vision of the public good, which truly enabled its individual citizens to flourish, see Rowan Williams, 'Politics and the Soul: A Reading of *the City of God*', *Milltown Studies*, no. 19/20 (1987): 55–72.

17. Williams, *Wrestling with Angels,* 44. Williams argues that such an account of the self is embedded for Hegel in Trinitarian theology.

18. A point made in a discussion of William Stringfellow. See Rowan Williams, 'Being a People: Reflections on the Concept of "Laity"', *Religion, State and Society* 27, no. 1 (1999): 11–12. See also Williams, *Faith in the Public Square,* 306.

19. Williams, 'Mission and Christology', 8–10.

Hegel, 'is not to be thought of as a historical subject'.[20] In this sense, it is an end pulled into the conceptual orbit of *non aliud* – it is not *an*-other state of affairs.

This eschatological inflection arguably saves Williams from the 'bad' Hegelianism some of his interrogators fear. The end proposed is essentially a generative *non*-presence, which is another way of describing the *non aliud* God. Just as in the previous chapter a 'bad' teleology was avoided, so here – in the light of this generative *non*-presence – a 'bad' politics of reconciliation is avoided. For Williams's Hegel, the church adumbrates, but does not realize, the optimal form of sociality.[21] For Williams himself, it is the instantiation – as God's pilot project – of a reparative and kenotic politics, but it is *not* the political fruition of that project. This ecclesiology travels with a studied eschatological underdetermination, and even an intuition that an over-determined 'end', one that has become *an*-other potential presence in time, has a satanic aspect.[22] Standing where Christ stands, the church holds the place of the 'last word' for creation. It is not a word that finishes the conversation, because it is never made uncomplexly present. It is, instead, that 'presence with whom ultimately every speaker may discover an exchange that is steadily and unfailingly life giving and free of anxiety'.[23] That word and end which appears in the middle is 'the eternal "Logos"', at work in the church to make history, not stop it.[24] It is in this way generative because it is no simple presence; its *non aliud* character is its vivifying power.

Eschatology: 'End Without End'

Williams's eschatology is underdetermined because its end is underdetermined. Another way to put this is to say that he proposes an 'end without end'. This is both the title of a key chapter in *The Wound of Knowledge*, in which Gregory of Nyssa is discussed, and a phrase from Augustine's *The City of God* (XXII.30), quoted in *Tokens of Trust*.[25] This coincidence of Gregory and Augustine is not accidental. To Williams, they both propose an 'end' that entails an endless movement towards

20. Rowan Williams, 'Review of Hans Küng, *The Incarnation of God: An Introduction to Hegel's Theological Thought as Prolegomena to a Future Christology*', *Journal of Theological Studies* 42, no. 1 (1991): 405.

21. Williams, *Wrestling with Angels*, 49. Williams recognizes a tension he has with Hegel's higher estimation of state.

22. See Williams's discussion of the over-realized eschatology of Shigalyov and Shatov in Rowan Williams, *Dostoevsky: Language, Faith and Fiction* (London: Continuum, 2008), 86–93.

23. Ibid., 139.

24. Rowan Williams, *Choose Life: Christmas and Easter Sermons in Canterbury Cathedral* (London: Bloomsbury, 2013), 66–7.

25. Rowan Williams, *Tokens of Trust: An Introduction to Christian Belief* (Norwich: Canterbury Press, 2007), 154.

God as a good never ultimately had. This eschatology repeats the rendering of creation as a comedic drama in its infinite movement towards its last word. It is tied to the grammar of God as *non aliud*, not a 'thing' that can be had. An end with *no* end is the correlate eschatology to that divine grammar, its endless nature the mode in which it is a generative *non*-presence.

Gregory and Augustine appear side by side in *The Wound of Knowledge*, in two chapters that, in both content and juxtaposition, are arguably theologically programmatic. Following Jean Daniélou, Williams places the idea of *epektasis* – an endless straining forward towards God – at the heart of Nyssa's thought. It is ('perhaps') his most vital theological contribution.[26] Correlate to it is an accent on desire. In a 'markedly "eschatological"' conception, the Christian journey is for Nyssa a movement, in this world and the next, 'always marked by *desire*'.[27] Desire, in the chapter that follows, is also placed at the heart of Augustine's thought. To be human is to desire, to be 'naturally passionate, vulnerable, mobile', and an Augustinian account of salvation entails the right alignment of desire towards God. This alone grants coherence to humanity's mobile vulnerability.[28] Such a reading of Augustine was already alluded to in the previous chapter. What is significant in *The Wound of Knowledge* is the way in which convergences are drawn between Nyssa and Augustine. Williams notes the congruity of Augustine's descriptions of 'the never-ceasing pilgrimage of the heart or spirit or *mens*' with Gregory's *epektasis*. For Augustine, desire is an impulsion to 'strain forward', a subtle echo by Williams, taken from *Enarrationes in Psalmos* 38.6, of the 'straining forward' implied in *epektasis*.[29]

This convergence between Augustine and Nyssa is, in fact, drawn as early as Williams's doctoral thesis. There, Augustine's *imago Dei* persists as a ' "God-directed intentionality" not very different from Gregory of Nyssa's *epektasis*'.[30] Language reminiscent of *epektasis* can also be found, again connected to the Augustinian *imago*, in Williams's 1989 essay on *De doctrina*: 'To know the difference between *res* and *signum* is, for the Christian believer, to know the difference of God, and so be equipped for life in God's image, the *unending expansion of love*.'[31] Nyssa is not mentioned here,

26. Rowan Williams, *The Wound of Knowledge: Christian Spirituality from the New Testament to St John of the Cross*, 2nd Rev. edn. (London: Darton, Longman and Todd, 1990), 54–5. *Epektasis*, Williams notes, is the noun 'straining forward' derived from the verb *epekteinō* employed by Paul in Phil. 3:13. For Jean Daniélou, 'perfection considered as continual progress' is Nyssa's 'most characteristic doctrine'. See his *From Glory to Glory: Texts from Gregory of Nyssa's Mystical Writings*, trans. H. Musurillo (New York: St Vladimir's Seminary Press, 2001), 47.

27. Williams, *The Wound of Knowledge*, 58.

28. Ibid., 75–6.

29. Ibid., 79.

30. Rowan Williams, 'The Theology of Vladimir Nikolaievich Lossky: An Exposition and Critique' (Doctoral Thesis, University of Oxford, 1975), 122.

31. Rowan Williams, 'Language, Reality and Desire in Augustine's *De Doctrina*', *Journal of Literature and Theology* 3, no. 2 (1989): 147, emphasis mine.

but *epektasis* is implicit. A more straightforward convergence is found again in the essay 'To Stand Where Christ Stands' (1999), which recapitulates the lineaments of much in *The Wound of Knowledge*. Nyssa's *Life of Moses* is there read as portraying the spiritual life as 'always in motion', and marked by desire.[32] Augustine is then read as re-presenting this insight 'with unparalleled imagination and depth'.[33] Thus, both theologians are read as proposing an end without end that entails endless desire.

This endless eschatology is, importantly and demonstrably, carried from Nyssa and Augustine into Williams's own thought. To quote *The Truce of God*:

> Real desire is about recognizing that I have no resting place: my home is what I must look for, eagerly, attentively, as I grow and journey. And – the Christian will add – my journey only 'ends' when it reaches God – and even then it does not come to a comfortable full stop because God is himself a region of unending new discovery and reappraisal and fresh vision.[34]

Elsewhere, Williams describes talk of 'heaven' as speech about 'the fulfilment and *enlargement without end* that we can receive as God's partners, as the objects of an endless attentive regard'.[35] What is rejected by Williams is anything that looks like an eschatological stasis, for 'it is a strange, contradictory thing, to desire the ending of desire – to desire stasis, frozenness'.[36] Such a frozen end, almost an eschatology of aberration, would be a last word that closes conversations, passing from a generative *non*-presence into a deadening continuous present. If the end is *non aliud*, this cannot be, and this is why an eschatology of stasis tends, for Williams, to diabolism, an insight born out profoundly in *Dostoevsky*. There the Devil is a spirit of stasis, whose work is the instillation of silence and the ending of narratives,[37] whereas a Dostoevskian vision of immortality has, as an essential component, a 'conviction that the narratives of growth, conflict and attention that characterize life here are not fated to come to an end'.[38] What Williams affirms within *Dostoevsky* is congruent with what he is attracted to in the *epektasis* of

---

32. Rowan Williams, 'To Stand Where Christ Stands', in *An Introduction to Christian Spirituality*, eds R. Waller and B. Ward (London: SPCK, 1999), 6–7.

33. Ibid., 9.

34. Rowan Williams, *The Truce of God* (London: Fount, 1983), 85. Repeated verbatim in *The Truce of God* (2005), 90.

35. Rowan Williams, 'Heaven and Hell: A Modern Embarrassment?', *Epworth Review* 21, no. 2 (1994): 17 (emphasis mine). Even purgatory falls under the rubric of *epektasis*. While sceptical of the idea of a post-mortem 'remand prison', Williams sees the impetus behind purgatory as the idea of 'a continuing journey with God as we become acclimatized to the fullness of love'. See Williams, *Tokens of Trust*, 148–9.

36. Rowan Williams and Philip Sheldrake, 'Catholic Persons: Images of Holiness. A Dialogue', in *Living the Mystery: Affirming Catholicism and the Future of Anglicanism*, ed. J. John (London: Darton, Longman & Todd, 1994), 88.

37. Williams, *Dostoevsky*, Ch. 2 *passim*. See especially pp. 79, 88 and 93.

38. Ibid., 80–1.

Nyssa and the thought of Augustine: our end is ultimately endless. This is, in turn, congruent with his repudiation of Myshkin's *static* timelessness, which entails a parodic eschatology where 'time will be no more'. Such an eschatology travels with the parodic icon of a corpse with no narrative future. This is the dark counterpoint to what is eschatologically central to Williams.

Endlessness and Apophaticism

As stated above, Williams's eschatology is correlate with the grammar of *non aliud*. This is itself demonstrable in a discussion that, at first sight, has little to do with eschatology – apophaticism. For Williams, Christian apophaticism is governed by an intuition of unending progress. Revelation is to him, by nature, generatively propulsive; it fractures 'existing frames of reference' and 'extends debate'.[39] He makes clear, in a 2008 lecture, that the negative theology that emerges in response to this propulsive force understands that no set of linguistic formulae can fix or still this process. There is 'always more to say (even in heaven)', and 'this "more" is always more compelling and wonderful'.[40] In other words, negative theology is, for Williams, coded in language that connotes a comedic *epektasis* in the process of theological description. Its negativity arises not from a stasis of infinite separation, wherein God's unknown-ness is a fixed and irreparable given, but from an infinite movement in knowing which always intuits an excess that has not yet been spoken.

This insight is echoed in the explorations of Nyssa's thought within *The Wound of Knowledge*. For Gregory, God is unknowable because knowing God is interminable. There is no datum-like divine essence where knowledge *can* terminate.[41] If there is an 'end' to knowing God, as Williams relates in a 1993 article on Nyssa, it is the attainment of an endless state of 'strictly *objectless* attention, love without projection or condition, moving and expanding but not restless'.[42] The language of '*objectless* attention' recalls my discussion in Chapter 1 of a *non aliud* grammar implying a God who is never *an*-other determinate object. Yet, this One who is *no* object is still the object of an ever-expansive but non-restless love. Williams also discusses Nyssa and apophaticism in *Arius*. Recapitulating the point about the elusivity of any datum-like divine essence, he notes the impossibility for Gregory of creatures attaining knowledge of the divine *ousia*. Creaturely knowledge of God is, rather, participative and Christological – 'living the life of the Son in faith and love'. This is a non-exhaustive, and *non-exhaustible*, knowing *in via*. It is 'always

39. Rowan Williams, *On Christian Theology* (Oxford: Blackwell, 2000), 134.

40. Williams, *Faith in the Public Square*, 73–4.

41. Williams, *The Wound of Knowledge*, 54, 62.

42. Rowan Williams, 'Macrina's Deathbed Revisited: Gregory of Nyssa on Mind and Passion', in *Christian Faith and Greek Philosophy in Late Antiquity: Essays in Tribute to George Christopher Stead*, eds L.R. Wickham and C.P. Bammel (Leiden: Brill, 1993), 242. Emphasis mine.

developing and never reaches conclusion.'[43] Overarchingly, in *Arius*, post-Nicene apophaticism (exemplified by *both* Nyssa and Augustine) is not, again, a negativity of static distance, but of intimate engagement. For those *in via* in discipleship, neither perspective nor distance is possible; God's 'everlasting act is as little capable of being a determinate object to our minds as the wind in our faces and lungs can be held still and distant in front of our eyes'.[44] Thus, God's unknowability persists in the intimate presence of one who is *not*-other to us, and not as an infinite distance. But this presence can never be a determined datum, never *an*-other object. This, again, is the grammar of *non aliud*.

This intimate presence is never a determined end because, for all its closeness, it maintains a tantalizing elusiveness that draws us on. In 'To Stand Where Christ Stands' Williams reprises Nyssa's vision of discipleship *in via*: 'The goal is, in a strange way, not being in the place of Jesus, but being never quite in the place of Jesus, always being taken along the road that his life in eternity and history defines.' This journey is one of infinite deferral, following Christ's traces but never quite arriving, of being 'swept up into the Son's journey towards the Father, his eternal and temporal pouring of his life into the life of the Father who eternally pours his life into the Son'. [45] Thus, Jesus perpetually escapes our grasp, but also leads us into an endless course set by the inner life of God. If negative theology is about the infinitude of a reparative movement of knowing, that unending movement has a Christological and Trinitarian mark upon it. It is a christomorphic journey into the life of God, Father, Son and Spirit.

The endlessness of *epektasis* in knowing is thus premised on the endlessness of God. It is a Christologically mediated induction into that Trinitarian life explored in Chapter 1 as a never terminating round of deflected desire, wherein God is *non aliud* even to God – intimate presence and infinite evasiveness, *not*-other and yet never *an*-other. The transcription of that life into the Christian's knowing is a perpetual, decentring, journey. This is the content of that 'always compelling and wonderful' more that negative theology proposes, although it comes also, as Williams reminds us through John of the Cross in 'Deflections of Desire', as a trauma of unknowing. To quote that essay, *epektasis*

> expresses the process of 'finding our way' within the life of the three divine agencies or subsistents. It is grounded in the endlessness of the movement from Son to Father, Father to Son, Father to Spirit, and so on: the endlessness of self-bestowal, which never reaches a terminus, never exhausts the otherness of the other.[46]

43. Rowan Williams, *Arius: Heresy and Tradition*, 2nd edn. (London: SCM, 2001), 207–8.
44. Ibid., 242–3.
45. Williams, 'To Stand Where Christ Stands', 6–7. See also *The Wound of Knowledge*, 62–3.'
46. Rowan Williams, 'The Deflections of Desire: Negative Theology in Trinitarian Disclosure', in *Silence and the Word: Negative Theology and Incarnation*, eds O. Davies and D. Turner (Cambridge: Cambridge University Press, 2002), 134. Williams also notes that to bring this out properly from Nyssa's conception requires some supplementation to fully locate it in a Trinitarian framework; in 'Deflections' this is found in John of the Cross.

This endlessness in knowing is inseparable from an endlessness in eschatology; there is always more to speak, 'even in heaven'. An eschatology of stasis, on the other hand, could only imply that our knowing comes to an end – meeting either an impossible fullness of knowledge (capturing, perhaps, the divine *ousia*) or facing an ultimately irreparable stasis of unknowing.

The Eschatology of Creation

But *epektasis* does not simply inflect Williams's understanding of the believers' eschatological fate, or their journey in knowing God. It also governs Williams's understanding of creation in the concrete freedom of its whole. This was hinted at in my discussions, under the aegis of Augustine and Rose, of creation being perpetually in a reparative movement towards its never-temporally attained end. But this vision is also intriguingly set out, from a different angle, in both *Grace and Necessity* and *Dostoevsky*. *Grace and Necessity*'s concluding chapter is, ostensibly, about the ontological implications of artistic creation. That said, it is also laden with theological import. For Williams, art (both literary and plastic) persists as what it is because the world is not yet what it will be. Creation's meaning is *in via*, in a process of being generated and unfolded, in part through being *known*. The process of knowing, or perception, is one whereby creation is 're-presented' in non-identical repetition by the knower. Because we always think things in terms of other things, in thinking we are transposing creation's forms into other media – and, insofar as art is the deliberate imaginative transposition of forms into new media, it is a particularly pointed and expressive mode of thinking in general. What Williams conjures in the pages of *Grace and Necessity* is the vision of a created manifold wherein things are not discreet objects separable from the thinking of them. Rather, in the process of being perceived, they betray an excess, an inner life provoked into definition in being re-presented in new forms. Things must, in this way, pass out of themselves to obtain the fulsomeness of their meaning. The role of artistic representation in this, as a deliberate activity and a species of thinking that unfolds creation's as yet undefined meanings, is art's dignity and import.[47]

A vision is implied here of creation as a process whose meaning – and, therefore, goodness – is emergent, akin to the Augustinian vision explored earlier.

---

47. Rowan Williams, *Grace and Necessity: Reflections on Art and Love* (London: Continuum, 2005), 135–70. Some of these themes also reappear in Williams's later book *The Edge of Words* (London: Bloomsbury, 2014). There he is keen to stress that material reality and the thinking of it interpenetrate one another. Matter is not 'dead' but 'inherently symbolic'. It is 'structured as a complex of patterns inviting recognition and constantly generating new combinations of intelligible structures' (103). Representation, for instance in language, discerns 'significant' and 'intelligible clusters' within the flow of reality, and each cluster opens 'out on such a wide assortment of connections that its representation is *never finalised*' (106–8, *italics* mine).

This world is 'always asymptotically approaching its fullness by means of the response of the imagination'. This 'asymptotic' language, with its implication of an infinite non-meeting between a line and a curve, evokes the idea of a constant deferral of that fullness's arrival. Already, there is a hint of *epektasis*. But there is also a connotation of *kenosis*. Creational reality is a 'shedder of forms, *dispossessing itself* of this or that shape to be understood and remade'.[48] This applies both to the 'endless environmental adjustment' that is the process of evolution, and the human artistic unfolding of meanings within that process.[49] Williams is explicit about the theological overtones of this kenotic aspect, drawing upon Bulgakov's idea of the self-devastation that occurs between the Father and Son, both in the incarnation and within the intra-Trinitarian life. It is the prototype for creation's dispossessive movement. The world which 'makes itself other' in the process of finding its integrity, dependently and non-identically repeats this divine 'making other', which is the 'wisdom' that 'radically grounds' creation.[50] This is consonant with Williams's point, discussed in the previous chapter's treatment of his Augustinianism, that the grammars of Christ and creation are interlocking. Wisdom incarnate is the 'definitive clue' to creation's processes, and Wisdom incarnate is he who sheds his form in non-defensive self-giving.

The idea that creation, and creatures, must be made other to become what they are in an unending process ultimately characterizable as *epektasis*, reappears in *Dostoevsky* – even if that discussion is more oriented towards the becoming of individual agents than of creation as a material whole. It is also a discussion, marked by a motif of misrecognition, that evokes the spirit of Rose.[51] In a consideration of Dostoevsky's literary methods, which doubles as an unconcealed essay in theology and ontology, Williams argues that to engage in dialogue is to engage in a process, even a drama, in which one is going to be mistaken by others. One is then faced with a choice. One can simply repeat, like some obtuse monoglot tourist, what was previously said, or one may attempt to non-identically re-present what was said in a new form, finding new words to move the conversation towards recognition.[52]

Simple repetition is the conversational analogue to an eternal return, or a Rosean aberrated mourning; the conversation or drama becomes pathologically stuck in such repetition. But finding new words parallels that dispossesive

48. Williams, *Grace and Necessity*, 153–4. Emphasis mine.

49. Ibid., 156.

50. Ibid., 158–64. Bulgakov is referenced in note 26, p. 163. He is something of an animating presence in the entirety of the chapter's discussion. His intuition that humanity's task is to humanize the world, and thereby to realize it as a work of art and bring to fullness its sophianic potential, is congruent with what Williams says about art's role in unfolding creation. See Rowan Williams, *Sergii Bulgakov: Towards a Russian Political Theology*, trans. Rowan Williams (Edinburgh: T&T Clark, 1999), 212–3.

51. Although Rose is not cited in the pages of *Dostoevsky* under discussion, she *is* cited in the previously discussed section of Williams's *Grace and Necessity* (p. 140, note 5).

52. Williams, *Dostoevsky*, 132.

non-identical repetition discussed in *Grace and Necessity*; it sheds pervious verbal forms to re-present itself. This is an intrinsically kenotic self-staking in the face of prior misrecognition. It parallels that kenotic self-staking earlier spoken of as necessary, in Hegel's thought, for sensible politics.[53] It could be called a 'catholic' act, wherein a stolid and defensive territorialization of the self is refused by seeking a good that cannot be had without the other. It is also an act that opens up the possibility for growth. To Williams, it denies the self as a fixed, self-defined entity. It is rather 'dependent for its definition and realisation on dialogue extended in time'. Following Bakhtin, this dialogue is the space for agents to become, for the first time, what they truly are.[54] So, just as things, in *Grace and Necessity*, cannot remain inert particulars but must pass out of themselves to obtain their meaning, so too it is with sentient agents in *Dostoevsky*.

Importantly, in *Dostoevsky*, the search for new words has an ' "unfinalizable" character' which 'projects the idea of a continuation of growth and self-definition *beyond death*'.[55] As stated earlier, in Williams's reading a Dostoevskian vision of eternal life is not one of stasis, but one of endless narratival growth. Thus, to argue, in relation to Dostoevsky, that 'my identity is in the future, unfolding itself as it is formed in speech and, thus in encounter',[56] is to imply a limitlessness to that futurity of the self. Ultimately, this is because the self emerges in a dialogue not merely with immanent others, but with that vivifying 'last word' to whom it is eternally exposed.[57] In its *non aliud* nature, this word is never had, but it always presents the generative gift of more time. This is a re-presentation, in a different medium, of *epektasis*.

To synthesize the thrust of the arguments in *Grace and Necessity* and *Dostoevsky*, together with what has already been said, creation, and the sentient selves within it, become what they are in a process characterized as both kenotic and endless. In being known, thought, re-presented artistically, and dialogued with, reality comes to itself; an inchoate, but not predetermined, potential of excess is expanded in unforeseen ways. Ultimately, it is in being known and dialogued with by a *non aliud* Self, a 'last word' that has no end, that creation and creatures come to their selves. Because this Self has no end, it facilitates an endless vivifying conversation. Reality, distended towards this endless end, infinitely grows and deepens in meaning and fullness. The endlessness of God implies, then, that creation, and created selves, become dependently endless and endlessly meaningful – not because they hold this quality in themselves, but because of their movement towards a fullness they can never have. *Epektasis* is not merely a way of conceiving of an endless

---

53. The Hegelian underlay of Williams's concept of representation in this discussion is, in fact, hinted at in an appendix to his later work *The Edge of Words* (pp. 186–97).

54. Williams, *Dostoevsky*, 132–3. See also Mikhail Bakhtin, *Problems of Dostoevsky's Poetics*, trans. C. Emerson (Minneapolis: University of Minnesota Press, 1984), 252.

55. Williams, *Dostoevsky*, 133–4. Emphasis mine.

56. Ibid., 136.

57. Ibid., 138–9.

progression in discipleship, or of the individual's eschatological fate; it implies an eschatological ontology for all of creation in its concrete freedom, an endless ripening of reality in relation to its Creator. Some of this is implicit in the previous chapter's discussions. It is possibly a more eudaemonic vision than Rose – with her language of mourning and misrecognition – might allow, even if the argument that she is a fundamentally *non*-tragic thinker holds. It is arguably, even, more eudaemonic than Williams himself is comfortable with. But it is the implication of, at least, aspects of his thought. It also returns us to look anew at some of the questions that have arisen in this book.

The Endlessness of the Question

To revisit the problem of Christological mediation, and the heightened mode it takes in relation to Christ's innocence, I affirmed that these issues could only be eschatologically determined; only then would it be clear that life-giving possibilities enfold the deathly consequences attendant upon Jesus's authorship of a human agency. The *endlessness* of Williams's eschatology shifts the frame of possibility when it comes to this eschatological determination. It also shifts the parameters of how we might think about the more general, but related, question of the mending of creation's tragic aspect by the end proposed. These questions are related because Christ is the appearance of that end in creation's middle. Creation's tragedies are not healed by a finalized happy ending, but by creation having *no* ending. The very *unsettledness* of the question posed by tragedy is transposed into the solution. Tragedy does not triumph, because there is always more made possible. God, to recall the previous chapter's discussion of 'The Health of the Spirit' is the one who *perpetually* re-opens possibilities foreclosed by the failure and finitude of his creatures.[58]

It is worth looking at remarks made in the essay in dialogue with McCord Adams that I have already cited. Considering the possibilities of post-mortem healing for grievous suffering, Williams urges discretion in a discussion that can become dangerously glib. Yet, if there is a theological significance to post-mortem existence in this respect, it is 'to try and imagine a context ample enough for the subject of profound injury to grow into a different kind of self-perception'. In an 'unlimited time scale', there is always more resource for healing. The caution added is that such an infinite reparative time cannot imply the dissolution of the subject through infinitude or a maximally positive experience such that the self, as a meaningful subject, ceases.[59] Such an eschatology would have too much in common with the timeless privation of Myshkin's idiotic euphoria.

58. Rowan Williams, 'The Health of the Spirit', in *Public Life and the Place of the Church: Reflections to Honour the Bishop of Oxford*, ed. Michael Brierley (Aldershot: Ashgate, 2006), 218.

59. Williams, *Wrestling with Angels*, 263–4.

Importantly, post-mortem healing also cannot be through an

> unmediated experience of the divine love – as if the love of God could now be
> bestowed on an individual subject without the intervention of a 'world'; as if we
> could make sense of a notion of experience that bypassed the world – our entire
> environment, our history and language, our essential interconnectedness with
> other subjects.[60]

Such an *unmediated* experience would not be 'catholic'; it would not acknowledge that our good is bound up in the concrete freedom of creation as a whole, and that our life and death is with our neighbours. Salvation, even post-mortem, must be according to that whole, and the tragedies dealt with must not be deracinated from the manifold in which they occur. This is where the argument that Williams proposes an endless *epektasis* for the whole of creation finds its biting point. It is in the eternal ripening of creation that a *mediated* healing is possible. It does not remove creatures from the contexts that make them what they are. Thus, we forever come to ourselves in relation not only to God, but also to one another and the world. No tragic damage can outpace this ever-expanding horizon.

Significantly, this must include the damage caused by Jesus. This *could* be an argument that the possibilities his life opens enfold and outpace tragic consequence because, in a world caught up in *epektasis*, that is what lives do. This would open Williams to the charge that what is specifically Christian, and Christological, about his thought has been loosely pinned onto a more generalized hopeful ontology, even a 'Hegelian' one. What protects him from this charge are the theological moves foregrounded in this book: his insistence that the particular life of Jesus is the mending appearance within history's broken middle of its unending end, and, thereby, that this particular life is, *itself*, the animating force within history of its movement towards that end. If Jesus is the one whose note-perfect performance decouples tragedy from necessity, and transposes stuck mourning into an inaugurated movement towards God, then his human life is the efficient cause of history's unending movement, as well as being the transcription of its endless final cause. This is what it is for Christ to be 'the key and centre of the whole series', or history's 'definitive clue'. If Jesus's history is everlasting Wisdom in speech and action, this is a kenotic Wisdom that finds its culmination in the heightened *syncrisis* of the dereliction. He makes 'an empty space in the world for God to come in'[61]; he sheds his form. But this can only be vouchsafed as *divine* if this dispossession issues into an unending opening up of possibilities, a resurrection proleptic for the created manifold and pointing towards an *epektasis*. Only if *kenosis* travels with *epektasis*, death with resurrection, may the life-giving

---

60. Ibid., 264.

61. Rowan Williams, *Open to Judgement: Sermons and Addresses* (London: Darton, Longman and Todd, 1994), 69. The sermon this quote is taken from, 'Risen Indeed' (pp. 67–71), emphasizes Jesus's kenotic obedience.

possibilities inaugurated enfold and outpace the damage done. Only then is there a possibility for Christ to be 'innocent', and Christological mediation 'successful' – and with this, we move from a general consideration of Williams's eschatology, towards that particular historical series that makes it thinkable. We have to talk about the resurrection.

Williams's Positive Doctrine of the Resurrection

In a 2005 Easter sermon, Williams effectively ties the grammar of *epektasis* to Jesus's resurrection. The Christian hope is understood there to be concerned with 'growth into an unimaginably greater dimension'. Death is an existential threat to such growth, but it is answered in a resurrection that allows us to 'stand with and in Jesus Christ looking into the inexhaustible depths of God's reality – the sea we must learn to swim in but will never cross over'.[62] Williams here implies the grammar I discerned earlier: that of standing in Christ's place and being brought into the endless 'sea' of the Trinity's life. He makes explicit the contention that only in a movement from the dispossession of death to a resurrection reversal is *epektasis* possible. This is true not only for individuals, but also for the whole created order.

The recurrence of the language of *ex nihilo* around the locus of the resurrection was noted in Chapter 2. It generates an expectation that the resurrection has some import for creation. In a 2004 lecture, Williams addresses this point explicitly. *Ex nihilo* language is necessary because death – 'a descent into dark nothingness' – can only be answered by the coming to be of 'something out of nothing, just like creation the first time around'. This 'something out of nothing' is not the provision of an instantaneous resolution, but the ignition of a process, 'a journey which goes on through history, in the material world'. Thus, recreation, like creation, is coded as process, and what is first brought to be, as I have said, is a community. Recalling the narrative of Jn. 21, the resurrection establishes a renewed relationship with the group of those whom Jesus called friends. But it 'is a relationship that in principle involves the whole world in which his friends live. The significance of the things of the world begin to change.'[63]

We can recall, at this point, *Grace and Necessity*'s discussion of the role of perception and representation in unfolding reality. The process by which the things of the world have their 'significance' changed in relation to a human community cannot be reduced to an act of surface nominalism. Rather, the implication is that things *really* grow into a new fulsomeness in their new signification, their re-presentation, by the community. The resurrection is, then, the ignition of a

---

62. Williams, *Choose Life*, 139–41. The imagery in the last sentence is taken from a hymn by the Welsh poet Ann Griffiths.

63. Rowan Williams, *Thoughts on the Resurrection*, vol. 12, Great St Mary's Papers (Cambridge: Great St Mary's Church, 2004), 3–5. See also Williams, *Open to Judgement*, 78.

journey by a community (God's 'pilot project') in history and materiality, which passes into a journey of growth in meaning for the material and historical order. This is why, as Williams makes clear in a 2008 lecture, the resurrection inaugurates a novel and final phase of history.[64] But, as will be clear from what's been argued so far, this finality cannot – if Williams is a consistent thinker – be a terminus.

It is worth noting that Williams has, in some ways, quite a traditional doctrine of the resurrection. In a 1996 essay, when considering whether belief in the empty tomb is necessary, Williams responds with punctuating brevity: 'Actually, yes.' The post-Easter Jesus has a *'material'* continuing agency, not reducible to 'mental operations on the part of believers'. Yet, while rejecting such a Bultmannian possibility, Williams is still hesitant to engage in any 'quasi-scientific discussion of the character of the risen body'[65] (and I will return to the importance of this). In *Resurrection*, however, he notes the continuity of Jesus's continuing material agency with the human being the disciples had known. Although not unambiguously so, Jesus is recognizable. His appearances are not of a figure who has sloughed off the human condition. They occur within that condition, and involve conversation and food. And this human continuity is inseparable for Williams from the intuition that the resurrection recreates a community, a set of friendships.[66]

That human continuity is not sloughed off is an intuition that travels in Williams's thought from Jesus's resurrection to the doctrine of a general eschatological resurrection, and even to the world's eschatological future. In the Q&A session of his 2008 lecture, he affirms that human destiny is a resurrection in psychosomatic wholeness: 'the whole of our memory, the whole of our temperament, the whole of who we are – body, mind and spirit'; 'God is free to remake us in our wholeness on the far side of death'.[67] The repetition of 'whole' and 'wholeness' flags up previous discussions of Williams's catholic logic of the whole. The doctrine of the resurrection abides by this logic. It understands that the 'whole' of who we are includes our concrete freedom within the created manifold. To quote *Tokens of Trust*:

> If we believe in life with God that does not just evaporate at our physical death, it must still be life in a community and context, life in a world where all our relationships with things and persons are fully anchored in the Trinitarian love of God and fully transparent to that love.[68]

64. Rowan Williams, ' "Risen Indeed": The Resurrection in the Gospels – Bishop of Winchester's Lent Lectures, Part 1', http://rowanwilliams.archbishopofcanterbury.org/articles.php/1380/risen-indeed-the-resurrection-in-the-gospels.

65. Williams, *On Christian Theology*, 194–5. The essay is 'Between the Cherubim: The Empty Tomb and the Empty Throne', pp. 183–96.

66. Rowan Williams, *Resurrection: Interpreting the Easter Gospel*, 2nd Rev. edn. (London: Darton, Longman and Todd, 2002), 91–4.

67. Williams, 'Risen Indeed', Part 1.

68. Williams, *Tokens of Trust*, 141.

If the resurrection of Jesus creates the novel possibility of an eternal enlargement of all that we are in relation to God, it is an enlargement that encompasses the material order in which we subsist.

That material order is one of irreducible embodiment: 'We are not who we are without bodies, ours or others,' a point made in an essay already cited in Chapter 4. To recall, for Williams 'the body *is* the soul', and life in the body is already social and symbolized.[69] This intuition is recapitulated, in a different tenor, in 2003's *Silence and Honey Cakes*:

> Only the body saves the soul. It sounds rather shocking put like that, but the point is that the soul (whatever exactly that is) left to itself, the inner life or whatever you want to call it, is not capable of transforming itself. It needs the gifts that only external life can deliver: the actual events of God's action in history, heard by physical ears, the actual material fact of the meeting of believers where bread and wine are shared. ... Only in this setting do we become holy – in a way entirely unique to each one of us[70].

This is an anthropological analogue to the creational ontology of *Grace and Necessity*. The soul in separation from the body (if such a thing even makes sense) is inert. It can only grow into holy uniqueness, the fullness of itself, in the risks of a negotiated material life – a realm of symbol and re-presentation, and orientation to other bodies. To switch registers, a disincarnate soul is the truest instance of a 'beautiful soul', abnegating its agency by refusing the distinctly corporeal drama of misrecognition. What this chimera cannot acknowledge is that 'our life and death is with our neighbour, the actual here and now context in which we live – including the unique neighbour who is my own embodied self'.[71] This is why the resurrection of the body, both Jesus's and ours, is significant. It is the only way to save the 'whole' of who we are in its potential ever-emergent fullness. That fullness is only what it is in the concrete freedom of the material world. Thus, *epektasis* for the soul entails *epektasis* for the body, and for the 'whole' manifold in which we come to be.

'Talking to a Stranger'

But the material human continuity of Jesus cannot be the whole story. For Williams, the Gospel accounts also present a countervailing witness of discontinuity, a Jesus not at first recognizable. On one level, the resurrection re-establishes a community

69. Rowan Williams, 'On Being a Human Body', *Sewanee Theological Review* 42, no. 4 (1999): 406–7.

70. Rowan Williams, *Silence and Honey Cakes: The Wisdom of the Desert* (Oxford: Lion Hudson, 2003), 94–5.

71. Ibid., 96.

of friendship, but on another, the risen Christ is 'not a dead friend but a living stranger'.[72] A chapter of the book *Resurrection* is even entitled 'Talking to a Stranger', and it opens with a quote from Iris Murdoch: 'The Christ who travels towards Jerusalem and suffers there can be made into a familiar. The risen Christ is suddenly something unknown.'[73]

This sense of discontinuity is also present in the 2004 lecture discussed above. While the risen Christ is 'recognisably' the same 'material historical being', there are 'signs of strain':

> Yes, this is the life we knew. Yes, this is the flesh we recognise, the flesh that sat on the other side of the table from us. And no, it is not a resuscitated corpse and it is not another item in the universe, and no, we have no idea how to make sense of this, but this is what we have to tell you – and that is what the Gospels are saying.[74]

In the affirmation that Christ is not a 'resuscitated corpse' is replicated the earlier-noted hesitancy to engage in any 'quasi-scientific discussion' of the risen body. In the statement that he 'is not another item in the universe' is a programmatic hint of discussions to come, for it is redolent of the concept of *non aliud*. Essentially, for Williams, the risen Christ is a 'living stranger' because the humanity he holds in continuity with before-Easter has experienced what might be called (although this is not language Williams uses) a post-resurrection communication of the attributes. That divine *non aliud* quality that the pre-Easter Jesus mediated rather opaquely now re-presents itself with a new intensity. In a new way he is not *an*-other.

It is this intensified quality of Jesus's participation in divine difference that, for Williams, makes the resurrection 'worth believing in'. Its motive force is that 'here is what we cannot master and which will always be ahead of us in our understanding. ... We shall grow in resurrection faith precisely as we walk with the risen Jesus, never quite catching up.'[75] Christianity is not, fundamentally, retrospective towards a Jesus present in the simple past: 'We do not look back to a founder; we look now, around, within, for a presence that has authority over our lives and is active today.'[76] To speak so of Jesus's continuing agential presence is to speak in the ambit of the

---

72. Williams, *Resurrection*, 74–5.

73. Ibid., 68. The quote is from Iris Murdoch, *The Red and the Green* (Chatto & Windus: 1965), 230. This passage seems to be in mind in what appears to be an elided quotation in Williams's lecture on 'Little Gidding'. He notes Murdoch's contention that ' "the risen Christ, hidden with God" is as puzzling, as much of a *skandalon* as the crucified Christ, or more, more inaccessible, certainly, even less open to concept or system'. See Williams, 'The Four Quartets', (1975), lecture 3, 8. 'Little Gidding' is also referred to in Williams, *Resurrection*, pp. 74, 77.

74. Williams, *Thoughts on the Resurrection*, 5.

75. Ibid., 8.

76. Williams, 'Christian Identity and Religious Plurality', 70.

resurrection, but coding even this as an un-complex presence, a returned friend without an evasive remainder, cannot provide the propulsive power Williams discerns in the resurrection. What is existentially important is not so much an – admittedly not *un*important – sense of material continuity. It is the discontinuity, and the deferral of presence, that functions as the engine of an Easter vitality that opens out into *epektasis*. The language of a Christ with whom we never quite catch up recalls Christ as the one who summons us on a never-ending journey into God, a presence always ahead of us, even a generative *non*-presence.

This new intensity of difference is tangible in the comparative theological weight Williams places on the empty tomb. It is the evocative locus of a generative *non*-presence, the symbolic transcription of the *non aliud* end that Christ mediates. This is marked in the essay 'Between the Cherubim' (1996), organized as it is around the image of the tomb's vacant shelf. It is an emptiness flanked, in the Gospel of John, by two angels. This is a deliberate commentary by allusion upon the empty mercy seat of the Ark, flanked by cherubim. It signifies a particular sort of divine presence in absence, a space where God both is and is not, a gap between images that is almost a visual wound analogous to a *syncrisis* of silence.[77] In one sense, this is the perfect iconic representation of the *non aliud* God who will never be *an*-other in our world – and, importantly, to Williams this 'image of an absence', and not any one of Jesus's resurrection appearances, is the central and controlling image of the Easter accounts.[78] The scene most iconic of the resurrection is one where Jesus does not appear. This is not Williams doubting the resurrection; it is Williams marking what is theologically central to it.

Something similar is conveyed when he draws attention to the refusal of the Eastern iconographic tradition to depict the actual event of resurrection. It is, like the moment of creation itself, an undepictable 'simple act of God'.[79] This foregrounds, again, the pairing of resurrection and creation, further equating both with a 'simple' divine act. To recall the discussions in our first chapter, creation *ex nihilo* and the grammar of *non aliud* are mutually implicated. God is the generative possibility of creation's manifold as a whole, but not mappable within creation's causalities. Thus, the divine act of creation cannot be so mapped, only its effects discerned. Similarly, now, the resurrection is framed as an unplaceable divine act of generativity. This is true, as Williams notes elsewhere, even for the Gospel writers. The resurrection does not appear in the Gospels because it 'does not and

---

77. Williams, *On Christian Theology*, 186–7. See also the sermon 'Holy Space' in Williams, *Open to Judgement*, 101–4.

78. Williams, *On Christian Theology*, 195–6.

79. Rowan Williams, *The Dwelling of the Light: Praying with the Icons of Christ* (Norwich: Canterbury Press, 2003), 23–4. Williams concedes that the resurrected body, the effect of the event, can be portrayed. He has also commented on a (Western) portrayal of the resurrection, Piero della Francesca's painting in the Borgo San Sepolcro. See Williams, *Thoughts on the Resurrection*, 14–15, as well as his poetic meditation in Rowan Williams, *Headwaters* (Oxford: Perpetua, 2008), 26.

cannot belong to history: it is not *an* event, with a before and an after, occupying a determinate bit of time'. Like creation, it is only discernible in its effects: 'We can speak of it only as the necessary condition for our living as we live.' Thus, it persists as a generative possibility that cannot be found *within* the word. It is 'hidden in God's eternal act'. [80]

If the moment is beyond depiction, and best symbolized as an absence, its most immediate effect, a risen material identity, has communicated to it something of that moment's *non aliud* quality. Christ's body is, again, no longer 'another item in the universe', and certainly not a simple presence compelling belief. Even appearing to his friends, he maintains the discomforting aspect of a stranger, opaque to instantaneous recognition – and there are no 'evidential appearances to an indiscriminate public or to Pilate and Caiaphas'.[81] The risen Christ remains an ambiguous sign, not assimilable to the world's truths. He is not even easily assimilable to the church's purposes, something elucidated in 'Between the Cherubim'.

The empty tomb and the motif of elusiveness in the resurrection function to prevent a totemic absorption of Jesus into any ecclesial agenda. This is 'part of what its confession of the divinity of Jesus amounts to in spiritual and political practice'. Insofar as the risen Jesus is enfolded into the divine *non aliud,* he cannot be territorialized as a possession. Just as an empty throne between the cherubim was 'a deliberate repudiation of a graspable image, an absence reflected in the strange formulation of the divine name in Exodus 3', so there is an 'ungraspability' to the risen Jesus as the source of the community's life.[82] Transposing to another Easter lacuna, the missing end of Mark's Gospel is also read by Williams as a chastening absence, signifying that Jesus's narrative cannot be decisively finished, even by '"authorised" tellers of the story'. He persists as that creative *non*-presence, not 'exhausted in any text or ensemble of texts, in any performance or ensemble of performances'.[83]

This *non*-presence is the mode in which Christ is a 'last word' to us, engendering perennial growth. A resuscitated corpse, one that can be itemized in the world, might provide a more *determining* word. But, as Williams puts it in a 2003 Easter sermon, there is 'no going back to the Jesus who is humanly familiar'. Such a retrospective view is, in fact, a temptation, one exemplified by the account of Mary Magdalene in the garden. She 'wants Jesus back as she remembers him; failing that, she wants his corpse in a definite place'. But he is on his way to the Father, and what is needed is a vision that looks 'forward to where Jesus leads, to that ultimate being-at-home with God that he has brought to life in the history of

80. Williams, *Resurrection*, 89–90.

81. Rowan Williams, 'Looking for Jesus and Finding Christ', in *Biblical Concepts and Our World*, eds D. Z. Phillips and M. von der Ruhr (Basingstoke: Palgrave MacMillan, 2004), 151–2.

82. Williams, *On Christian Theology*, 192–3.

83. Ibid., 193.

our world'. To look back is, in fact, to desire a manageable datum, a totem for our rightness.[84] It is also to evade that movement towards its true end that Jesus's life instantiates within creation. The elusiveness of the risen Christ is thus vital for keeping the church's political practice ironic, and, therefore, reparative and catholic. His mediation of the end remains a *non*-presence that draws his people onwards and de-centres them from any territory within the world they might wish to occupy safely. In the Easter intensification of Jesus's participation in divine difference lies the possibility for the community he creates to mirror that *non aliud* life – *not*-other to the broken middle in which it lives, but generatively so because it always slips the bonds of being located as *an*-other competitive territory. The risen Jesus 'cannot be trapped in the coils of my unreconstructed desire', and it is in this elusiveness that he 'begins to take on more and more clearly the tone and character of what we say about God'.[85] He is more palpably divine, insofar as he is less graspable as *an*-other in our world, and the confession of that divinity entails a certain kind of politics.

It also entails a certain kind of theological negativity: 'A theology of the risen Jesus will always be, to a greater or lesser degree, a *negative theology*, obliged to confess its conceptual and imaginative poverty – as is any theology which takes seriously the truth that God is not a determinate object in the world'.[86] It is worth recalling that theological negativity is not a matter of static distance, but of infinite movement into intimacy. Thus, insofar as the elusiveness of Jesus post-Easter is the provocation to a prospective vision, the intensification of divine difference in the risen Christ is also an invitation to the church, and the world, to move forward in *epektasis*. It is in the resurrection that Jesus decisively becomes that generative *non*-presence underwriting Williams's endless eschatology. This is why reducing Christ to familiarity is an error, and why he must always maintain something of the stranger's aspect. Reduced to a resuscitated corpse, the *dénouement* of a story comfortably told, Jesus becomes as parodic a vision in its own way as that *non*-resuscitated corpse found in Holbein's painting. In both of these imaginings, movement stops. Holbein's Christ is safely cadaverous, the locatable body Mary wished for if she couldn't have a simply returned friend, but he is a static icon who cannot move mourning out of its aberrated register. Yet, neither can a familiar risen Christ. He remains a triumphant given, the end of a story where there is *an*-other divine king between the cherubim. To return to discussions in *Dostoevsky*, the truth of such an ending would be like that 'of defensible propositions, a truth demanding assent as if belief were *caused* by facts'. There is no gratuity in such belief, and it attains to a diabolical mode that proffers a Christ who is ultimately 'another variant of trying to stop history'.[87]

84. Williams, *Choose Life*, 111–14.
85. Williams, *Resurrection*, 83.
86. Ibid., 84.
87. Williams, *Dostoevsky*, 43–4.

Habeas Corpus?

Yet, if there is a question that arises from these discussions, particularly the idea that there is a post-resurrection communication of the attributes that intensifies the participation of Jesus in the divine *non aliud*, it is this: 'Whither his humanity?' This book has argued that the incarnation is best understood as a *human* performance, one to which God is generatively *not*-other. In my discussions of the parodic Myshkin, and of the complex unfallenness of Jesus, I have suggested that this performance was deeply implicated in a conflictual world, and that this was the source of an opacity in Christological mediation. At first glance, for Williams, this opacity seems lightened in the resurrection. From the first, Christians found the risen Jesus 'a place where the meaning of "God" and the meaning of "humanity" overlapped'. Williams is careful to stress that this 'does not cancel or call into question his identity as a member of the human race',[88] but it must be asked if the dramatic flow of his account does not, in fact, travel in that direction. After all, the controlling image of the resurrection is a missing body.

It is important to add caveats. Even if the mediatorial opacity of the risen Jesus recedes, he does not compel belief. Christ's divinity, and the resurrection itself, are not data *in* the world that can do so. Rather, the opacity of a human performance passes over in the resurrection into an elusiveness that enfolds even Jesus's physical body, his human recognizability. Christ is no 'given', either before or after Easter, but the mode of his not-being-given changes. In neither mode, opacity or elusiveness, is his divine nature *an*-other item to be mapped. But his post-resurrection elusiveness is a lure to engage in a journey of perpetually deferred arrival into God – the engine of *epektasis*. The logic of *epektasis* also implies that the revelation of Jesus's divinity in the resurrection cannot be an instantaneous given. It is the ignition of a process whereby the questions of Christ's innocence – and, thus, of Christological mediation – and the mending of creation's broken middle are cast against an endless horizon of vivifying possibility. The answers that would confirm divinity never arrive, but precisely in their never arriving, Jesus's divinity is obliquely shown. It is revealed in the transformative journey for the whole created manifold he makes possible. But this journey seems to imply, at certain points, a moving beyond Jesus's material humanity.

In several places, Williams considers the question of Jesus's humanity as an appropriate object of devotion. In *Resurrection,* he notes the examples of thinkers like Origen, Cassian and Eckhart, who encouraged the spiritually mature to abandon the contemplation of that humanity. While recognizing the potential for an elitism and incipient docetism in such an approach, Williams refuses to entirely eschew it – for, in Jesus, 'we have to reckon with an historical life that itself urges us away from its historical limits, that opens onto immense horizons'.[89] There is something about this humanity that will not let our gaze

88. Williams, *Resurrection*, 87–8.

89. Ibid., 85. For additional commentary on Eckhart, see Williams, *The Wound of Knowledge*, 134–5.

comfortably settle upon it. In the essay 'A History of Faith in Jesus' (2001), Williams emphasizes that Jesus's humanity both 'is and is not' a proper end for devotion. It *is* so because through the particular historical series of that life, a new relation with God is made possible. It is *not* so because that relation is only had by inhabiting 'the relation Jesus always and already has to God'. An orientation to the human Jesus must slip *through* that humanity, to stand where he stands in relation to the divine. But, when we look to take hold of that humanity in itself, we find instead 'an *absence* at the centre of Christian imagination, a space opening up to the final otherness and final intimacy of encounter with the Father'.[90] Essentially, the grammar at work in the resurrection is also at work in spirituality: when we go looking for a familiar, we find, instead, an iconic absence.

A similar point is made, in relation to John of the Cross, in 'Deflections of Desire'. Jesus, in his self-giving to the point of dereliction, 'renders himself absent as a simple terminus of piety'.[91] In *kenosis,* he becomes that self-effacing 'absence' at the centre of devotion, but *kenosis* passes over into *epektasis,* just as death cedes to resurrection, and it is not accidental that Williams goes on to speak once more of Mary in the garden, finding that the human Jesus has ceased to be a simple terminus for *her* devotion. He is no longer a 'steady object', or 'an historical other in the past'. He is now a space to be stood in where we are 'deflected towards the absence of any static divine object so that the divine life may be lived in us as subjects'.[92]

Arguably, in these discussions, Jesus's human body loses its status as 'object', or at least its objectivity is greatly complexified[93] – and if the point already made in this book about psychosomatic unity stands – that the body *is* the soul, the place where the self is unfurled – then a body losing its status as an object is a whole human self that is losing its status as an object. Yet, this slipping of objectivity is not, in and of itself, deemed a problem by Williams. It is, rather, the process where the human Jesus is becoming a generative *non-presence* and invitation to *epektasis.* It is not accidental that he immediately follows the above discussions in 'Deflections' with a rumination on Rublev's icon as the 'graphic representation' of the endless deflection that Jesus's human

---

90. Williams, 'A History of Faith in Jesus', in *The Cambridge Companion to Jesus,* ed. M. Bockmuehl (Cambridge: Cambridge University Press, 2001), 230.

91. Williams, 'The Deflections of Desire', 128. See also the (already quoted) sermon on John where Jesus 'makes himself an empty space in the world for God to come in' (Williams, *Open to Judgement,* 69).

92. Williams, 'The Deflections of Desire', 128.

93. Williams notes that even John's ally, Teresa (who opposed spiritualities she feared bypassed Jesus's humanity), acknowledged his body as not 'a physical object like others'. See Rowan Williams, *Teresa of Avila* (London: Geoffrey Chapman, 1991), 70. Her allegiance to the humanity of Christ demarcates her from John, but Williams notes that this can be overplayed (Williams, 'A History of Faith in Jesus', 229).

life invites us into.[94] This coincidence of an icon with the complexification of Jesus's objectivity is, in itself, a theological tell.

It is worth recalling the discussion of icons in the first chapter of this book – that they are Christologically underwritten, and that they are objects that shed their normal objectivity in relation to what they signify. In view of their Christological determination, it is not inappropriate to say that there is a communication of the attributes between icons and what they depict, just as there is between the iconic risen humanity of Jesus and the *non aliud* difference of God; both icon and iconic humanity tread the borders of ceasing to be *an*-other object in the world – and, to return to the discussion of Holbein's painted corpse, that rendering is parodic because it is a limit case of the cessation of movement, and, thereby, in a certain way it is *utterly* an object. There is no *epektasis* after *kenosis* in a cadaver to which nothing has been communicated, just a stasis of decay. Icons do not do this – and yet, an icon is still *an* object that can be handled, and the humanity of Jesus both is not, and yet still *is*, an end of devotion and a body in continuity with what we knew. While the accent in Williams's discussions is on the generative absence of Jesus, there is still a friendship renewed with a flesh that sat across the table. This body does not utterly cease but, to recall another earlier discussion, its presence is that of a *signum*.[95]

In Williams's reading of Augustine's *De doctrina*, there is 'one "point in the world" entirely transparent to God', an 'authorized "sign" which we cannot mistake for anything *but* a sign' – the humanity of Jesus.[96] This humanity *is* still a worldly 'point', but refuses to remain simply so. It restlessly pushes our attention beyond itself, representing 'the absence and deferral that is basic to *signum* as such'.[97] It does not leave the world of created things so much as transform it, manifesting 'the essential quality of the world itself as "sign" or trace of its maker'. Thus, the Word embodied recasts all bodies as words, and no longer is anything in creation a stopping point in itself, *no* object is purely *an* object anymore.[98] Williams is potentially doing something quite extraordinary here. What could be read as the de-realizing of the humanity of Jesus is pivoted into the transformation of all things. The question is no longer 'Whither the body?', but 'Whither *every* body?' Everything is de-realized in itself, but also made real in a new way – it is re-presented. If Jesus's humanity

---

94. Williams, 'The Deflections of Desire', 128–9.

95. Paradoxically, in his *The Edge of Words*, Williams argues that this is a body that becomes a *signum* precisely in a certain *sort* of cessation of movement. By moving towards 'silence and motionless within the human world', through death and dereliction, this body 'represents the unrepresentable God', fleshing out divine power as dispossessive. Yet, following the theme already established in this book of *kenosis* giving way to *epektasis*, it is in the resurrection that his becomes a body '*significantly* absent' (176–7, Emphasis mine).

96. Williams, 'Language, Reality and Desire', 140–1.

97. Ibid., 148.

98. Ibid., 141.

utterly gives itself up to performing God's life, it becomes utterly significant of what it is not. Yet, to Williams, this was never an operation involving the loss of human integrity; rather, this humanity became more intensively real. In being de-realized *in itself*, one could say in a kenotic passing out of itself, it gained in reality in relation to what it is not, and entered into an endless fulsomeness of meaning. In Williams's essay on *De doctrina*, this Christological possibility is sketched, by implication, as a possibility for the whole created manifold. It is arguable that this sketch finds its fulfilment in the *epektasis* of all things.

If one insists that any created thing, including the humanity of Jesus, is a *res* without remainder, one is, by Williams's logic, saying that such a thing is a determinate point, a proper terminus for desire. It is where movement can cease, as it need not signify onwards. As Susannah Ticciati has pointed out in her work on Williams's reading of *De doctrina*, this implies a world where relations between creatures are essentially dyadic, reductive and even abusive. The reason for this is that no thing *can* be a *res* without remainder – for, when we stop our desire on another creature, and treat it as an end, we still engage in a truncated form of signification. We insist that the object (for it is in this instance only an object) has a significance, but only in relation to our desires; we exhaust its significance in terms of our desires.[99] To use language already employed in this book, we turn everything into a parodic and static icon, rendering it a corpse in the process and refusing to allow its movement into greater meaning.

For Ticciati, what occurs when things are allowed to signify in relation to God, when the world becomes *signum* in relation to Christ, is that relations between creatures become triadic and non-reductive. Every *res* is now *signum* in relation to God, and thus evinces an element of its life that we cannot control in terms of the truncated signification of our own needs. There is always an inexhaustible third term in every relation.[100] Interestingly, Williams makes an argument along very similar lines in a 2002 lecture, where he describes a non-reductive 'un-secular' viewpoint as one where we look upon others as those who are already seen from another perspective, which is not ours and which we cannot finalize. This way of seeing acknowledges something inaccessible about the other, an extra that only 'time and understanding' can begin to unfurl.[101] Then there is the argument in *The Edge of Words*, towards the end of a chapter in which (under the aegis of C. S. Peirce and Walker Percy, and drawing upon Aquinas) a parallel differentiation to Ticciati's dyadic/triadic distinction is explored: the limited structures of creation are 'inseparable' from the limitless God who is their cause. In that relation, that which is finite escapes reductive explanation. There is 'always more to be said about it'.[102]

---

99. Susannah Ticciati, 'The Castration of Signs: Conversing with Augustine on Creation, Language and Truth', *Modern Theology* 23, no. 2 (2007): 166.

100. Ibid., 167–9.

101. Williams, *Faith in the Public Square*, 17–18.

102. Williams, *The Edge of Words*, 64–5. For the earlier discussion of Peirce and Percy, see pp. 52–6.

All this implies that a world where every body is a word, a *signum*, because the Word became a body, is also a world where every body is in an unfinalizable relation of signification. Everything is always *more* because it has ceased to be a static object, and evinces an excessiveness that it cannot have in itself, but only in being rendered significant of what it is not. This is a world where everything must pass out of itself to obtain the fullness of its life. This is a vision entwined with that laid out in *Grace and Necessity* and *Dostoevsky*, where things unfold in being known by, and related to, God, but also by being known by, and related to, their fellow creatures. This is the *epektasis* of all things in their concrete freedom. But, as argued earlier, this *epektasis* finds its efficient cause in the authorized *signum* that is Jesus of Nazareth. What looked like the de-realization of his humanity turns out to be its de-realization as a static object open to reductive significations and totemic usages. In ceasing to be *an*-other object, and being the definitive sign of the *non aliud* God, the reality of that humanity is not diminished, but expanded against an infinite horizon – and that expansion through signification is communicated as a possibility to the entirety of creation. In a sense, this is the *theosis* of the world by a communication to it of something of the divine *non aliud*.

Conclusion

In relation to Christ, all things – the catholic whole of reality – slip their moorings as objects and are drawn into a divine orbit. The world becomes endlessly iconic, but not less creaturely. Its endlessness is not its own, but had only in relation to the divine life into which it endlessly journeys, and of which it becomes endlessly significant. The cause of this journey is one consummately significant human performance, a life lived at the intersection of multiple pressures in body and society. In its refusal to live self-defensively, this life establishes evil's non-necessity, and mendingly transcribes time's *non aliud* end into its broken middle. As his *kenosis* cedes to resurrection, he becomes a *non*-presence that is ever more fully a transcription of that end, luring on the community formed by him in a reparative politics that re-presents the world. This is love's endless work in the midst of time's misrecognitions, and it is a comedic journey because, ultimately, it can never end but only grow more replete with meaning. Mourning is inaugurated to ignite endless joy. To call Jesus the 'last word' is, for Williams, to say something like this.

CONCLUSIONS

Recapitulation

To recapitulate the journey of this book, we began with an exploration – in various registers and idioms – of divine difference in Williams's work. God is *non aliud*, not *an*-other mappable among creaturely items or causes, but still generatively *not*-other to the whole created manifold. This account of difference, which is shot through even the Trinitarian life, was taken to both make possible, and complicate, Christology. In Chapter 2, I explored that Christology. What emerged was a vision self-consciously working within the parameters of traditional orthodoxy, wherein Christ is a perfect performance, in time and humanity, of the divine difference. The content of that performance offers transformative judgement, and creates novel possibilities. As *an*-other human life that uniquely instantiates the generative *not*-other of God, it mediates a divine disruption in the violent sameness of history. This led on to a discussion of the importance of the historical particularity of Jesus, and of history in general. Williams was cast as an 'incarnational historicist', for whom the incarnation is the centre of time that constellates history into meaning. That meaning, in turn, informs the theological content of the incarnation.

In Chapters 3 and 4, I initiated a more oblique exploration, one that began to foreground the complexity that Williams's account of difference brings to Christology. I argued that his use of parodic Christ figures, particularly Prince Myshkin, amounts to a negative Christology. Myshkin is portrayed as a privative 'beautiful soul' who, in a diabolical and parodic *kenosis*, abnegates his agency in time. Backlit by this, Christ emerges as the non-privative one, truly a human *an*-other, who engages in true *kenosis*, committing himself to time's '*drama of misrecognition*'. I underlined the necessity of Christ's being fully ensconced as *an*-other human agent within history. But, as I explored in Chapter 4, this stretches – and potentially garbles – God's grammar. In the history that we have, in which human lives are enmeshed in an agonized and opaque manifold, the innocence of Christ as *an*-other, the generativity of his life and, thereby, the possibility of Christological mediation, is a very difficult datum. If Jesus is truly human, he is hemmed in by a fallen manifold such that his own *un*fallenness can only be complex and 'polyphonic'. What emerges is a vision of Christ as the place of *syncrisis*, living an existence at the confluence of numerous pressures in body and society, and yet remaining unimaginably stable. Yet, there is a suspended quality to this stability – its success, and, thereby, Jesus's innocence and the success of Christological mediation, remains ultimately an eschatological datum. This vision is understood as a departure from aspects of the post-Chalcedonian tradition, especially the thought of Maximus. It is one in which God hazards a greater dramatic risk in the incarnation than some might wish to allow.

Chapter 5, in the light of these discussions, pulled back to take a more general look at the dynamics of mediation within Williams's work. Two tensioned, but intertwined, mediatorial logics were discerned – a pacific logic of the whole (dependent on God's *non aliud* grammar), and a logic of *syncrisis* (related to a tragic construal of contingency wherein God can only appear in dialectical contrasts). In explorations of Christological, but also poetical and scriptural mediation, the concern was raised that the latter logic might overcome the former, disabling the possibilities of mediation such that God's life can only appear to us as a wound in time's woundedness.

Chapter 6 began a repair of this situation. I employed theological resources already present within Williams's work: dialogues with Augustine, and with Rose's reading of Hegel. In continuity with his teacher Donald MacKinnon, Williams is seen as a theologian attuned to the tragic. In discontinuity with MacKinnon, he is seen as one who adopts an eschatological vision, which ameliorates, without dissolving, that tragedy. Mediation in time, thereby, becomes more thinkable, if not less complex. History is cast as an (ultimately) comedic drama, the efficient cause of which is the appearance in time's broken middle of Jesus as the one who mediates, opaquely, its end. This is how time is constellated into meaning, against an eschatological horizon. The final chapter engaged more fully with Williams's eschatological vision, beginning with the community emerging from the resurrection. What Williams proposes, if sometimes obliquely, is an 'endless end', an *epektasis* of all creation in the vivifying wake of a Christ whose participation in the difference of God has been intensified in the resurrection. Christ is now a generative *non*-presence, the 'last word' of creation, which summons it into ever new significance in relation to God.

Provocations

By way of completing this work, I want to highlight three areas of discussion that call for further comment, and perhaps point to further work. First, it is worth remarking on the degree to which Williams's Christ is implicated in the human condition, understood in its most agonized terms. To return to the logic of similarity and dissimilarity explored in Chapter 4, Williams's brave predications of similarity – to the point of rendering Christ's unfallenness 'polyphonic' – leave him a potential theological outlier. There is a deep soteriological impetus to this, a desire to assume our tragedy in order to heal it. The result, in at least one essay, is the injection of the language of dramatic *syncrisis* into the hypostatic union itself, suspending (as I have repeatedly noted) the possibilities of Christological mediation. This dramatic suspension extends even, as I also noted, into the divine life. Thus, a dialectical crisis is set up in Jesus, a risking of the divine life in maximal encounter with human vulnerability. This represents a forceful undercurrent within

Williams's theology, and perhaps, at times, a troublesome substrate. It pushes him, arguably, to the edges of acceptable Christian speech about Jesus's soteriologically necessary *dis*similarity to us, raising the question of his very capacity not to sin. If the logics of this book are correct, this in turn raises the question of creation's capacity to be anything other than tragically in enmity with itself and God. Perhaps here is the subterranean connection between this Christological *syncrisis* and the wider logic of *syncrisis* that I noted, a logic that at times threatens to undo mediation's possibilities. Both are based in a construal of temporal contingency as fraught and conflictual. Both bring Williams's project to the limits of its coherence, where the only word that can be spoken is a wound of silence.

If coherence is a possibility, and ultimately for Williams it is, it is eschatological. This brings us to the second area of consideration, the eschatology with which I concluded. For all its argued importance, and almost exuberant hopefulness, it is a remarkably *sotto voce* feature within Williams's writings. It is often expressed with diffidence, and only fully uncovered through some – almost archaeological – efforts by the reader. This, in itself, seems theologically significant. Perhaps it is tied to Williams's hesitancy about over-determined eschatologies, and their potentially diabolic aspect. It certainly seems connected with the powerful imaginary of the empty tomb, and a vacant seat, which governs his concept of the resurrection. Insofar as that resurrection is proleptic of the end, that image of absence is telling. It signifies an eschatological reserve that would not say or show too much – the end, or 'last word', is not a presence. But this hesitancy about presence opens up a lacuna in Williams's eschatology, and maybe even his Christology.

A seat that is *not* empty is implied in the New Testament, in the ascended Christ's enthronement in the Father's presence. As 'mythical' as such language must be, there is a notable absence in Williams's writings of concentrated attention on the ascension, and the ascended Christ's *presence* in that victorious 'space'.[1] Also lacking is discussion of the *parousia* of such a figure. Thus, in comparison to the traditional lineaments of Christian eschatology, there is arguably something missing from the drama that Williams presents. Is there room for a turning point, even a point of heightened *syncrisis* within history, which ends one phase of it? The *parousia* of Christ implies the coming possibility of a new, if possibly still complex, form of Christological presence, and a moment that tips inaugurated mourning (which is still mourning) into a register of greater comedic hilarity. At some point, the comedic nature of the drama must rise more distinctly to the surface, and

---

1. This has been commented upon by Andrew Stobart in his doctoral thesis ('A Constructive Analysis of the Place and Role of the Doctrine of Jesus' Resurrection within the Theologies of Rowan Williams and Robert Jenson', [Aberdeen: University of Aberdeen, 2011], 150). The ascension is not *absent* from Williams's work (see Rowan Williams, *Resurrection: Interpreting the Easter Gospel*, 2nd Revised ed. [London: Darton, Longman and Todd, 2002], 81, *Tokens of Trust: An Introduction to Christian Belief* [Norwich: Canterbury Press, 2007], 93, & *The Lion's World: A Journey into the Heart of Narnia* [London: SPCK, 2012], 134). Rather, its presence is arguably under-pronounced.

a series of recognitions occur within it. As Williams himself acknowledges, in our life and death with our neighbour, with all its demanding engagements, it is possible 'we shan't know who we are until Judgement Day'.[2] Arguably, Williams's eschatology might benefit from being supplemented by a more overt presence of that Day's possibility – assuming such a supplement avoids the dangers of proposing the advent of a simple Christological presence, and, thus, a 'last word' that provides a determinate and static end.

Attention to eschatology seems all the more necessary when one considers the weight that, at least implicitly, it comes to carry for Williams. In the intertwined grammars of Christ and creation, neither can have its goodness secured except eschatologically. This leads to my final area of consideration, the complex displacement of theological weight in Williams's thought away from primordial beginnings, and towards the middle and the end. If there is a historical datum for creation's goodness, and an account of evil that historicizes as opposed to radically ontologizing it, it is not found in some original undisarranged peace. Its basis is, arguably, in that consummately significant historical life that is Christ's, and his almost impossible refusal of temptation. Thus, there is a shift from the beginning to time's Christological middle. But that middle is broken, not holy. It is not the pre-determined recapitulation of primordial peace, but the staking of a contestable place in time. The already occurring drama is entered so as to make it a drama in movement towards the end. It is created *as* drama, and unfrozen from a violent eternal return, in that entry. But because the middle is broken, this unfreezing cannot be temporally obvious. The end appears in the middle obliquely, even in the frisson of *syncrisis*, and the meaning of that middle is only had in the end – thus a second shift, from the middle to the end.

The suspended drama that is Christ's life, to return to our first point, a suspension that enfolds even the divine integrity, can only have a resolution in the whole concrete and catholic freedom of creation coming to be in an endless end. It is only the 'last word' when life-giving possibilities enfold all, but the enfolding is unending. The consummation of Christ's goodness, and the entailed consummation of all goodness, is in endless deferral and constantly *in via*. It seems, for Williams, that deferral *itself* becomes the form of goodness, that goodness's medium is the gift of endless reparative time. After all, deferral itself, an eternal joyous distension, is inscribed into the divine life as an eternal deflection of desire. The goodness of creation, then, is the inscription of this dynamic of endless divine movement upon it in *epektasis*. This, in a sense, is the *theosis* of time's drama. Its concrete possibility, in time, is a broken Christological middle that is also a last word eliciting this divinizing movement.

The almost painfully naive question left is – 'What about Eden?' If, to return to the language of 'Resurrection and Peace', 'conflict' is primordial within creation, although tragic 'strife' not metaphysically ultimate, a pattern of thought that has powerfully shaped Christianity is potentially upended. The foil for my discussion

2. Rowan Williams, *On Christian Theology*, (Oxford: Blackwell, 2000), 286.

of this within this book was a stream of thought represented by Milbank and Hart. But the trope of a primordial peace or goodness disarranged is scattered far wider than Radical Orthodoxy and its fellow travellers. It is arguably *the* dominant explanatory 'myth' in these matters. The problem is that, while it maintains its power (arguably even in Williams's own thought) as a regulative idea, this 'myth' has an increasingly frail purchase within time and history. Whether it be the fossil record, or the genome, no Eden is empirically obvious. The question then raised is this: How can evil be 'historicized' (except mythologically) if there is no Edenic history? If the critique of Milbank implied in Williams's (and Rose's) thought is correct, his *mythological* historicization of evil in a primordial prehistory, one with no traction in the time we know, results in a perverse violence towards history itself. For all its departure from the common sense of much of the tradition, Williams's complex displacement of theological weight from the beginning, towards the middle and the end, points to a potential other way: a theology that *both* historicizes evil *and* attends to history emerges as a possibility. It is a theology that places its weight on Christology, and eschews counterfactual accounts of a primordial unfallen existence. The important Adam is the 'second' one, the last word as opposed to the first. That is a project which cries out for further work and exploration.

Bibliography

Part I Primary Works by Rowan Williams

Books and Theses

Arius: Heresy and Tradition, 2nd ed. London: SCM, 2001.
Choose Life: Christmas and Easter Sermons in Canterbury Cathedral. London: Bloomsbury, 2013.
Christ on Trial: How the Gospel Unsettles Our Judgment. Grand Rapids: Zondervan, 2000.
Christian Imagination in Poetry and Polity: Some Anglican Voices from Temple to Herbert. Oxford: SLG Press, 2004.
Dostoevsky: Language, Faith and Fiction. London: Continuum, 2008.
The Dwelling of the Light: Praying with the Icons of Christ. Norwich: Canterbury Press, 2003.
The Edge of Words: God and the Habits of Language. London: Bloomsbury, 2014.
Faith in the Public Square. London: Bloomsbury, 2012.
Grace and Necessity: Reflections on Art and Love. London: Continuum, 2005.
Headwaters. Oxford: Perpetua Press, 2008.
The Lion's World: A Journey into the Heart of Narnia. London: SPCK, 2012.
Lost Icons: Reflections on Cultural Bereavement. Edinburgh: T&T Clark, 2000.
A Margin of Silence: The Holy Spirit in Russian Orthodox Theology/Une Marge De Silence: L'esprit Saint Dans La Théologie Orthodoxe Russe. Québec: Éditions du Lys Vert, 2008.
On Christian Theology. Oxford: Blackwell, 2000.
Open to Judgement: Sermons and Addresses. London: Darton, Longman and Todd, 1994.
The Poems of Rowan Williams. Oxford: Perpetua Press, 2002.
Ponder These Things: Praying with Icons of the Virgin. Norwich: Canterbury Press, 2002.
Resurrection: Interpreting the Easter Gospel, 2nd Revised ed. London: Darton, Longman and Todd, 2002.
Sergii Bulgakov: Towards a Russian Political Theology, edited and translated by Rowan Williams. Edinburgh: T&T Clark, 1999.
Silence and Honey Cakes: The Wisdom of the Desert. Oxford: Lion Hudson, 2003.
A Silent Action: Engagements with Thomas Merton. Louisville: Fons Vitae, 2011.
Teresa of Avila. London: Geoffrey Chapman, 1991.
'The Theology of Vladimir Nikolaievich Lossky: An Exposition and Critique', Doctoral Thesis, University of Oxford, 1975.
Tokens of Trust: An Introduction to Christian Belief. Norwich: Canterbury Press, 2007.
The Truce of God. London: Fount, 1983.
The Truce of God: Peacemaking in Troubled Times. Norwich: Canterbury Press, 2005.
Why Study the Past? The Quest for the Historical Church. London: Darton, Longman and Todd, 2005.
The Wound of Knowledge: Christian Spirituality from the New Testament to St John of the Cross, 2nd Revised ed. London: Darton, Longman and Todd, 1990.
Wrestling with Angels: Conversations in Modern Theology, edited by M. Higton. Cambridge: Eerdmans, 2007.
Writing in the Dust: After September 11. Grand Rapids, MI: Eerdmans, 2002.

Articles, Essays and Lectures by Rowan Williams

'"Adult Geometry": Dangerous Thoughts in R.S. Thomas', in *The Page's Drift: R.S. Thomas at Eighty*, edited by M. Wynn Thomas, 82–98. Bridgend: Seren, 1993.

'Afterword: Knowing the Unknowable', in *Knowing the Unknowable: Science and Religions on God and the Universe*, edited by John Bowker, 257–62. London: I.B. Tauris, 2009.

'Analysing Atheism: Unbelief and the World of Faiths', in *Bearing the Word: Prophesy in Biblical and Qur'ānic Perspctive*, edited by M. Ipgrave, 1–13. London: Church House Publishing, 2005.

'Athanasius and the Arian Crisis', in *The First Christian Theologians: An Introduction to Theology in the Early Church*, edited by G. R. Evans, 157–67. Oxford: Blackwell, 2004.

'Augustine and the Psalms', *Interpretation* 58, no. 1 (2004): 17–27.

'Augustine's Christology: Its Spirituality and Rhetoric', in *In the Shadow of the Incarnation: Essays on Jesus Christ in the Early Church in Honor of Brian E. Daley, S.J.*, edited by P. W. Martens, 176–89. Notre Dame, IN: University of Notre Dame Press, 2007.

'Balthasar and the Trinity', in *The Cambridge Companion to Hans Urs Von Balthasar*, edited by E. T. Oakes and D. Moss, 37–50. Cambridge: Cambridge University Press, 2004.

'Being a People: Reflections on the Concept of "Laity"', *Religion, State and Society* 27, no. 1 (1999): 11–21.

'Being Biblical Persons', in *William Stringfellow in Anglo-American Perspective*, edited by A. Dancer, 184–7. Aldershot: Ashgate, 2005.

'Beyond Liberalism', *Political Theology: The Journal for Christian Socialism* 3, no. 1 (2001): 64–73.

'The Body's Grace', in *Our Selves, Our Souls and Bodies: Sexuality and the Household of God*, edited by C. Hefling, 58–67. Boston, MA: Cowley, 1996.

'Catholic Persons: Images of Holiness, A Dialogue' (with Philip Sheldrake), in *Living the Mystery: Affirming Catholicism and the Future of Anglicanism*, edited by J. John, 76–89. London: Darton, Longman & Todd, 1994.

'Christian Art and Cultural Pluralism: Reflections on *L'art De L'icone*, by Paul Evdokimov', *Eastern Churches Review* 8, no. 1 (1976): 38–44.

'Christian Identity and Religious Plurality', *The Ecumenical Review* 58, no. 1 (2006): 69–75.

'Christians and Muslims before the One God: An Address Given at Al-Azhar Al-Sharīf, Cairo on 11 September 2004', *Islam and Christian-Muslim Relations* 16, no. 2 (2005): 187–97.

'Creation', in *Augustine through the Ages: An Encyclopaedia*, edited by Allan D. Ftizgerald, 251–54. Grand Rapids: Eerdmans, 1999.

'The Deflections of Desire: Negative Theology in Trinitarian Disclosure', in *Silence and the Word: Negative Theology and Incarnation*, edited by O. Davies and D. Turner, 115–35. Cambridge: Cambridge University Press, 2002.

'Does It Make Sense to Speak of Pre-Nicene Orthodoxy?', in *The Making of Orthodoxy: Essays in Honour of Henry Chadwick*, edited by Rowan Williams, 1–23. Cambridge: Cambridge University Press, 1989.

'Eastern Orthodox Theology', in *The Modern Theologians: An Introduction to Christian Theology in the Twentieth Century*, edited by D. F. Ford, 499–515. Oxford: Blackwell, 1997.

'The Four Quartets', (unpublished lecture typescript), 1975.

'God', in *Fields of Faith: Theology and Religious Studies for the Twenty-First Century*, edited by D. F. Ford, B. Quash and J. Martin Soskice, 75–89. Cambridge: Cambridge University Press, 2005.

'God and Risk (2)', in *The Divine Risk*, edited by R. Holloway, 11–23. London: Darton, Longman and Todd, 1990.

'"Good for Nothing?" Augustine on Creation', in *Doctrinal Diversity: Varieties of Early Christianity*, edited by Everett Ferguson, 31–46. New York: Garland, 1999.

'The Health of the Spirit', in *Public Life and the Place of the Church: Reflections to Honour the Bishop of Oxford*, edited by Michael Brierley, 217–22. Aldershot: Ashgate, 2006.

'Heaven and Hell: A Modern Embarrassment?', *Epworth Review* 21, no. 2 (1994): 15–20.

'Historical Criticism and Sacred Text', in *Reading Texts, Seeking Wisdom*, edited by David F. Ford and Graham Stanton, 217–28. London: SCM Press, 2003.

'A History of Faith in Jesus', in *The Cambridge Companion to Jesus*, edited by M. Bockmuehl, 220–36. Cambridge: Cambridge University Press, 2001.

'Imagining Christ in Literature', in *The Oxford Handbook of Christology*, edited by Francesca A. Murphy and Troy A. Stefano, 488–505. Oxford: Oxford University Press, 2015.

'Insubstantial Evil', in *Augustine and His Critics: Essays in Honour of Gerald Bonner*, edited by R. Dodaro and G. Lawless, 105–23. London: Routledge, 2000.

'"Is It the Same God?" Reflections on Continuity and Identity in Religious Language', in *The Possibilities of Sense*, edited by J. H. Whittaker, 204–18. Basingstoke: Palgrave, 2002.

'Islam, Christianity and Pluralism: The Zaki Badawi Memorial Lecture, Lambeth Palace, London 26 April 2007', *Islam and Christian-Muslim Relations* 19, no. 3 (2008): 339–47.

'Jesus – God with Us' (with Richard Bauckham), in *Stepping Stones: Joint Essays on Anglican Catholic and Evangelical Unity*, edited by C. Baxter, 21–41. London: Hodder & Stoughton, 1987.

'"Know Thyself": What Kind of Injunction?', in *Philosophy, Religion and the Spiritual Life*, edited by Michael McGhee, 211–28. Cambridge: Cambridge University Press, 1992.

'Language, Reality and Desire in Augustine's *De Doctrina*', *Journal of Literature and Theology* 3, no. 2 (1989): 138–50.

'Looking for Jesus and Finding Christ', in *Biblical Concepts and Our World*, edited by D. Z. Phillips and M. von der Ruhr, 141–52. Basingstoke: Palgrave MacMillan, 2004.

'Macrina's Deathbed Revisited: Gregory of Nyssa on Mind and Passion', in *Christian Faith and Greek Philosophy in Late Antiquity: Essays in Tribute to George Christopher Stead*, edited by L. R. Wickham and C. P. Bammel, 227–46. Leiden: Brill, 1993.

'Making It Strange: Theology in Other(s') Words', in *Sounding the Depths: Theology through the Arts,* edited by J. Begbie, 19–32. London: SCM, 2002.

'Making Moral Decisions', in *Cambridge Companion to Christian Ethics*, edited by Robin Gill, 3–15. Cambridge: Cambridge University Press, 2001.

Mission and Christology (J. C. Jones Memorial Lecture 1994). Brynmawr: Welsh Members Council, Church Mission Society, 1994.

'The Nicene Heritage', in *The Christian Understanding of God Today*, edited by J. M. Byrne, 45–8. Dublin: The Columba Press, 1993.

'No-One Can Be Forgotten in God's Kingdom', *Anvil* 25, no. 2 (2008): 117–28.

'On Being a Human Body', *Sewanee Theological Review* 42, no. 4 (1999): 401–13.

'The Paradoxes of Self-Knowledge in the De Trinitate', in *Collectanea Augustiniana: Augustine, Presbytr Factus Sum*, edited by J. T. Lienhard, E. C. Muller and R. J. Teske, 121–34. New York: Peter Lang, 1992.

'Penance in the Penitentiary', *Theology* 95, no. 764 (1992): 88–96.

'"Person" and "Personality" in Christology', *The Downside Review* 94 (1976): 253–60.

'The Philosophical Structures of Palamism', *Eastern Churches Review* IX, no. 1–2 (1977): 27–44.

'Politics and the Soul: A Reading of the City of God', *Milltown Studies* 19/20 (1987): 55–72.

'Resurrection and Peace', *Theology* 92, no. 750 (1989): 481–90.

'Review of Hans Küng, The Incarnation of God: An Introduction to Hegel's Theological Thought as Prolegomena to a Future Christology', *Journal of Theological Studies* 42, no. 1 (1991): 403–6.

'Review of Peter Winch, *Simone Weil: The Just Balance*', *Philosophical Investigations* 14, no. 2 (1991): 155–71.

'"The Sadness of the King": Gillian Rose, Hegel, and the Pathos of Reason', *Telos* 173 (Winter 2015): 21–36.

'Sapientia and the Trinity: Reflections on the De Trinitate', in *Collectanea Augustiniana: Mélanges,* edited by T. J. van Bavel, B. Bruning, M. Lamberigts and J. van Houtem, 317–32. Leuven: Leuven University Press, 1990.

'Saving Time: Thoughts on Practice, Patience and Vision', *New Blackfriars* 73 (1992): 319–26.

'The Seal of Orthodoxy: Mary and the Heart of Christian Doctrine', in *Say Yes to God: Mary and the Revealing of the Word Made Flesh,* edited by Martin Warner, 15–29. London: Tufton, 1999.

'The Spirit of the Age to Come', *Sobornost: The Journal of the Fellowship of St Alban and St Sergius* 6, no. 9 (1974): 613–26.

'Suspending the Ethical: R.S. Thomas and Kierkegaard', in *Echoes of the Amen: Essays after R.S. Thomas,* edited by D. W. Davies, 206–19. Cardiff: University of Wales Press, 2009.

'Teaching the Truth', in *Living Tradition: Affirming Catholicism in the Anglican Church,* edited by J. John, 29–43. London: Darton, Longman and Todd, 1992.

'"Tempted as We Are": Christology and the Analysis of the Passions', in *Studia Patristica,* Vol XLIV, edited by J. Brown, A. Cameron, M. Edwards and M. Vinzent, 391–404. Leuven: Peeters, 2010.

'Theology in the Twentieth Century', in *A Century of Theological and Religious Studies in Britain,* edited by E. Nicholson, 237–52. Oxford: Oxford University Press, 2003.

'The Theology of Personhood: A Study in the Thought of Christos Yannaras', *Sobornost: The Journal of the Fellowship of St Alban and St Sergius* 6, no. 6 (1972): 415–30.

'Thoughts on the Resurrection', *Great St Mary's Papers*, Vol. 12, Cambridge: Great St Mary's Church, 2004.

'To Stand Where Christ Stands', in *An Introduction to Christian Spirituality,* edited by R. Waller and B. Ward, 1–13. London: SPCK, 1999.

'Troubled Breasts: The Holy Body in Hagiography', in *Portraits of Spiritual Authority: Religious Power in Early Christianity, Byzantium and the Christian Orient,* edited by J. W. Drijvers and J. W. Watt, 63–78. Leiden: Brill, 1999.

'What Does Love Know? St Thomas on the Trinity', *New Blackfriars* 82, no. 964 (2001): 260–72.

'What Is Catholic Orthodoxy?', in *Essays Catholic and Radical,* edited by R. Williams and K. Leech, 11–25. London: Bowerdean Press, 1983.

Web Resources by Rowan Williams

'The Bible Today: Reading and Hearing', http://rowanwilliams.archbishopofcanterbury.org/articles.php/2112/the-bible-today-reading-hearing-the-larkin-stuart-lecture (accessed 1 December 2014).

'Creation, Creativity and Creatureliness: The Wisdom of Finite Existence', http://rowanwilliams.archbishopofcanterbury.org/articles.php/2106/creation-creativity-and-creatureliness-the-wisdom-of-finite-existence (accessed 29 July 2013).

'The Church: God's Pilot Project', http://rowanwilliams.archbishopofcanterbury.org/articles.php/1779/the-church-gods-pilot-project (accessed 29 November 2013).

Letter to Lulu (a six year old child), as reported by Damien Thompson, http://blogs.telegraph.co.uk/news/damianthompson/100084843/a-six-year-old-girl-writes-a-letter-to-god-and-the-archbishop-of-canterbury-answers (accessed 1 February 2016).

'Living the Questions: An Interview with Rowan Williams's, http://www.christiancentury.org/article/%2Fliving-questions (accessed 30 January 2013).

'The Lutheran Catholic: The Ramsey Lecture, Durham', http://rowanwilliams.archbishopofcanterbury.org/articles.php/2102/ramsey-lecture-durham-the-lutheran-catholic (accessed 29 November 2013).

'"No Life Here – No Joy, Terror, or Tears" a Response to Bishop Spong', http://anglicanecumenicalsociety.wordpress.com/2010/06/10/bishop-spong-and-archbishop-williamss-response/ (accessed 3 March 2014).

'"Risen Indeed": The Resurrection in the Gospels – Bishop of Winchester's Lent Lectures, part 1', http://rowanwilliams.archbishopofcanterbury.org/articles.php/1380/risen-indeed-the-resurrection-in-the-gospels (accessed 12 October 2013).

'Scriptures in Monotheistic Faith', http://rowanwilliams.archbishopofcanterbury.org/articles.php/2114/paper-for-seminar-scriptures-in-monotheistic-faith-at-st-egidio-conference-naples-italy (accessed 29 November 2013).

'Theology in the Face of Christ', http://rowanwilliams.archbishopofcanterbury.org/articles.php/2100/addresses-given-to-celebrate-the-centenary-of-the-birth-of-archbishop-michael-ramsey-i.-theology-in- (accessed 29 November 2013).

Part II Secondary Literature

Adams, Nicholas. *Eclipse of Grace: Divine and Human Action in Hegel*. Oxford: Wiley-Blackwell, 2013.

Andrews, James A. 'Relevant Augustine: What *De Doctrina Christiana* Says Today', in *Studia Patristica*, vol. 50, edited by A. Brent and M. Vinzent, 309–20. Leuven: Peeters, 2011.

Andrews, James A. *Hermeneutics and the Church: In Dialogue with Augustine*. Notre Dame: Notre Dame University Press, 2012.

Augustine. *Teaching Christianity (De Doctrina Christiana),* translated by E. Hill. New York: New City Press, 1996.

Bakhtin, Mikhail. *Problems of Dostoevsky's Poetics*, translated by C. Emerson. Minneapolis: University of Minnesota Press, 1984.

von Balthasar, Hans Urs. *Cosmic Liturgy: The Universe According to Maximus the Confessor,* translated by Brian Daley. San Francisco: Ignatius Press, 2003.

von Balthasar, Hans Urs. *The Glory of the Lord: A Theological Aesthetics, Vol. 5: The Realm of Metaphysics in the Modern Age,* translated by O. Davies, A. Louth, B. McNeil and R. Williams. Edinburgh: T&T Clark, 1991.

Bathrellos, Demetrios. *The Byzantine Christ: Person, Nature, and Will in the Christology of Saint Maximus the Confessor*. Oxford: Oxford University Press, 2004.

Bauerschmidt, F. C. 'The Abrahamic Voyage: Michel De Certeau and Theology', *Modern Theology* 12, no. 1 (1996): 1–26.

Begbie, Jeremy (ed.), *Sounding the Depths: Theology Through the Arts*. London: SCM Press, 2002.

Bonhoeffer, Dietrich, 'Lectures in Christology (student notes)', in *Dietrich Bonhoeffer Works, Volume 12: Berlin 1932-3*, edited by C. Nicolaisen and E. A. Scharffenorth, L. L. Rasmussen (ed. English edition), translated by I. Best and D. Higgins, Minneapolis: Fortress Press: 2009.

Bouchard, Larry D. *Tragic Method and Tragic Theory: Evil in Contemporary Drama and Religious Thought*. University Park, PA: Pennsylvania State University Press, 1989.

Burrell, David B. *Knowing the Unknowable God: Ibn-Sina, Maimonides, Aquinas*. Notre Dame: Notre Dame Press, 1986.

Burrell, David B. *Towards a Jewish-Christian-Muslim Theology*. Oxford: Wiley Blackwell, 2014.

Casarella, Peter. 'Cusanus on Dionysius: The Turn to Speculative Theology', in *Re-Thinking Dionysius the Areopagite*, edited by S. Coakley and C. M. Stang, 137–48. Oxford: Wiley-Blackwell, 2009.

Coakley, Sarah. *God, Sexuality, and the Self: An Essay 'on the Trinity'*. Cambridge: Cambridge University Press, 2013.

Daley, Brian. 'Anhypostasy', in *Encyclopaedia of Christian Theology*, edited by Jean-Yves Lacoste, 40–2. London: Routledge, 2005.

Daniélou, Jean. *From Glory to Glory: Texts from Gregory of Nyssa's Mystical Writings*, translated by H. Musurillo. New York: St.Vladimir's Seminary Press, 2001.

de Certeau, Michel. *The Certeau Reader*, edited by G. Ward, Oxford: Blackwell, 2000.

de Certeau, Michel. 'The Gaze: Nicholas of Cusa', *Diacritics* 17, no. 3 (1987): 2–38.

Dostoevsky, Fyodor. *The Best Short Stories of Fyodor Dostoevsky*, translated by D. Magarshack. New York: The Modern Library, 2001.

Dostoevsky, Fyodor. *The Brothers Karamazov*, translated by R. Pevear and L. Volokhonsky. London: Vintage, 2004.

Dostoevsky, Fyodor. *Devils*, translated by M. R. Katz. Oxford: Oxford University Press, 1992.

Dostoevsky, Fyodor. *The Idiot*, translated by David McDuff. London: Penguin, 2004.

Florovsky, Georges. 'The Predicament of the Christian Historian', in *Religion and Culture: Essays in Honour of Paul Tillich*, edited by Walter Leibrecht, 140–66. New York: Harper & Brothers, 1959.

Frei, Hans W. *The Identity of Jesus Christ: The Hermeneutical Basis of Dogmatic Theology*. Philadelphia: Fortress Press, 1975.

Girard, René. *Resurrection from the Underground: Feodor Dostoevsky*, translated by J. G. Williams. New York: Crossroad, 1997.

Hart, David Bentley. *The Beauty of the Infinite: The Aesthetics of Christian Truth*. Grand Rapids, MI: Eerdmans, 2003.

Hegel, G. W. F. *Aesthetics: Lectures on Fine Art, Volume I*, translated by T. M. Knox. Oxford: Clarendon Press, 1975.

Hegel, G. W. F. *Phenomenology of Spirit*, tanslated by A. V. Miller. Oxford: Oxford University Press, 1977.

Higton, Mike. *Difficult Gospel: The Theology of Rowan Williams*. London: SCM, 2004.

Hobson, Theo. 'Rowan Williams as Anglican Hegelian', *Reviews in Religion and Theology* 12, no. 2 (2005): 290–7.

John of Damascus, 'Exposition of the Orthodox Faith', in *Nicene and Post-Nicene Fathers Series Two, Vol IX*, translated by S. D. Salmond, edited by P. Schaff and H. Wace. Grand Rapids: Eerdmanns, 1988–91.

Kapic, Kelly. 'The Son's Assumption of a Human Nature: A Call for Clarity', *International Journal of Systematic Theology* 3, no. 2 (2001): 154–66.

Kroeker, P. T. and Ward, B. K. *Remembering the End: Dostoevsky as Prophet to Modernity*. London: SCM Press, 2001.

Lang, U. M. 'Anhypostatos-Enhypostatos: Church Fathers, Protestant Orthodoxy and Karl Barth', *Journal of Theological Studies* 49, no. 2 (1998): 630–57.

Lossky, Vladimir. *The Mystical Theology of the Eastern Church*, translated by Fellowship of St Alban and St Sergius. London: James Clarke, 1957.

Louth, Andrew. *Maximus the Confessor*. London: Routledge, 1996.

MacKinnon, Donald. 'Aristotle's Conception of Substance', in *New Essays on Plato and Aristotle*, edited by R. Bambrough, 97–119. London: Routledge & Kegan Paul, 1965.

MacKinnon, Donald. *Borderlands of Theology and Other Essays*. London: Lutterworth Press, 1968.

MacKinnon, Donald. *Explorations in Theology 5*. London: SCM Press, 1979.

MacKinnon, Donald. *The Problems of Metaphysics*. Cambridge: Cambridge University Press, 1974.

MacKinnon, Donald. 'Some Reflections on Hans Urs Von Balthasar's Christology with Special Reference to Theodramatik II/2, III and IV', in *The Analogy of Beauty: The Theology of Hans Urs Von Balthasar*, edited by John Riches, 164–79. Edinburgh: T&T Clark, 1986.

MacKinnon, Donald. *Themes in Theology: The Three-Fold Cord*. Edinburgh: T&T Clark, 1987.

MacKinnon, Donald. 'Theology and Tragedy', in *The Stripping of the Altars: The Gore Memorial Lecture and Other Pieces*, 41–51. London: Fontana, 1969.

McCurry, Jeffrey. 'Towards a Poetics of Theological Creativity: Rowan Williams Reads Augustine's *De Doctrina* after Derrida', *Modern Theology* 23, no. 3 (2007): 415–33.

McFarland, Ian A. *In Adam's Fall: A Meditation on the Christian Doctrine of Original Sin*. Oxford: Wiley-Blackwell, 2010.

McGuckin, John. *Saint Cyril of Alexandria and the Christological Controversy: Its History, Theology and Texts*. Crestwood, NY: St Vladimir's Seminary Press, 2004.

Madden, Nicholas. 'Composite Hypostasis in Maximus Confessor', in *Studia Patristica Vol. XXVII*, edited by E. A. Livingstone, 175–97. Leuven: Peeters, 1993.

Mathewes, Charles T. *Evil and the Augustinian Tradition*. Cambridge: Cambridge University Press, 2001.

Milbank, John. *Being Reconciled: Ontology and Pardon*. London: Routledge, 2003.

Milbank, John. 'Between Purgation and Illumination: A Critique of the Theology of Right', in *Christ, Ethics and Tragedy: Essays in Honour of Donald Mackinnon*, edited by Kenneth Surin, 161–96. Cambridge: Cambridge University Press, 1989.

Milbank, John. 'Scholasticism, Modernism and Modernity', *Modern Theology* 22, no. 4 (2006): 651–71.

Milbank, John. 'The Second Difference', in *The Word Made Strange: Theology, Language and Culture*, 171–93. Oxford: Blackwell, 1997.

Milbank, John. *Theology and Social Theory*, 2nd ed. Oxford: Blackwell, 2006.

Moody, Andrew. 'The Hidden Center: Trinity and Incarnation in the Negative (and Positive) Theology of Rowan Williams's', in *On Rowan Williams: Critical Essays*, edited by Matheson Russell, 25–46. Eugene: Cascade, 2009.

Moseley, Carys. 'Rowan Williams as Hegelian Political Theologian: Resacralising Secular Politics', *Heythrop Journal* 53, no. 3 (2012): 362–81.

Myers, Benjamin. *Christ the Stranger: The Theology of Rowan Williams.* London: T&T Clark, 2012.

Nicholas of Cusa. *Nicholas of Cusa on God as Not-Other: A Translation and Appraisal of De Li Non Aliud,* translated by J. Hopkins. Minneapolis: University of Minneapolis Press, 1979.

O'Connor, Flannery. *Mystery and Manners: Occasional Prose.* New York: Noonday, 1970.

Oenning Thompson, Diane. 'Problems of the Biblical Word in Dostoevsky's Poetics', in *Dostoevsky and the Christian Tradition,* edited by George Pattison and Diane Oenning Thompson, 69–99. Cambridge: Cambridge University Press, 2001.

Pascal, Pierre. *The Religion of the Russian People,* translated by Rowan Williams. London: Mowbrays, 1976.

Peace, Richard. *Dostoyevsky: An Examination of the Major Novels.* Cambridge: Cambridge University Press, 1971.

Phillips, D. Z. 'A Realism of Distances (Flannery O'Connor)', in *From Fantasy to Faith: The Philosophy of Religion and Twentieth-Century Literature,* 212–21. Basingstoke: Macmillan, 1991.

Poole, Adrian. 'Simone Weil: Force, Tragedy, and Grace in Homer's Iliad', in *Christian Theology and Tragedy: Theologians, Tragic Literature and Tragic Theory,* edited by Kevin Taylor and Giles Waller, 119–31. Farnham: Ashgate, 2011.

Prinkhod'ko, Irina. 'Review Article: Rowan Williams. Dostoevsky: Language, Faith and Fiction', *Sobornost: The Journal of the Fellowship of St Alban and St Sergius* 32, no. 2 (2010): 73–81.

Quash, Ben. *Found Theology: History, Imagination and the Holy Spirit.* London: Bloomsbury, 2013.

Quash, Ben. 'Four Biblical Characters: In Search of a Tragedy', in *Christian Theology and Tragedy: Theologians, Tragic Literature and Tragic Theory,* edited by Kevin Taylor and Giles Waller, 15–33. Farnham: Ashgate, 2011.

Quash, Ben. *Theology and the Drama of History.* Cambridge: Cambridge University Press, 2005.

Ricoeur, Paul. *Time and Narrative: Volume I,* translated by K. McLaughlin and D. Pellauer. Chicago: Chicago University Press, 1984.

Rose, Gillian. *The Broken Middle.* Oxford: Blackwell, 1992.

Rose, Gillian. *Judaism and Modernity: Philosophical Essays.* Oxford: Blackwell, 1993.

Rose, Gillian. *Love's Work.* New York: New York Review Books, 1995.

Rose, Gillian. *Mourning Becomes the Law: Philosophy and Representation.* Cambridge: Cambridge University Press, 1996.

Russell, Matheson. 'Dispossession and Negotiation: Rowan Williams on Hegel and Political Theology', in *On Rowan Williams: Critical Essays,* edited by Matheson Russell, 85–114. Eugene, OR: Wipf and Stock, 2009.

Schmidt, Dennis J. *On Germans and Other Greeks: Tragedy and Ethical Life.* Bloomington: Indiana University Press, 2001.

Shanks, Andrew. *Against Innocence: Gillian Rose's Reception and Gift of Faith.* London: SCM Press, 2008.

Shanks, Andrew. *God and Modernity: A New and Better Way to Do Theology.* London: Routledge, 2000.

Shanks, Andrew. *Hegel's Political Theology.* Cambridge: Cambridge University Press, 1991.

Shortt, Rupert. *God's Advocates: Christian Thinkers in Conversation.* London: Darton, Longman and Todd, 2005.

Steiner, George. *Errata: An Examined Life.* New Haven, CT: Yale University Press, 1997.

Steiner, George. *Tolstoy or Dostoevsky: An Essay in the Old Criticism,* 2nd ed. New Haven, CT: Yale University Press, 1996.

Stobart, Andrew J. 'A Constructive Analysis of the Place and Role of the Doctrine of Jesus' Resurrection within the Theologies of Rowan Williams and Robert Jenson', Doctoral Thesis, University of Aberdeen, 2011.

Symmons Roberts, Michael. 'Libretto for Parthenogenesis', in *Sounding the Depths: Theology through the Arts*, edited by J. Begbie, 41–6. London: SCM Press, 2002.

Tanner, Kathryn. *God and Creation in Christian Theology: Tyranny or Empowerment?* Oxford: Blackwell, 1988.

Ticciati, Susannah. 'The Castration of Signs: Conversing with Augustine on Creation, Language and Truth', *Modern Theology* 23, no. 2 (2007): 161–79.

Turner, Denys. 'Dionysius and Some Late Medieval Mystical Theologians of Northern Europe', *Modern Theology* 24, no. 4 (2008): 651–65.

Volpe, Medi Ann. *Rethinking Christian Identity: Doctrine and Discipleship.* Chichester: Wiley-Blackwell, 2013.

Wainwright, Geoffrey. 'Rowan Williams on Christian Doctrine', *Scottish Journal of Theology* 56, no. 1 (2003): 73–81.

Waller, Giles. 'Freedom, Fate and Sin in Donald Mackinnon's Use of Tragedy', in *Christian Theology and Tragedy: Theologians, Tragic Literature and Tragic Theory*, edited by Kevin Taylor and Giles Waller, 101–18. Farnham: Ashgate, 2011.

Weinandy, Thomas. 'Cyril and the Mystery of the Incarnation', in *The Theology of Cyril of Alexandria: A Critical Appreciation*, edited by T. G. Weinandy and D. A. Keating, 23–54. London: T&T Clark, 2003.

Weinandy, Thomas. *In the Likeness of Sinful Flesh: An Essay on the Humanity of Christ.* Edinburgh: T&T Clark, 1993.

Williams, Garry. *The Theology of Rowan Williams: An Outline, Critique and Consideration of Its Consequences.* London: The Latimer Trust, 2002.

Index

Note: Page locators followed by 'n' indicate footnotes.